EDMUND BURKE
AND THE PRACTICE OF POLITICAL WRITING

EDMUND BURKE
AND THE
PRACTICE OF
POLITICAL WRITING

CHRISTOPHER REID

GILL AND MACMILLAN
ST. MARTIN'S PRESS

Published in Ireland by
Gill and Macmillan Ltd
Goldenbridge
Dublin 8
with associated companies in
Auckland, Dallas, Delhi, Hong Kong,
Johannesburg, Lagos, London, Manzini,
Melbourne, Nairobi, New York, Singapore,
Tokyo, Washington
© Christopher Reid, 1985
0 7171 1038 9

First published in the United States of America by
St Martin's Press, Inc., 175 Fifth Avenue, New York, NY 10010.
ISBN 0-312-23696-4

Library of Congress Cataloging in Publication Data
Reid, Christopher, 1952-
    Edmund Burke and the Practice of Political Writing.
    Bibliography: p. 227
    Includes index.
    1. Burke, Edmund, 1729?-1797—Contributions in Political Science. 2. Great
Britain—Politics in Government—18th century. I. Title.
JC176.B83R45 1986   320'.092'4   85-22261
ISBN 0-312-23696-4

Print origination in Ireland by Galaxy Reproductions Ltd
Printed in Great Britain by
Biddles Ltd, Guildford and King's Lynn

For Sara

Contents

Abbreviations

The following abbreviations and short titles are employed in this study:

PRINTED WORKS

Corr.   *The Correspondence of Edmund Burke*, edited by T. W. Copeland and others, 10 vols (Cambridge and Chicago, 1958-78).

PE   *A Philosophical Enquiry into the Origin of Our Ideas of the Sublime and Beautiful*, edited by J. T. Boulton (London, 1958).

PH   *The Parliamentary History of England, from the Earliest Period to the Year 1803*, edited by W. Cobbett, 36 vols (London, 1806-20).

Writings and Speeches

    The Writings and Speeches of Edmund Burke, edited by P. Langford and others; in progress (Oxford, 1981-). (When complete this will be the most authoritative and comprehensive edition of Burke.)

MANUSCRIPT COLLECTIONS

Eg. MSS   Egerton Manuscripts, British Library, London.

Fitzwilliam MSS (Northampton)

    Burke papers in the Fitzwilliam (Milton) collection, on deposit at the Northamptonshire Record Office.

Fitzwilliam MSS (Sheffield)

    Burke papers in the Wentworth Woodhouse Muniments, on deposit at the Sheffield City Libraries.

Prefatory Note

1. REFERENCES AND TEXTS

In order to reduce the number of notes to an absolute minimum, references are wherever possible inserted into the text.

Unless otherwise indicated, all references to Burke's writings and speeches are to *The Works of the Right Honourable Edmund Burke*, edited by French Laurence and Walker King, 16 vols (London, 1803-27). Volume and page number are cited in parenthesis after each quotation.

With works by authors other than Burke, the date of publication of the edition concerned, page reference, and author's name (where this is not obvious from the context) are noted after each quotation, e.g. (Boswell, 1934-50, I, 261-2). Full details of works cited in this way are included in the bibliography, 2 (ii).

Pamphlets discussed in the third part of the study are listed separately in the bibliography, 2 (iii). Page references to quotations from these pamphlets are again included in the text.

2. TRANSCRIPTION FROM MANUSCRIPTS

In almost every case my readings of Burke manuscripts follow those of Langford (*Writings and Speeches*, Vol. II). I have generally followed his principles of transcription. Illegible words or phrases are indicated thus: (. . .)

Readings supplied from deleted phrases are enclosed in square brackets.

The Cavendish Diary presents particular problems of transcription. When Cavendish was unable to supply words or phrases of a speech, he left gaps of various lengths in his report. Deliberate omissions of this kind are indicated by a sequence of dashes, thus: —————.

In most cases I have expanded Cavendish's numerous abbreviations and attempted to supply punctuation where the original is seriously deficient. In quoting from manuscript and pamphlet material I have generally avoided the use of the term *sic*, which would soon become intrusive.

Acknowledgments

In writing this book, and the doctoral thesis on which it is based, I have incurred a number of debts: to the late Earl Fitzwilliam for permission to consult and quote from the Burke papers deposited in the Northamptonshire Record Office; to the Director of Sheffield City Libraries and the Trustees of the Fitzwilliam (Wentworth) Estates for permission to make use of the Burke papers in their custody; and to Dr Postles and Mr King, archivists at Sheffield and Northampton respectively, for their assistance. Grateful acknowledgment is also made to The Clarendon Press, Oxford, for permission to quote material from *The Writings and Speeches of Edmund Burke*, Vol. II, edited by Paul Langford, 1981.

I have received valuable criticism and support from many colleagues and friends. Professor J. T. Boulton, Professor John Chalker, Dr Howard Erskine-Hill, Mr Basil Greenslade, Dr Paul Langford and Dr Paul Stigant were each kind enough to read earlier drafts of this study, either in whole or in part. I am grateful to them for their comments and advice.

For financial assistance which helped me in the preparation of the second part of this study, I am indebted to the Committee of the Central Research Fund of the University of London.

1

Introduction: Literary Criticism and the Political Text

For the ruling classes of Britain and much of Europe the second half of the eighteenth century was a period of sustained and intensifying political crisis. Throughout this troubled period, from the Wilkite alarms of the 1760s to the ideological emergency of the French Revolution in the 1790s, there was scarcely a controversy of significance to which Edmund Burke failed to respond or which he failed to enliven. In the course of a career of enormous intellectual and literary labour he generated an ideological energy which has yet to ebb away. On one hand, Burke's writings and speeches continue to nourish the language and thought of modern conservatism. On another, they remain capable of provoking powerful feelings of hostility and rejection. The debate on Burke, disputed with sufficient heat during his own lifetime, has never quite been allowed to settle down or to resolve itself into a comfortably academic affair. Thus in the great revival of interest in Burke's career which was witnessed in the 1950s, interpretations of his political thought were presented quite openly as contributions to the ideological struggle against Marxism.

If Burke's standing as an ideologist and political thinker remains high, it has at times almost been matched by his literary reputation, the consequence of imaginative resources and a gift for polemic which make his political writings among the richest and most vibrant in the language. It is difficult historically, and even for the purposes of analysis, to separate these literary and political elements in Burke. What we may now wish to recognise and study as a literary achievement was in the 1790s devised, experienced and felt as a series of political acts, dedicated to the repression and ultimate defeat of the radical movement. At the moment of their greatest peril the monarchies and aristocracies of Europe could take comfort in Burke. In the writings of Godwin, Paine and their circle English radicalism forged a distinctive style in politics and letters, but it failed to find (or perhaps was prevented from finding) a spokesman with quite Burke's rhetorical talents and sense of history. This was to prove a serious, perhaps even a decisive weakness.

The literary components of Burke's writings, their styles, structures and forms of address, can therefore be said to have had definite political and historical consequences. The purpose of the following chapters is to examine this relationship between literary form and political practice. Burke, as I have said, has long been regarded as a distinguished literary figure as well as a statesman. In view of this, and given the growth of interest in his career, it may seem surprising that so few literary studies of his work have appeared. Recent work on Burke has, for the most part, been biographical or historical in character. In addition, there have been several important and controversial accounts of his place in the history of political ideas. Few literary studies have proved as rigorous, as extensive or as provocative as these.[1] One might be forgiven for concluding that, with some brave exceptions, literary criticism is not yet sure quite what to do with Burke. Notwithstanding his reputation as one of the great masters of English prose, he seems destined to remain an essentially marginal figure in literary history. This is not a verdict which need particularly surprise us. Of all the great writers of his time, Burke was the one whose works were furthest removed both in form and circumstance from the condition of *belles-lettres* — ever subject to the demands of party and of office and cast in the pragmatic forms of the pamphlet and the speech. As a great *political* writer he is perhaps less assured of his place in the literary canon than most of his contemporaries. My aim in this introduction is not to enter a claim on Burke's behalf for a more secure place in that canon, but rather to consider his writings in the light of recent debates about the nature and compass of literary discourse. By so doing I hope to extend our understanding of the manner in which a political writer such as Burke might be studied and read.

Literary appreciations of Burke have from the very outset been tinged with regret, as if he had somehow been too fine a writer to soil his hands in the mire of party politics. The rebuke which Goldsmith administered in his poem 'Retaliation', when he accused his friend of being one

> Who, born for the Universe, narrow'd his mind,
> And to party gave up, what was meant for mankind
>
> (ll. 31-2)

established a way of understanding Burke's writings and career which has never quite lost its force in literary study. A variation of this attitude has been to value his works in so far as they failed, or are supposed to have failed, to secure practical political objectives. Political defeat can then be seen as almost a prerequisite for a literary triumph. In these responses to Burke one senses the embarrassment literary criticism sometimes suffers when faced by works written for specific occasions and with a view to obtaining particular ends. Such works do not obviously fulfil the criteria of permanence and universality which are so often held to distinguish literature worthy of serious critical attention, a category from which works of political argument, with their concern for immediate issues and possibilities of action, have generally been excluded. If Burke's political writings have been regarded as exceptional, it has usually been on the grounds that, unlike the works of other controversialists of his time, they are universal in their application and appeal.

There may not, on the face of it, appear to be anything particularly contentious in this assessment. Some works, after all, are simply more serious, interesting and durable than others. Yet in seeking to emphasise what is of permanent value in Burke's writings it is easy to detach them from the crises and contingencies which lent them their particular urgency, form and colour. Such an approach would no doubt succeed in highlighting their most humane, liberal and rational elements, those which may continue to move, inspire or make us think. The outcome, however, would be a highly selective reading of Burke, one which would risk misrepresenting his historical role and even his literary manner. For in the works on which his reputation now largely rests, the counter-revolutionary tracts of the 1790s, humanity and sympathy are at a premium. These writings reverberate with an extraordinary rhetorical violence. Burke came early to the conclusion that the revolution in France should be crushed by military force. In his last years it was largely in urging this course of action that he exercised his formidable literary talents.

This immediate and practical rhetorical function is at the heart of Burke's enterprise, and seems to set his writings apart from the more customary objects of literary study. His works took root in conditions which differed in many respects from those in which more recognisably literary producers — novelists, playwrights and poets — are accustomed to write. On his election to the House of Commons in 1765 Burke, an expatriate Irish intellectual of middle-class parentage, dedicated himself to the political advancement of the Rockingham Whigs, a predominantly aristocratic parliamentary group in whose interests he was to write and speak for thirty years. In most cases, and in furthering those interests, his works address themselves to a definite political occasion or crisis — a riot, a debate, the appearance of a rival pamphleteer, and so forth. His literary craft could not therefore develop at its own pace, according to some aesthetic of its own. It took forms which were chosen as much for their political utility as for their literary decorum. In this way Burke's writings, like those of any other pamphleteer, were shaped in form, mode and meaning by institutional constraints and the pressures of circumstance. Novels, plays and poems are not less tied to their own conditions than pamphlets are, though they may sometimes seem self-enclosed. In political discourse, however, those conditions, towards which the writer constantly gestures and responds, are presented directly as the very *raison d'être* of the work.

These conditions give rise to particular literary forms and methods. Since many of these are unfamiliar, and to some, perhaps, uncongenial, it is not surprising that they have been little discussed in literary studies of Burke. His political writings are often read indiscriminately, as if they were virtually identical in form, or at least as if their formal differences were unimportant. In reality they are formally complex and diverse. The *Works* of Burke, a collection of writings which may at first sight seem uniform in purpose and manner, is, on closer inspection, a somewhat miscellaneous set, made up of a variety of literary modes: letters of advice and instruction, political memoranda, motions and resolutions, practical works of political economy, committee reports, articles of charge, parliamentary orations and addresses, platform speeches, and so on. Although these modes of writing may appear routine and unpromising in comparison to the spectacular passages of rhetoric they sometimes introduce, they are, like any other group of literary forms and conventions, fundamental to the writer's art, laying down, as it were, a framework of rhetorical possibilities within which the orator and pamphleteer can speak or write.

This diversity makes Burke a difficult writer to classify and understand. In particular, it complicates any attempt to determine the exact contents and confines of his text, the object of literary study. The problem of unfamiliarity, in other words, is closely related to one of definition. It is a precondition of literary criticism that we should possess as accurate and complete a text of an author's works as possible. But when faced with a writer such as Burke, the methods according to which a literary text is usually established are likely to break down. His writings present a host of empirical difficulties, practical editorial considerations, bibliographical problems of attribution, transcription, revision, and so on. These problems, which have been discussed authoritatively in William B. Todd's *A Bibliography of Edmund Burke*, may not be unfamiliar in themselves. Indeed, they offer the kind of challenge to which editors and bibliographers have become quite accustomed. In Burke's case, however, they are more than textual accidents or bibliographical puzzles which, given good empirical research and a measure of luck, might be resolved once and for all. These difficulties originate in the very nature of Burke's practice of writing. In order to come to terms with them, we need to examine the distinctive features and functions of political discourse itself, and to consider its relationship with those modes of writing which we are more accustomed to think of as 'literary'.

Political writing is often a collective craft. I suppose that all literary works can be said to be collaborative in the sense that they will be indebted to occasional influence, assistance and advice. In exceptional cases literary collaboration may, of course, be more deliberate and extensive than that. For the political writer, however – or at least for the party spokesman that Burke was for much of his career – collaboration is a regular and essential *modus operandi*. His practical commitment to the cause of the Rockingham Whigs meant that a good deal of his literary effort was likely to be of a collaborative nature. Thus the early pamphlets, the *Short Account of a Late Short Administration* (1766), the *Observations on a Late Publication, intituled, 'The Present State of the Nation'* (1769) and the *Thoughts on the Cause of the Present Discontents* (1770), were all, to a greater or lesser degree, party ventures. In each case Burke was no doubt the prime mover behind the work, and largely responsible for its final form, but the authorial control he enjoyed was by no means exclusive. His most recent editor concludes that in writing the *Observations* Burke 'was essentially marshalling and co-ordinating the collective materials at the command of his friends' (*Writings and Speeches*, II, 106). The *Thoughts* was more decisively Burke's own production, and yet his correspondence with other members of the Rockingham group shows how closely they were involved in the formulation of strategy and argument. I am not suggesting that Burke was ever a mere mouthpiece, the tame philosopher of his aristocratic employers. The experience of the 1790s demonstrates that he was quite capable of writing and speaking independently when he chose. The more important point – one which lies behind some of the textual problems I have just described – is that as a pamphleteer Burke was engaged in one of the more collective forms of writing, one which is not always easily reconciled with more traditional ideas of the nature of literature and the author's role.

There is another sense in which Burke's practice of writing tends to cut across the categories which are commonly used to characterise a literary text. Perhaps the single most important element in any political communication is its form of address, since this defines and gives notice of the kind of audience it is seeking to persuade. In Burke's writings that audience is often addressed by means of a printed letter which may have a single figure as its formal recipient. In this form of address, one of the central conventions of political writing in the eighteenth century, the character, reputation and social status of the addressee are by no means incidental to the work. Rather, they provide the essential authority upon which its politics and rhetoric will rest. A letter will be addressed to an intelligent, inquisitive but inexperienced young gentleman in order to justify a paternalistic and pedagogical approach to political affairs. A letter will be addressed to a statesman of mature years, sober tempera-ment and aristocratic class in the hope that some of his dignity and consequence will be conferred upon the pamphlet-eer and his work. This convention, by which an individual addressee becomes the literary representative of a wider audience, can make it difficult to distinguish formally between Burke's private correspondence and 'public' works. In the letter, one of his most favoured forms of political argument, the concerns and protocols of public and private life begin to coalesce. This is noted in a study of Burke's correspondence by J. T. Boulton, who draws attention to the 'formal and weighty epistolary style' of many of the private letters. He adds that 'political necessity frequently required [Burke] to correspond with influential men on the edge of or outside the central Rockingham group. For them the private-formal mode had to give away to the near-public voice. And yet again there were occasions when Burke addressed a large audience through the medium of the personal letter.' (1966a, p. 193)

When we refer to Burke's political writing, then, we are speaking of a literary practice which incorporates but may not be confined to the celebrated public works. Many of the latter are cast in forms and styles identical with those in which, for thirty years, he conducted everyday political business. Publication may sometimes have been almost as much the result of political expediency as of artistic design. Only a handful of Burke's parliamentary speeches, for instance, were ever published on his own authority, and it is probable that the decision to publish — if the political climate seemed favourable, and the necessary drafts and reports could be assembled — was often taken after the speech had been delivered. No doubt the printed letters were more usually selected for publication at the outset, and yet there were other occasions when a private correspondence grew under Burke's hand, and perhaps without his realising it, into a public address. Describing the composition of the *Reflections on the Revolution in France*, the author recalled that 'having thrown down his first thoughts in the form of a letter, and indeed when he sat down to write, having intended it for a private letter, he found it difficult to change the form of address, when his sentiments had grown into a greater extent, and had received another direction' (V, 27-8). We need not take this statement quite at face value. Burke was determined to take a public stand on the French Revolution, and the correspondence he had been conducting with a young Parisian, Charles-Jean-François Depont, provided a convenient forum, together with a ready-made rhetorical strategy. Even in the *Reflections*, however, where the epistolary form is stretched to its furthest limits, the personal address is more than a mere device. The work did, after all, originate in a real exchange of letters.

Occasionally the exact status of a letter, its public or private character, must remain in doubt. Burke's 5,000-word letter to William Weddell (31 January 1792), in which he defends his record as one faithful to the principles of the Rockingham/ Portland Whigs, is both formal and informal by turns. Although never published by Burke, it was evidently intended to reach an audience beyond Weddell himself, as Burke's closing remarks suggest:

> This long Letter my dear friend is for you; but so for you, as that you may shew it to such of our friends, who, though they cannot, in prudence, support, will not, in Justice, condemn me.   (*Corr.*, VII, 63)

In this instance, and indeed in many others in Burke, public and private forms of address are combined, a procedure which can make his works difficult to classify. Should the letter to Weddell, for instance, be regarded as less worthy of critical attention, than, say, the *Letter to Samuel Span* (1778) simply on the grounds that, unlike the latter, Burke did not choose to issue it in print? Historically some 'private' letters have certainly been granted literary status: the letters of Chesterfield and Walpole are among the most important eighteenth-century examples. In addition, the study of an author's correspondence has often played a significant role in literary scholarship. In such cases, however, the letter is not generally read in and for itself, but as an aid to the interpretation of the literary text. Its function is to throw light on, resolve difficulties in, and provide a background for the more important public writings. This auxiliary status is perhaps confirmed by the custom whereby editions of correspondence are issued separately from the *Works* which they complement. It is not difficult to account for this arrangement. The novels of George Eliot, for instance, may be considered as qualitatively distinct from her private correspondence. They were destined to reach a large and unknown audience, while the letters were usually addressed to a familiar individual. There is no doubt that different conventions and assumptions moulded the two modes of writing. It would not therefore seem unreasonable to suggest that they should be read according to different procedures — that they should, if you like, be studied at different levels of seriousness.

Yet in the case of Burke, as I have indicated, distinctions of this kind do not always hold. His political works do not slot neatly into the categories which have become customary in literary study. In this respect the most problematical of all his writings are the 'official' works he undertook in his capacity as a parliamentarian. Of these, the *Reports of the Select Committee of the House of Commons on India* (1781-83) are probably the best known. These reports present a number of problems of attribution. Their most recent editor is able to ascribe most of the *First* report to Burke, together with the *Ninth* and *Eleventh* in their entirety, but concludes that 'Burke's contribution to the writing of the reports . . . is in general hard to determine.' (*Writings and Speeches*, V, 144, 626-8) Although this appears to be another purely editorial and bibliographical difficulty, its implications are again wider than that. We are uncertain of the extent of

Burke's responsibility for the *Reports* not only because we lack the information required to determine their authorship, but also, and more radically, because we are unsure of the terms in which works such as these should be read. In other words, the question of attribution is at root a theoretical one which arises from the particular mode of writing in which the reports engage, the character of the institution in which they evolved, and the political occasion which prompted them.

Formally speaking, the reports represented the collective view of the committee rather than the opinions of any individual member. It is as 'your Committee' that Burke and his colleagues address the House and report their findings and recommendations. It might be said that this is simply a matter of protocol, a device which barely masks Burke's intellectual and artistic ascendancy over the other members of the committee. It would be wrong, however, to underestimate the influence of parliamentary etiquette and procedure on the rhetoric and argument of the reports. They were presented as exclusively parliamentary publications, printed, according to the *Journals of the House of Commons*, for the 'Use of Members of the House'. Given this function, it is not surprising that the reports should adopt a distinctly parliamentary style and method. Even those which have been most confidently identified as 'Burke's' tend to fall back upon the stylistic neutrality of official discourse. It is not that these reports are uniformly bland in tone. They are enlivened by moments of considerable irony, and even of passionate denunciation, but these occur within (and are perhaps occasioned by) what is at heart an impersonal and collective mode of writing.

Although at least one critical study of the rhetoric of the reports has appeared (Speer, 1971), their style is not one which especially endears itself to literary criticism. My emphasis on this style, and, more generally, on the special conditions which shape Burke's political writings, might then be seen as confirmation of the essentially 'non-literary' character of his work. I would prefer to think that serious political writers such as Burke, the full force and significance of whose work can only be felt through a close scrutiny of its language and forms, call into question the relatively narrow conceptions of the 'literary' which have sometimes held sway.

Definitions of literature are notoriously contentious, and in the end may not always be very helpful. Those based primarily upon aesthetic criteria, on considerations of literary quality, verified by the reader's taste, are particularly unreliable, since of all the possible definitions they are the least capable of demonstration. Preferable, in this respect at least, are historical and institutional approaches to the problem which seek to identify those modes of writing which have been regarded as literary in the past.

The range of activities required of the writer in the eighteenth century was generally wider than we would expect of an author today. This diversity has often been recognised as an obstacle to our understanding of writers like Burke. Thomas Copeland has described some of the dilemmas it poses for the literary critic:

> Though he has certainly the right to be called a man of letters, Burke ranged into more semirelated and downright non-literary fields than perhaps any single man of letters who ever wrote in English. He was an orator, a pamphleteer, a political philosopher, an aesthetician, a historian and a journalist — if we go no farther. Naturally such multifariousness increases the difficulty of passing judgments upon him. Unless the critic is as protean as Burke, he will find it impossible to judge in all fields at once; if on the other hand he attempts to disentangle and examine a piece of Burke's work in some single department, he will surely find that his judgment is blurred and confused by the co-existence of all the other departments.
>
> (1949, pp. 5-6)

Most modern readers of Burke will have encountered the difficulties Copeland describes. There have been many moments during the writing of this book when I have been aware of stepping dangerously beyond the limits of my competence. And yet critics of Burke are not alone in their exposure to such risks. From an historical point of view, the diversity of Burke's achievement need not be seen as singular. It may, indeed, be quite characteristic of the eighteenth-century 'man of letters'.

It is in the expectations a society has of the writer's role —

including his or her functions, duties and privileges — that its conception of the 'literary' is made most clearly apparent. In the eighteenth century, it would seem, the division of intellectual labour had yet to reach an advanced stage. Many of the great writers of the period operated in a number of diverse fields. We sometimes obscure this fact by classifying their careers in a more specialised way. Thus Adam Smith, lecturer in rhetoric and *belles-lettres*, successively Professor of Logic and of Moral Philosophy at Glasgow, and author of the *Theory of Moral Sentiments* as well as the *Wealth of Nations*, is now almost without hesitation described as an 'economist'. Joseph Priestley, now celebrated for his achievements as a chemist, was also a noted theologian, philologist and political writer. It is not my intention to dispute the judgment that Priestley's greatest advances were made in chemistry and Smith's in economics. But this emphasis on a single discipline can be misleading. It can conceal the complex interaction between the various intellectual endeavours in which Priestley and Smith were engaged. In the case of Smith, for instance, it would be unwise to attempt to isolate the economics of the *Wealth of Nations* from the moral and social philosophy which underpins it. In a similar way, it would be difficult to abstract an essentially 'literary' element from the works of many of the great eighteenth-century writers without doing violence to their principles of form and cohesion. Defoe, Swift and Johnson are obvious examples of writers whose work would not respond kindly to such treatment. Burke himself is another. It is evident that the 'man of letters' in the eighteenth century was one whose writings could encompass a number of disciplines. An 'economist' like Smith, a 'philosopher' like Hume, an 'historian' like Gibbon and a 'political writer' like Burke would all have been regarded as literary figures. Indeed, the term 'literature', as used to denote a select corpus of works, is less often encountered in eighteenth-century writings than the phrase 'the republic of letters', with its suggestion of a community of intellectuals and disciplines.

A helpful account of these changing attitudes towards literary discourse is to be found in the recent work of Raymond Williams. In his view, the dominant modern con-

ception of literature as an 'imaginative' or 'creative' mode of
writing, distinguished from other forms by its freedom from
the realm of fact, began to gather force early in the nine-
teenth century. In the eighteenth, he suggests, literature
could have been defined more broadly, and more helpfully,
as 'a group of written works of a certain level of seriousness,
capable of sustaining an attention that others could not'
(1979, p. 325). Although the generality of this statement
may render it imperfect as a definition – the criteria according to which a work may be judged to have attained 'a certain
level of seriousness' are not made entirely clear – in a sense
that is its virtue and its strength. For as Williams argues, the
modern emphasis on literature as the exclusive domain of
creativity and aesthetic response has had damaging consequences, leading on one hand to the abstraction of literature
from its social reality and, on the other, to a belief that it is
unnecessary to examine the processes of writing and composition of supposedly 'non-literary' works.

Williams's remarks have a number of implications for the
study of Burke. If we accept his claim that 'from the 19th
century onwards, the definition of literature has rested on
an ever firmer separation between imagination and reality,
fiction and fact' (ibid., p. 326), then it is clear that to read
Burke in terms of such a definition would be to falsify the
manner of his writing. It would involve the extraction of
passages which, taken in isolation, would be quite unrepresentative of his rhetorical art. To understand Burke it
is necessary to follow the interaction of different modes of
writing across the whole range of his work. Williams indicates
how this might be done in a passage in which he expresses his
dissatisfaction with the conventional opposition between
'factual' and 'imaginative' forms:

> Argument . . . can be distinguished from narrative or char-
> acterizing forms, but in practice certain forms of narrative
> (exemplary instances) or forms of characterization (this
> kind of person, this kind of behaviour) are radically em-
> bedded in many forms of argument. Moreover, the very
> fact of address – a crucial element in argument – is a
> *stance* (at times sustained, at times varying) strictly com-

parable to elements that are elsewhere isolated as narrative or dramatic. This is true even of the apparently extreme case, in which the stance is 'impersonal' (the scientific paper), where it is the practical mode of writing that establishes this (conventional) absence of personality, in the interest of the necessary creation of the 'impersonal observer'.   (1977, pp. 148-9)

In effect, Williams is arguing that conventions, received and determining forms of presentation and composition, radically shape every mode of writing. Narrative and character, the basic constituents of the novel and the drama, may also animate political writing, together with other non-fictional forms. The texts of Burke might almost have been designed as a test case for this argument. It would be possible to analyse Burke's diverse endeavours in terms of the formal elements which Williams describes. For instance, we might examine the use of narrative and characterisation in Burke's writings and speeches (the *Speech on American Taxation*, with its chronicle history of colonial policy, and its famous portraits of Townshend, Grenville and Chatham, would be a good example). Or we might look at Burke's assumption of a stance or *persona* both in his pamphlets and in formally 'objective' or 'impersonal' works like the *Reports of the Select Committee*. In the chapters which follow I explore some of these possibilities, extending a formal and rhetorical analysis to areas of Burke's writing which have generally been overlooked in literary study.

The account of Burke I have to offer remains a highly selective one. His complex Irish and Indian writings, together with other important texts, receive only cursory attention. For it is not my aim here to provide a fully authoritative critical and biographical study of Burke, but rather to examine some of the ways in which a political discourse such as his was constituted and put into effect.[2] Thus in the first part of the book I look at the rich and complex language in which Burke responds to events and argues his politics, annexing and combining terms, concepts and forms of address drawn from diverse modes of writing and thought. In the second part I investigate more minutely the methods of composition and delivery of a particularly durable form of political argument – the parliamentary speech. In the third part I undertake an historical and contextual reading of Burke's *Thoughts on the Cause of the Present Discontents*. The pamphlet debate on John Wilkes and the Middlesex Election is surveyed in some detail in order both to account for the distinctive features of Burke's tract and, more widely, to reach an understanding of the literary dynamics of a political crisis.

What this amounts to is an attempt to read Burke historically: to relate the 'external' history of politics and power to an 'internal' history of composition, convention and form. Studies of Burke have sometimes been criticised for paying insufficient regard to the particular circumstances which occasioned his writings. This criticism certainly carries weight when applied to some of the work produced in the 1950s. At that time there was a vigorous attempt to promote Burke's worth as a moral and political philosopher. Scholars such as Stanlis, Parkin and Canavan elevated the religious and ethical elements of his work above all others. They pictured him as a Christian statesman who throughout his career honoured the principles and pursued the logic of a natural moral law which transcended the political, socioeconomic and legal conditions of his period. It is true that these studies lack a sense of the social and political contexts of Burke's work. What has been less often recognised, and is perhaps more surprising, is that in celebrating the 'universal' relevance of Burke's writings they pay little heed to the particularity of the idioms, images and forms in which those writings are cast. These literary elements – the conventions of Burke's writing – are as 'historical' (though not necessarily as important) as the riots, revolutions, wars, schisms and scarcities which occupy so much of his attention. Conventions might be described as the socially and historically modifiable elements at the core of any literary practice. Literary scholarship has had much of importance to say about the conventions which have shaped the history of poetry, the drama and the novel. The study of these conventions has extended our understanding of the historical development and great internal complexity of literary forms. But because political writing has often been regarded as formally unproblematic, its conventions have generally gone undetected, or at least unexplained. The 'substance' of an argument is more often discussed than the style, stance or form of àddress in which it is communicated. It is with the conventions which inform Burke's political writings — with what might be called their literary-historical modes of existence — that I shall be primarily concerned in the following chapters.

PART ONE

The Languages of Politics

2

The Legal Idiom

'The thought of Burke', writes J. G. A. Pocock, '. . . is largely
an examination of what languages have been, and what
appropriately may be, employed in English political debate.'
(1971, pp. 25-6) The identification of these 'languages', the
various idioms which come into play in Burke's political
writing and which lend it its extraordinary range and effect,
remains an important task for those who wish to understand
his ideological and historical role. One major strand has been
unravelled by Pocock himself. In his study of the British cult
of the 'ancient constitution' (ibid., pp. 202-32) he highlights
Burke's reverence for the customs and precedents bound up
in common law. Burke's attitude towards law, and his use of
its idioms, can be understood in a number of ways. While
Pocock considers the common law to be one of Burke's
foremost political 'languages', others have found in his
writings a steady belief in a metaphysical framework of
Natural Law, in relation to which all secular legal systems
are held to be subordinate and declaratory. My own concern
is more rhetorical than jurisprudential. In what follows I
shall consider Burke's use of legal discourse as an element
in his art of persuasion. In his pamphlets and speeches he
turns to the law as an authoritative medium for political
argument, one which provides him with a set of judgments
and positions from which he can characterise and respond
to the most pressing political circumstances.

This manner of understanding and engaging in politics is
part of a larger pattern of thought and feeling. In the
eighteenth century the conventions and idioms of law are a
familiar component of texts of a literary character. Presented
as more than a naked instrument of power, the law appears

to define and inform the identities of individuals and the activities of social life. It is in the social commentary of the novel that this pattern is most marked. David Punter has observed that 'whereas the universe of the seventeenth-century romance was bounded and controlled by cosmic justice, reflected in already given quasi-mythic narrative structure, the universes of Defoe, Fielding, Radcliffe, Godwin are limited by various manifestations of human law' (1982, p. 47). It is possible to identify moments at which the old and new modes of seeing intersect. In Defoe's *Moll Flanders*, for instance, the institutions which enforce the criminal law perform the theological function once discharged by images of hell-fire and the like. An essentially social and secular landscape can still be experienced in religious terms. When Moll reports her first sight of Newgate prison, she interprets the experience within an overtly emblematical and Christian frame of reference:

> the hellish Noise, the Roaring, Swearing and Clamour, the Stench and Nastiness, and all the dreadful crowd of Afflicting things that I saw there; joyn'd together to make the Place seem an Emblem of Hell itself, and a kind of an Entrance into it.   (Defoe, 1971, p. 274)

As Douglas Hay remarks in his study of the eighteenth-century criminal law, 'The secular mysteries of the courts had burned deep into the popular consciousness, and perhaps the labouring poor knew more of the terrors of the law than those of religion.' (1975, p. 30)

The narratives of Fielding, in which the consciousness is more decisively secular and humanist, find an authoritative language in the law. In one sense they offer a criticism of the contemporary administration of justice, of an abuse of power which in *Joseph Andrews* can incarcerate the hero and heroine for the theft of a twig. In a less obvious, but perhaps equally important way, the law provides Fielding's novels with an imagery capable of organising fiction itself. The most cursory reading of *Tom Jones* would recognise it as a novel strewn with legal metaphor. Tom Jones is presented as the principal defendant, assisted or arraigned by counsel for the defence and prosecution, while the narrator himself is the magistrate who presides over events, sums up the evidence, and sits in judgment. At times the narrative strategies of the novel appear to be modelled on the procedures of a court of law. Thus a moral debate can be presented in the form of a 'Discussion . . . in the Court of Conscience' (Fielding, 1974, I, 316-20).

As one might expect, this familiarity with legal thinking and practice is reflected in much of the political writing of the period, Burke's included. But it would be inaccurate to describe Burke's approach to politics, at least in his earlier works, as *legalistic*. His writings on America, in particular, are strongly opposed to the kind of thinking which understands political issues as problems of abstract legal right. In the *Letter to the Sheriffs of Bristol* (1777), for instance, he distinguishes between the duties of those who make law and the functions of those who interpret or enact it:

> legislators ought to do what lawyers cannot; for they have no other rules to bind them, but the great principles of reason and equity, and the general sense of mankind. These they are bound to obey and follow; and rather to enlarge and enlighten law by the liberality of legislative reason, than to fetter and bind their higher capacity by the narrow constructions of subordinate artificial justice.
> (III, 144-5)

This is essentially the position Burke had developed in his published speeches on America. An over-legalistic approach to political affairs was seen there as incompatible with the principles of good government. Thus the determination of Lord North's ministry to prosecute the colony of Massachusetts as if it were an individual possessed with criminal intent was condemned by Burke as ineffectual, unstatesmanlike and politically inept. It was the response of pettifoggery rather than statecraft. Reiterating his opposition to the American penal acts of 1774, Burke declared in the *Speech on Conciliation* that

> It looks to me to be narrow and pedantick, to apply the ordinary ideas of criminal justice to this great publick contest. I do not know the method of drawing up an indictment against an whole people. (III, 69)

An expansive survey of the commerce, finance, education, religion and manners of the inhabitants of America, discursive in style and blessed with a characteristic rhetorical sweep, the *Speech on Conciliation* is opposed, even at a level of its methods and form, to a 'narrow and pedantick', excessively legalistic, conception of affairs of state.

At the same time Burke's political writing remains deeply versed in the language and practice of the law. They are understood as essential elements in the political culture of his time. This is evident even in the *Speech on Conciliation* when, in proposing the resolutions which were the formal object of the speech, Burke is careful to adopt the forms and conventions of the laws of parliament. Addressing the House, he claims to speak in 'the language of your own ancient acts of parliament', for

> Determining to fix articles of peace, I was resolved not to be wise beyond what was written; I was resolved to use nothing else than the form of sound words; to let others abound in their own sense; and carefully to abstain from all expressions of my own. What the law has said, I say. In all things else I am silent. I have no organ but for her words. This, if it be not ingenious, I am sure is safe.

> (III, 94-5)

The style and even the thought of an individual give way at this point to the public, august and long-sanctioned discourse of the law. In this usage, and in many similar instances in Burke's writings, the law is not simply a coercive instrument applicable only to those actions which threaten the security of the state. It is more than a series of statutes designed solely to protect existing property rights. As a customary form of address, a set of definitions, and a fund of imagery, the law is a richly traditional medium for political argument. More than an agent of social control, it is one of the major languages of politics.

A good deal of Burke's oratory is, of course, explicitly forensic in form. The painstaking research into the affairs of the East India Company, conducted in the cramped committee rooms of the House of Commons, was ultimately presented in Westminster Hall, to the highest court in the land.

There the House of Lords, sitting in its judicial capacity, heard Burke and his fellow-managers deliver a formal legal indictment: the impeachment of Warren Hastings. A considerable — if not the best-known — proportion of Burke's collected writings is made up of the juridical apparatus of the impeachment: articles of charge, speeches for the prosecution, and so on. But a good many of Burke's tracts which are not directly legal in purpose are themselves written according to legal or quasi-legal conventions. Occasionally this formal relationship between legal and political discourse is apparent in the title of a particular text. The *Appeal from the New to the Old Whigs* (1791) is a case in point, a defence of Burke's political conduct heard before a tribunal of contemporary readers, above whom, as the title suggests, the Whig grandees of the Revolution settlement sit as the final court of appeal. In this pamphlet Burke adopts a familiar rhetorical strategy. Introducing a legal metaphor which allows him to conduct his own defence in an apparently impersonal manner, he writes in the guise of an attorney who has been hired to argue his client's case:

It is certainly well for Mr. Burke that there are impartial men in the world. To them I address myself, pending the appeal which on his part is made from the living to the dead, from the modern Whigs to the antient. (VI, 75-6)

It is a tactic of impersonation which he sustains throughout the *Appeal*.

In this mode of writing there is no doubt a trace of Burke's own experience of the law (he studied at the Middle Temple in the early 1750s) and, more immediately, of the legislative procedures of parliament itself. In his capacity as private secretary to Lord Rockingham, Burke was often required to draw up formal addresses, petitions, parliamentary resolutions, and the like. I have already suggested that Burke's own pamphlets may adopt the quasi-legal form of such transactions, a strategy to which he resorts most frequently in his writings of the 1790s. The *Observations on the Conduct of the Minority* (1793) — a title which seems to promise a detached review of politics, couched in the idiom of a statesman — is in fact drawn up as a legal indictment of Fox's parliamentary conduct. Burke's fifty-four 'objections' to the activities of the New Whigs are framed, listed and numbered just as the articles of charge against Warren Hastings had been. An early and unauthorised edition of the *Observations* was even advertised as 'Containing Fifty-Four Articles of Impeachment against the Right Hon. C. J. Fox'. There is a tendency for Burke to characterise diverse political events according to a common vocabulary of crime and accusation. In *Thoughts on French Affairs* (1791) the radicals of France, as venal, in Burke's opinion, as the officers of the East India Company, are upbraided in the language which had brought Hastings himself to trial. In either case the indictment is one of avarice and corruption. Condemning the Jacobins for a Hastings-like ambition, Burke fuses the politics of France and Bengal in a single metaphor. 'A bribe,' he charges, 'great without example in the history of the world, was held out to them — the whole government of a very large kingdom.' (VII, 21)

This manner of presenting politics — this use of judicial language, imagery and address — is never a purely 'formal' affair. It corresponds in some way to the ideological character of each crisis Burke was seeking to understand and resolve. Thus Burke's advocacy of legal reprisal, and his assumption of a punitive style of address, become more marked in the writings on India and France. It is as if the *persona* of the parliament man, which had been dominant in the earlier works, has given way to the guise of the magistrate, a change which involves a distinct modulation of voice, gesture and attitude. As O'Gorman points out, 'Burke's earlier Whig theories of limited government tended to give way in the 1790s to an emphasis on the powers of state.' (1973, p. 139) Consequently there is less concern with law as the cement of the constitution and the guarantee of liberty than with executive justice as the means of quelling dissent and maintaining order.

In other words, Burke tends increasingly to think of political crises as if they were primarily problems of legal enforcement. Unwilling to conceive of the commonwealth itself as criminal, he elects to prosecute certain of the agents within it, those individuals whom he holds responsible for administrative malpractice and the onset of civil commotion.

In a letter of January 1786 he declared that

> As to the Gentlemen who serve in India, as a *body*, I have
> nothing to say to them; because I have nothing to say to
> men in *bodies*. I attach myself to the guilty, where alone
> guilt can lie, *individually*. . . .   (*Corr.*, V, 256)

Thus in the parliamentary orations on *Fox's East-India Bill*
(1783) and the *Nabob of Arcot's Debts* (1785) the criminal
agents within the body politic are identified as Warren
Hastings and Paul Benfield. In a sense these political speeches
are preliminary statements of — indeed, rehearsals for — the
impeachment proceedings themselves. Political discourse contains within it the material for a detailed recitation of crime.

As a means of dealing with the affairs of the East India
Company, this approach may seem entirely appropriate; but
when applied to a crisis of the magnitude of the French
Revolution it has the effect of limiting Burke's historical
understanding and of inhibiting his political response. In his
Remarks on the Policy of the Allies (1793) Burke reiterates
his belief that 'the body and mass of the people never ought
to be treated as criminal' and adds that 'This is one of the
few fundamental and unalterable principles of politicks.' And
yet he is equally emphatic that none of 'the leaders of jacobin
clubs . . . should escape a punishment suitable to the nature,
quality and degree of their offence, by a steady but a measured justice' (VII, 190, 192). The indictment of individual
agents is indeed a feature of Burke's writings on the French
Revolution. Condorcet, Lafayette, Sieyès and Brissot, or, on
the domestic front, Priestley, Paine and Gordon, are charged
with inciting the subversion of the state. More often, however,
Burke's writ is directed against larger associations of men.
Constitutional societies and Jacobin clubs are denounced in
a legal vocabulary which depicts their members as a con-
spiratorial 'banditti', preying on an uncomprehending and
helpless people. Thus in the *Letter to a Member of the
National Assembly* (1791) Burke claims that 'the powers
and policies' of the Jacobins

> are not those of great statesmen, or great military com-
> manders, but the practices of incendiaries, assassins, house-

breakers, robbers, spreaders of false news, forgers of false orders from authority, and other delinquencies, of which ordinary justice takes cognizance.... They act more in the manner of thieves who have got possession of a house, than of conquerors who have subdued a nation. (VI, 64-5)

Such allegations read more like a digest of Blackstone's *Commentaries* than a classical specimen of political prose. Refusing to afford the Jacobins the conventional courtesies of diplomacy, or even party politics, Burke figures them as a gang of revolutionary outlaws. Increasingly, in his anti-Jacobin writings, Burke adopts this vindictive and magisterial voice. Indeed, in the *Letters on a Regicide Peace* (1796-97), perhaps the most punitive of all his works, Burke invokes all the rigours of the Black Act against the revolutionary senators of France. He refutes the suggestion that the French constitution of 1795 had ushered in a more moderate phase in the revolution. Far from it. The representatives of the Directory are the same 'bold brave banditti' of old, hard-hearted Jacobins decked out in unaccustomed finery. As such they are no better than felons in disguise, assassins and housebreakers masquerading in senatorial garb. They should therefore be subject to the full force of Whig justice:

The Parisians, (and I am much of their mind) think that a thief, with a crape on his visage, is much worse than a bare-faced knave; and that such robbers richly deserve all the penalties of all the black Acts. (IX, 48)

The Black Act itself, as Blackstone tells us, was 'occasioned by the devastations committed in Epping forest, near Waltham in Essex, by persons in disguise or with their faces blacked'.[1] Directed against criminal gangs alleged to have plundered the king's forests, this statute, as Thompson (1975) relates, introduced over 250 capital offences. In this sense it virtually constituted a penal code in its own right. For Burke's purposes it is both an instrument of discipline and a legal metaphor which can be exploited and explored in political writing.

In this reference to the Black Act, Burke recalls the penal legislation introduced and extended in the early years of the Hanoverian Whigs. Such overt and uncritical demands for legal redress are characteristic of his counter-revolutionary writings. It is almost as if in the periodic domestic disquiet of the reign of George I Burke finds a precedent for the more serious crises of the 1790s. The pressure of the French Revolution gives rise to a political discourse which marshals a coercive imagery within an increasingly legalistic framework. But neither Burke's politics nor his writings always shared this structure. As late as 1789 he declared in parliament that he considered 'the whole system of the penal laws in this country' to be 'radically defective'. Promising that he would 'continue to resist their intended multiplication', he 'recommended a revision of the whole criminal law, which, in its present state, he thought abominable'. In many cases, he added, 'a civil was preferable to a criminal remedy'.[2]

In the *Letters on a Regicide Peace*, however, this position is transformed. Even the civil law is found to have coercive potential. It is on an analogy drawn from civil precepts, for instance, that Burke's proposals for military intervention in France are justified. In an elaborate disquisition he explores in detail the ways in which legal terminology might be used in political argument and for the definition of a political object. The analogy which Burke is intent on developing is one which will compare the political struggle against France with the conduct of a civil lawsuit. He reminds us that

> It has ever been the method of publick jurists to draw a great part of the analogies on which they form the law of nations, from the principles of law which prevail in civil community. Civil laws are not all of them merely positive. Those which are rather conclusions of legal reason, than matters of statutable provision, belong to universal equity, and are universally applicable. Almost the whole praetorian law is such. There is a *Law of Neighbourhood* which does not leave a man perfect master on his own ground. When a neighbour sees a *new erection*, in the nature of a nuisance, set up at his door, he has a right to represent it to the judge; who, on his part, has a right to order the work to be staid; or if established, to be removed. On this head the parent law is express and clear; and has made many wise provisions, which, without destroying, regulate and restrain

the right of *ownership*, by the right of *vicinage*. No *innovation* is permitted that may redound, even secondarily, to the prejudice of a neighbour.   (VIII, 185-6)

Burke's emphasis on the word 'innovation' is not accidental. A term with powerful (and, for Burke, pejorative) political associations, it clinches the analogy, allowing him to proceed as if the principles of civil law and grand diplomacy were strictly comparable. This is a claim we may wish to contest. Burke's general point, that Jacobin France is answerable to the community of Europe for its actions, is certainly an important one. But the language he adopts is somehow inadequate to its object. Legalistic in character, it dulls the sense of crisis which the *Letters* were designed to inflame. Burke was no doubt aware of this problem himself. For, having pursued the analogy relentlessly, he effects an abrupt change in tone. His learned disquisition on law gives way to an altogether more vindictive and vulgar form of abuse:

> In describing the nuisance erected by so pestilential a manufactory, by the construction of so infamous a brothel, by digging a night-cellar for such thieves, murderers, and house-breakers, as never infested the world, I am so far from aggravating, that I have fallen infinitely short of the evil.   (VIII, 188)

The transition from an abstruse legal discourse to this extravagant and emotional piece of rhetoric is not an easy one. One senses here (and elsewhere in the counter-revolutionary writings) the difficulty Burke experienced in finding an idiom which would sufficiently engage his audience, do justice to the complexities of the occasion, and satisfy his own overwhelming feelings of crisis.

Burke's use of the civil law in political argument illustrates some of these difficulties. For to compare the creation of the revolutionary French state to the erection of a 'nuisance' likely to offend the sensibilities of a landowner is to risk a descent into bathos. It is to the principles of civil law that the man of property has resort when his estate is threatened by a rival claim. Burke himself was involved in such a lawsuit in the summer of 1774, when an 'insolent neighbour' claimed the rights to a wooded lane that bounded his farm (*Corr.*, III, 11-12). His application of a 'law of neighbourhood' to the conduct of international affairs seems to have more in common with the language of this local dispute than with the sagacious generalities of the opening paragraphs of the *Letters on a Regicide Peace*. I see this discrepancy as more than an incidental lapse in Burke's response to the crisis of Jacobinism. For there is a curious sense of instability, a characteristic unevenness of tone, in many of his writings of the 1790s. At one level, the French Revolution is apprehended as an event on an apocalyptic scale. At another, it is regarded as a derisory criminal act, demanding the exertion of a discipline both local and severe. Address and tone shift from the reflective to the executive. At his most impassioned, Burke will condemn the Jacobins for a truly luciferian ambition. Replete with 'the cold malignity of a wicked spirit', these disciples of 'the principle of evil himself' (VIII, 56) have 'made a schism with the whole universe' (VIII, 184) – an infernal phrase which suggests that if the revolutionary crisis is to be resolved it will be a metaphysical rather than a political transaction. Almost at once, however, Burke will revert to the language of criminal accusation and invoke those ordinances of the law by means of which the magistrate is empowered to arrest the agents of civil strife.

In the post-war history of Burke scholarship the first of these 'languages' has often been stressed. 'Natural Law' interpreters of Burke have identified him as, above all, a Christian statesman who owes his pre-eminent position in the history of English political thought to the grandiose, prophetic and 'philosophical' manner of his anti-Jacobin writings. Yet Burke's liking for an imagery and address drawn from legal practice suggests that his rhetoric often has extremely local objectives. At many points political thought will be presented in a language dedicated to the anticipation, prevention and suppression of felony and riot. In the processes of political writing that language may be used to forge a link between local manifestations of disorder and the great public issues of the day. The particular occasion of the *Thoughts on the Cause of the Present Discontents* (1770), for example, was the controversy concerning the Middlesex Election and the civil disturbances which followed it. Reflecting on this material, Burke raises it to a certain level of generality, transforms it into an historical review of cabinet government, and ultimately fashions it into the 'political Creed of our Party' (*Corr.*, II, 136).

It is the purpose of the *Thoughts* to reject coercive and penal measures against the discontented in favour of the purgation of a malignant form of government. We have already seen, however, that in many parts of the Indian and counter-revolutionary writings Burke is determined to present political issues as problems of legal enforcement. Those passages which depict the Jacobins as rioters, assassins and felons have a good deal in common with one of Burke's earlier 'executive' works, the memorandum entitled *Some Thoughts on the Approaching Executions*. In this short tract Burke addresses himself to immediate problems of crime and punishment, and in so doing enunciates a set of terms and principles which he will later apply to the loftiest affairs of state. The executions to which Burke refers in his title are those which were to follow the Gordon Riots of 1780. In the most obvious sense these disturbances, partly provoked by Sir George Savile's measure for Catholic relief, were of a violently sectarian character. But they also challenged the authority of parliament and threatened or destroyed Newgate and the Bank of England, those most august of Whig institutions. Burke's recommendations on this occasion are notable for their combination of lenity and restraint. Punishment itself must observe a kind of decorum if order is to be restored. Judging the people to be 'in a very critical disposition, and such as ought to be managed with firmness and delicacy', Burke rejects both 'injudicious severity' and 'weak measures, on the part of Government'. In his determination to strike a judicial balance, he weighs the abatements of mercy against an exemplary and well-regulated terror. In Burke's view, the executions 'ought to be such as will humble, not irritate' the people. 'Nothing will make Government more awful to them than to see, that it does not proceed by chance or under the influence of passion.' (IX, 269)

Burke's plea for mercy, proposed and argued with eloquence throughout the pamphlet, is certainly worthy of note.

Equally significant are his demands for precision in the deciding of a sentence and his awareness of execution itself as a spectacle. Estimating that a maximum of six of the rioters of 1780 ought to be hanged, Burke seems intent on refining punishment into a logical art, on presenting it as a regular and orderly performance. The six condemned, he suggests, 'ought to be brought out and put to death, on one and the same day, in six different places, and in the most solemn manner, that can be devised' (IX, 270). In this way punishment will be inflicted with a kind of dramatic economy. Indeed, Burke writes of public execution as if it were primarily a theatrical experience. His interest in the theatre had been evident in the early dramatic criticism of the Dublin *Reformer* and in the remarks on tragedy he had included in the *Philosophical Enquiry into the Origin of Our Ideas of the Sublime and Beautiful*. Perhaps drawing on this critical discourse, he remarks in *Some Thoughts on the Approaching Executions* that 'I have ever observed, that the execution of one man fixes the attention and excites awe; the execution of multitudes dissipates and weakens the effect.' (IX, 271) While urging the need for a classical clarity and precision, Burke continually finds his concept of punishment caught up in images of a sublime and awe-inspiring theatre. Anxious to avoid unnecessary severity, he nevertheless remains convinced that the authority of government depends upon the sense of dignity and power it can project.

I have dwelt on this admittedly minor work because in its strictly judicial proposals Burke works out a language which he will later use to characterise the most momentous political events. Its images and ideas of punishment are the local manifestations of a more general political theory. Arguing that outright coercion would be inappropriate (indeed counter-productive) in the present crisis, Burke declared to Sir Grey Cooper that 'Justice and Mercy have not such opposite interests as people are apt to imagine.' (IX, 266) Similar pronouncements, delivered in an equally sagacious tone, abound in Burke's writings of the 1790s. In the *Remarks on the Policy of the Allies*, for example, he considers at some length the principles involved in restoring order in France. Justice, he declares again, must be administered with humanity, with a quality of mercy which will distinguish the Whig from the Jacobin. To his way of thinking, those guilty of civil or political crimes ought to be spared. Only those who have 'rebelled against the law of nature, and outraged man as man' (VII, 191) should be punished — a grandiloquent and apparently merciful decree which in practice ushers in a most punitive policy. For Burke remains strongly opposed to any general act of indemnity. A large number of Jacobins and radicals will be included among those to be prosecuted as rebels against human nature. Burke would not only act against the regicides but would punish other ideological adversaries, 'all men concerned in the burning and demolition of houses or churches, with audacious and marked acts of sacrilege and scorn offered to religion; in general, all the leaders of jacobin clubs' (VII, 192). Orders of crime are drawn up, degrees of offence classified, and cases worthy of acquittal or prosecution are identified. In this way Burke continually picks up the terms he had introduced in his memorandum of 1780. 'In all these punishments,' he urges,

> any thing which can be alleged in mitigation of the offence should be fully considered. Mercy is not a thing opposed to justice. It is an essential part of it; as necessary in criminal cases, as in civil affairs equity is to law. It is only for the jacobins never to pardon.   (VII, 192-3)

'Mercy is not a thing opposed to justice' — the repetition of this idea in unrelated contexts suggests that there may be a language of jurisprudence, a concept of legal and political authority, which binds together the apparently diffuse elements of Burke's career. The crisis of the French Revolution is often understood — like the Gordon Riots of 1780 — as an event which may be shaped, informed and finally encompassed by the discourse of the jurist. While in the *Reflections on the Revolution in France* (1790) Burke had made an effort to understand the revolutionary crisis in theoretical terms, in his later writings that crisis tends to be regarded more and more as an 'executive' problem, to be countered pragmatically, through military intervention and criminal justice, rather than intellectually, through social, political and economic analysis.

Burke's powerfully historical imagination allows him to apprehend and communicate the novelty and scale of the crisis; but he often responds to it in terms of the familiar legal apparatus of Whig rule. He turns to the model of the Black Act, recalls measures taken to repress civil discontent, or recommends mercy in the judicial form of the pardon. It is not, then, that he understands political issues as questions of abstract legal right. But he does see them, almost intuitively, within a legal framework, as questions of judicature and police. When the customs and institutions Burke most values come under threat, his mode of argument hardens into a rhetoric of coercion. He strikes an attitude, and speaks a language, which may seem new in his work but which had long been part of the Whig repertoire, part of the vocabulary of public order.

3

The Politics of Taste

*Your admiration of Shakspeare would be ill sorted indeed, if
your Taste (to talk of nothing else) did not lead you to a perfect abhorrence of the French Revolution, and all its Works.*
Burke to Edmund Malone, 5 April 1796

Until recently Burke's *Philosophical Enquiry into the Origin
of Our Ideas of the Sublime and Beautiful* (1757) could be
expected to receive at the most a bare mention in discussions
of his political thought. It was seen as an exception among
his writings, the sole product of his early and unfulfilled
literary ambition. It was thought of as more relevant to the
history of British aesthetics than to the development of
Burke's own outlook. More recently, however, the *Philosophical Enquiry* has been identified as the primary source
of ideas and attitudes which were to shape Burke's political
thinking throughout his life. His aesthetics and politics, it is
now often said, are intimately allied.[1] This new emphasis
reflects a more general readiness to extend the range of meanings and applications available to politics. The boundaries of
the 'political' have been revised so as to take in areas of
experience which lie well beyond the traditional political
spheres of statecraft and public affairs. If authority were
needed for this change, it is provided by Burke himself, in
his response to the French Revolution. The extreme urgency
of that response was prompted by his perception that more
was at stake than an alteration in a system of government. In
order to counter the threat of revolution, Burke touches on
a wide range of feelings and attachments, drawing his readers'
experience of a whole way of life into the arena of political
struggle.

Such appeals were based upon Burke's understanding of

the principles of human nature, principles which he had first laid down systematically in the *Philosophical Enquiry*. The aim of that work was not only to formulate aesthetic categories but also to put them on a 'natural' basis, to trace back our ideas of the sublime and beautiful to their origins in the mechanisms of sensation, perception and response. The *Philosophical Enquiry* can therefore be related to the political works which followed it both at the general level of category and concept and at the level of Burke's own perception, apprehension and presentation of particular political events. In a discussion of the first kind of relation Neal Wood has argued that 'Burke's two basic aesthetic categories, the sublime and the beautiful, inform and shape several of his fundamental political ideas'. He suggests that 'these aesthetic categories are a unifying element of Burke's social and political outlook' (1964, p. 42). Thus the pattern of authority I described in the preceding chapter finds a counterpart in Burke's aesthetics. In the well-tempered state the principles of justice and mercy will act in unison, but their modes of operation will remain quite distinct. In the realm of aesthetics the *Philosophical Enquiry* presents a similar set of oppositions. Elements of aesthetic experience are classified in two categories, according to the ideas of the sublime and beautiful. This division in aesthetics is not simply analogous to the one which governs social and political life. For the sublime and beautiful are, by virtue of their definition, based on the relationship between the individual and society. The sublime, Burke tells us, is associated with those 'passions which belong to SELF-PRESERVATION'; it is the expression in aesthetics of our fears for our own safety. The beautiful, on the other hand, is associated with 'the passions which belong to SOCIETY'; it is the expression of our sociality and sympathy (*PE*, pp. 38, 40).

Most of the *Philosophical Enquiry* is devoted to the detailed illustration of the various physical and psychological sources of the sublime and beautiful — terror, obscurity, vastness, smoothness, delicacy, sweetness, and so on. These qualities, as we shall see, find a place in the language and imagery of Burke's political writing. But even in the course of the *Philosophical Enquiry* itself Burke will occasionally afford them a political significance. Perhaps the most striking instance occurs in the section entitled 'Power' (*PE*, pp. 64-70). Admitting that he knows 'of nothing sublime which is not some modification of power', Burke proceeds to examine power in both its natural and political manifestations. In the former, as found in the lion, the tiger and the wolf, it is awe-inspiring and terrible. Likewise, 'The power which arises from institution in kings and commanders, has the same connection with terror. Sovereigns are frequently addressed with the title of *dread majesty*.' A few years earlier William Hogarth had remarked in his own æsthetic treatise, *The Analysis of Beauty*, that 'The robes of state are always made large and full, because they give a grandeur of appearance, suitable to the offices of the greatest distinction. The judge's robes have an awful dignity given them by the quantity of their contents. . . .' (1753, p. 30) In the *Philosophical Enquiry* Burke systematises this occasional semiotics of power. The range of qualities he associates with the sublime — terror, astonishment, reverence, admiration and awe — seems to anticipate the coercive style of authority he invokes in his counter-revolutionary tracts.

In this way the *Philosophical Enquiry*, projected as a treatise on the mechanisms of the sensibility, sometimes shifts its ground to take up moral, social and political issues. In section X of the third part these issues are brought together in a disquisition on the nature of virtue. Burke decides that, in effect, the virtues are of two kinds. Those which belong to authority and the power to command are described as 'sublime'. Those which operate in personal life, and consort with the means of charity, compassion and love, are defined as 'beautiful'. Although Burke's discussion of these virtues is organised on aesthetic principles, their relation to a legal and political structure of authority could hardly be more explicit:

Those virtues which cause admiration, and are of the sublimer kind, produce terror rather than love. Such as fortitude, justice, wisdom, and the like. Never was any man amiable by force of these qualities. Those which engage our hearts, which impress us with a sense of loveliness, are the softer virtues; easiness of temper, compassion, kindness and liberality; though certainly those latter are of less immediate and momentous concern to society, and of less dignity. But it is for that reason that they are so amiable. The great virtues turn principally on dangers, punishments, and troubles, and are exercised rather in preventing the worst mischiefs, than in dispensing favours; and are therefore not lovely, though highly venerable. The subordinate turn on reliefs, gratifications, and indulgences; and are therefore more lovely, though inferior in dignity. Those persons who creep into the hearts of most people, who are chosen as the companions of their softer hours, and their reliefs from care and anxiety, are never persons of shining qualities, nor strong virtues. It is rather the soft green of the soul on which we rest our eyes, that are fatigued with beholding more glaring objects.   (*PE*, pp. 110-11)

Here Burke not only affords his aesthetic categories a moral and social meaning, but also establishes a hierarchy among them in which the 'sublime' virtues take precedence over the 'beautiful'. The latter, however, are by no means useless in social life. As Wood (1964, pp. 52-7) argues, the 'beautiful' qualities (sympathy, affection, friendship, and the like) are the modes in which society, in most circumstances, is able to cohere. They appear to establish a series of 'lateral' alliances, while the political relations of the sublime are essentially those of subordination.

In a well-ordered society these virtues will be combined, for, as Burke tells us in his political tracts, justice and mercy have the same interests. It is in the aesthetics of the *Philosophical Enquiry* that Burke seems to develop this pattern of authority for the first time. In the second edition of the work (1759) he was at pains to point out that the sublime and beautiful are categorically distinct, and related in most cases only by way of opposition:

If the qualities of the sublime and beautiful are sometimes found united, does this prove, that they are the same, does it prove, that they are any way allied, does it prove even that they are not opposite and contradictory? Black and white may soften, may blend, but they are not therefore the same. (*PE*, pp. 124-5)

The final part of this remark is important. It is true that the conjunction of the two categories may culminate in the destruction of the weaker one, but it may also lead to modification and restraint:

> There is something so over-ruling in whatever inspires us with awe, in all things which belong ever so remotely to terror, that nothing else can stand in their presence. There lie the qualities of beauty either dead and unoperative; or at most exerted to mollify the rigour and sternness of the terror, which is the natural concomitant of greatness.
>
> (PE, p. 157)

In general Burke's aesthetic categories are rigidly, even mechanistically applied. It is his aim in the *Philosophical Enquiry* to determine what he calls 'the logic of Taste'. The passage I have just quoted does not in itself contradict this, but Burke leaves himself a little room for manoeuvre. Although in natural objects (and presumably in works of art) he dislikes the combination of sublime and beautiful qualities, he at least allows for the possibility of interaction. In an abstract concept such as society or the state, as opposed to physical objects of the kinds discussed in the *Philosophical Enquiry*, the functions of the sublime and beautiful virtues may even be complementary. In periods of stability the beautiful may act 'to mollify the rigour and sternness' of the magisterial sublime. But in extreme circumstances, when the state is faced by war and revolution abroad and by the threat of subversion at home, it must be allowed to exercise its powers unqualified and undiminished.

In this respect Burke's counter-revolutionary tracts (indeed, his political writings in general) might be read as an attempt to work out the respective roles of the sublime and the beautiful in politics. It is not, I think, too much to claim that Burke perceives the French Revolution in aesthetic terms. When it is experienced in its magnitude and its terror as a sublime event, the only effective response on the part of its opponents must itself be a politics and rhetoric in the grand style. In the *Letters on a Regicide Peace*, to which I shall refer throughout this chapter, a foremost concern is the stress on the national sensibility caused by the war against a Jacobinised France. Terror, in the *Philosophical Enquiry*, had been the quintessentially sublime emotion, one which 'robs the mind of all its powers of acting and reasoning' (*PE*, p. 57). Following the disasters which had dogged the campaign against France, Burke is anxious lest this fear should become the ruling passion in government and the nation at large:

> There is a courageous wisdom: there is also a false reptile prudence, the result not of caution but of fear. Under misfortunes it often happens that the nerves of the understanding are so relaxed, the pressing peril of the hour so completely confounds all the faculties, that no future danger can be properly provided for, can be justly estimated, can be so much as fully seen.   (VIII, 86-7)

Burke images this state of moral inertia as a paralysis of the organs of sensation. Such is the power and military might of the Revolution that 'The eye of the mind is dazzled and vanquished' (VIII, 87), a remark which again seems to have its basis in the aesthetics of the *Philosophical Enquiry*. For in the section entitled 'Light' (II, xiv) Burke observes that while brightness is generally less productive of the sublime than darkness is, 'such a light as that of the sun, immediately exerted on the eye, as it overpowers the sense, is a very great idea' (*PE*, p. 80).[2]

The French Revolution is one of those 'glaring objects' which subdue the organs of sight, an event capable of exciting sublime sensations — fear, astonishment and awe. But Burke does not wish us to respond to it as we would to an awe-inspiring work of art. The connection between the political and the aesthetic does not always run along a line of simple analogy. In the *Philosophical Enquiry* he describes a group of emotions (terror, astonishment, awe, and so forth) associated with self-preservation and excited by the immediate prospect of pain. He also devises a category of aesthetic experience called the sublime which implies a distancing from the source of those emotions: 'terror is a passion which always produces delight when it does not press too close' (*PE*, p. 46). As Paulson (1983) reminds us, it was not Burke's purpose in his counter-revolutionary writings to distance his readers from the revolutionary threat or to instil in them that sense of security upon which the true sublime depends. On the contrary, he mobilises a kind of rhetoric of terror in order to alert them to the perils of the situation.

Yet there are times, in his presentation of revolutionary events, when Burke falls back (perhaps without realising it) upon the effects of distancing he had described in the *Philosophical Enquiry*. Paulson may be thinking of this when he remarks that 'Burke could come to terms with the Revolution by distancing it as a sublime experience, even while denying its sublimity and realizing that it might not keep its "distance".' (1983, p. 67) Burke is inclined to frame his response to the Revolution in dramatic terms.[3] It is when he presents the Revolution as tragedy, as he does in one of the best-known passages in the *Reflections*, that the aesthetic distancing of the sublime comes into its own:

> when kings are hurled from their thrones by the Supreme Director of this great drama, and become the objects of insult to the base, and of pity to the good, we behold such disasters in the moral, as we should behold a miracle in the physical order of things. We are alarmed into reflection; our minds (as it has long since been observed) are purified by terrour and pity; our weak unthinking pride is humbled, under the dispensations of a mysterious wisdom. Some tears might be drawn from me, if such a spectacle were exhibited on the stage. I should be truly ashamed of finding in myself that superficial, theatrick sense of painted distress, whilst I could exult over it in real life.   (V, 157)

Pity of this kind, genuine enough in itself, is unlikely to issue in immediate political action, since it confirms Burke and his reader in their role as spectators. The aesthetic model — tragedy — brings with it a sense of the inevitability of revolution, fused with a Christian acceptance of its place in a divine plan beyond human comprehension.

More often, however, Burke exposes us directly to the source of the terror and fuels those passions he considers most likely to quell it. He insists that the Revolution has declared war on the beautiful and social virtues. This is the symbolic significance of the celebrated portrait of Marie

Antoinette in the *Reflections on the Revolution in France*. The desecration of the queen's person signals the end of an era in which the exercise of power had been tempered by a respect for the softer passions. Thus the Revolution is charged with precipitating the demise of

> all the pleasing illusions, which made power gentle, and obedience liberal, which harmonized the different shades of life, and which, by a bland assimilation, incorporated into politicks the sentiments which beautify and soften private society. . . .   (V, 151)

Burke's task in the *Reflections* and other pamphlets of the 1790s is to devise a course of political action, and a style of political writing, capable of countering this threat. He gives us an intimation of what this style might comprise in a letter he wrote to Lady Elliot in December 1787, praising her husband's recent speech in the impeachment of Sir Elijah Impey. In this letter, one of the few examples of detailed rhetorical criticism in Burke, Elliot's speech is particularly commended for its range of emotional effects:

> This well combined piece was so very affecting, that it drew Tears from some of his auditory, and those not the most favourable to his Cause. In Truth the whole came from the heart, and went to the heart. At the same time, in some parts, and towards the End particularly, it was something awful and even terrible. It was humanity, compelled, even by the gentleness and mildness of its Character, to pass a stern Sentence upon Cruelty and oppression. It was Abdiel rebuking Satan. Look at the passage in your Milton, and you will conceive something of the Effect.
> (*Corr.*, V, 369)

In this analysis Burke draws upon the psychological and aesthetic vocabulary of the *Philosophical Enquiry*. He describes a composition in which the beautiful passions give way, of necessity, to a rhetoric of the sublime, but which provide the emotional impulse behind the entire oration. Elliot's manner and tone move from pity (in the realm of the beautiful) to a sublime attitude of command ('something awful and even terrible'). Pity, an emotion which Elliot's speech would appear to have inspired in its audience, finds its most powerful expression in Burke in the portrait of Marie Antoinette. Indeed, it is arguable that in that passage sympathy spills over into the sentimental, where the object of pity is valued for its ability to raise that passion. Defending himself against Philip Francis's charge that the description of the queen was 'pure foppery', Burke refused to apologise for the sentimentality of the portrait. Instead he insisted that

> the recollection of the manner in which I saw the Queen of France in the year 1774 and the contrast between that brilliancy, Splendour, and beauty, with the prostrate Homage of a Nation to her, compared with the abominable Scene of 1789 which I was describing did draw Tears from me and wetted my Paper. These Tears came again into my Eyes almost as often as I lookd at the description. They may again.   (*Corr.*, VI, 91)

Yet however sincere this may have been as an initial response, in the long run it is scarcely an adequate riposte to the challenge of the Revolution. In spite of — perhaps because of — Francis's charge of 'foppery' and Thomas Paine's derisive dismissal of the 'weeping effect' of his 'tragic paintings' (1969, pp. 71-2), Burke's stance in his pamphlets of the 1790s is more often 'awful' and 'terrible' than gentle and mild. His writings are characterised less by sympathy, conciliation and love than by the more rigorous virtues of the sublime. He feels compelled to cast himself as a defiant and heroic Abdiel, engaged in an epic war against Jacobinism. If we follow the advice Burke had offered to Lady Elliot, and turn to the passage in Milton, we find Abdiel warning Satan to expect a similar shift in the exercise of power:

> That golden sceptre which thou didst reject
> Is now an iron rod to bruise and break
> Thy disobedience.   (*Paradise Lost*, V, ll. 886-8)

In his anti-Jacobin writings Burke, like Elliot, casts aside the golden sceptre, an emblem of mercy, and picks up the iron rod of justice.

The qualities and passions required to sustain this stance are those which distinguish Burke's fine (and neglected)

Letter to William Elliot (1795). Burke calls there for a return
to the principles of the sublime in government. Before 1789,
he recalls, society could be both sublime ('august') and lovely.
He claims that 'never was so beautiful and so august a spectacle presented to the moral eye, as Europe afforded the day
before the revolution in France' (a comment in which, as so
often, Burke presents a concept – the culture and polity of
the *ancien régime* – as a scene, object of sight, or work of
art). But in the subsequent crisis 'it was necessary that in the
sanctuary of government something should be disclosed not
only venerable, but dreadful. Government was at once to
shew itself full of virtue and full of force.' (VII, 362-3, 364)
Burke resolves to add his voice 'to draw down justice, and
wisdom and fortitude from heaven' (VII, 368), just those
virtues which, in the *Philosophical Enquiry*, he had declared
to be most characteristic of the sublime: 'Those virtues
which cause admiration, and are of the sublimer kind, produce terror rather than love. Such as fortitude, justice, wisdom, and the like.' (*PE*, p. 110)

So far I have argued that Burke's response to the French
Revolution is shaped by, if not precisely modelled on, the
aesthetics and psychology of the *Philosophical Enquiry*. The
term which links the social and aesthetic spheres, and on
which many of Burke's judgments turn, is *taste*. For taste is
the social ratification of the individual aesthetic response; it
carries with it a set of moral, social and even political standards. In the second edition of the *Philosophical Enquiry*
Burke included an introductory chapter 'On Taste' in which
he sought to demonstrate that the potential for a uniform
standard of taste exists in all human beings. In the 1790s,
moving into the realm of aesthetic judgment, he accuses the
Jacobins of having violated this standard. Their 'barbarous
philosophy', he declares in the *Reflections*, 'is destitute of
all taste and elegance' (V, 152). Later, in a more detailed
piece of analysis, it is on aesthetic grounds that Burke attacks
Rousseau, whom he regards as the preceptor of the Revolution. He objects not only to the alleged naivety of Rousseau's
social theory and the immorality of his personal conduct,
but also to his disorderly and incorrect mode of writing.
Thus, in the *Letter to a Member of the National Assembly*

(1791), we are told that

> Taste and elegance, though they are reckoned only among
> the smaller and secondary morals, yet are of no mean im-
> portance in the regulation of life. A moral taste is not of
> force to turn vice into virtue; but it recommends virtue
> with something like the blandishments of pleasure; and it
> infinitely abates the evils of vice. Rousseau, a writer of
> great force and vivacity, is totally destitute of taste in any
> sense of the word. . . . We certainly perceive, and to a
> degree we feel, in this writer, a style glowing, animated,
> enthusiastick; at the same time that we find it lax, diffuse,
> and not in the best taste of composition; all the members
> of the piece being pretty equally laboured and expanded,
> without any due selection or subordination of parts.
>
> (VI, 36-7, 39)

Burke's literary criticism confirms the opinion he had already
reached of Rousseau's morals and politics. The Genevan's
style is 'glowing, animated, enthusiastick' (terms which are
not in themselves positively complimentary); but it is also,
like his sexual conduct and moral outlook, 'lax' and 'diffuse'.
Moreover, this apostle of equality lack any sense of literary
decorum. His literary works, like his vision of society, are
composed 'without any due selection or subordination of
parts'.

   In this way Burke's standard of taste and criterion of the
'correct' in writing contribute to a broader political argument. In the *Letters on a Regicide Peace* this occasional
critique is developed into a thoroughgoing rhetorical analysis
of political texts. Burke quotes extensively from various
official notes and royal declarations, compares their differences in style and address, and considers the relationship
between literary form and political function. The royal
declaration of 29 October 1793 is for Burke a model text.
It states, with clarity and panache, the objectives of the war
against France. There can be no question for Burke of a
contradiction between form and content, between the
correct political position and the proper form of address.
Belligerent in its sentiments, the declaration is also, Burke
notes with approval,

the most eloquent and highly finished in the style, the most judicious in the choice of topicks, the most orderly in the arrangement, and the most rich in the colouring, without employing the smallest degree of exaggeration, of any state paper that has ever yet appeared.   (VIII, 133-4)

As such it is worthy of comparison with the declarations of the great Whigs of the reign of William III. It shares, for instance, the 'manly, spirited, and truly animating style' (VIII, 155) of an address to the Crown delivered in 1697 by a House of Commons which remained resolute after eight years of war with Louis XIV.

It is upon similarly stylistic grounds that Burke approves of the Downing Street 'note' of 10 April 1796, but in subsequent ministerial pronouncements he can discern nothing but disorder and passivity, a degeneration not only in the practice of diplomacy but in the language of politics itself. In the third of the *Letters on a Regicide Peace* Burke subjects two specimens of this decline – the 'declaration' of 27 December 1796 and the ministerial speech which followed it – to a sustained and critical analysis. The declaration, Burke insists, transgresses both the principles of rhetoric and the elementary rules of politics. His reading of the paper reveals a flaw in its structure, a disparity between the exordium and the peroration. The declaration opens with a stark but accurate history of the humiliations suffered by Lord Malmesbury and other English diplomats during the recent negotiations with France. According to Burke, rhetorical practice and conventional expectations demand that such an introduction should be followed by a resolution to prosecute the war with renewed vigour. He even goes so far as to suggest the form that such an exhortation might take. Casting Pitt in a sublime and heroic role, he provides him with a selection of patriotic lines from *Henry V*, a play often plundered for its store of bellicose, anti-Gallic sentiments. The minister, Burke proclaims,

is placed on a stage, than which no muse of fire that had ascended the highest heaven of invention, could imagine any thing more awful and august. It was hoped, that in this swelling scene . . . he would have stood forth in the form,

> and in the attitude of an hero. On that day, it was thought
> he would have assumed the port of Mars. . . .   (VIII, 292)

But the declaration itself, devoid of the true language of
statecraft, is unable to rise to the occasion. It cannot sustain
the sublime style. It concludes with a tame pledge to resume
negotiations at the earliest opportunity, notwithstanding the
humiliating rebuffs Britain had already received. 'This exordium,' laments Burke, reviewing the entire declaration in its
formal aspect, 'as contrary to all the rules of rhetorick, as to
those more essential rules of policy which our situation
would dictate, is intended as a prelude to a deadening and
disheartening proposition.' (VIII, 294-5) The communications
of the state are marred by a formal collapse which Burke
regards as a symptom of the enfeebled and, as he would have
it, 'effeminate' spirit of Pitt's administration.

While Burke often resorts to aesthetic judgments in his
political tracts, this attention to the language of diplomacy
and political debate is particularly marked. In a sense the
principles of rhetorical criticism provide the terms in which
that debate is conducted. We have seen how, in the third of
the *Letters on a Regicide Peace*, Burke examines various notes,
declarations and speeches, the products of 'official' discourse.
In the *Letter to the Earl Fitzwilliam* (the so-called 'fourth' of
the *Letters on a Regicide Peace*) he casts his critical eye on
the writings of one of his political opponents. In this case the
victim is Lord Auckland, the author of a pamphlet entitled
*Some Remarks on the Apparent Circumstances of the War in
the Fourth Week of October 1795*. In his reply to Auckland,
whose pamphlet recommended the merits of peace with
France, Burke again introduces aesthetic criteria into the conduct of political argument. Auckland's work is ridiculed for
the unnecessary pedantry of its title, and for a political
passivity which scars its very sentence structure. Like the
later 'declaration' of 1796, which Burke discusses in the third
of the *Letters*, it is unable to emulate the grand style, declin-
ing, within the space of a sentence, from the heroic to the
banal:

> In the very womb of this last sentence, pregnant, as it
> should seem, with a Hercules, there is formed a little bant-

ling of the mortal race, a degenerate, puny parenthesis, that totally frustrates our most sanguine views and expectations, and disgraces the whole gestation. (IX, 82)

There is a powerful fusion here of detailed textual criticism, classical allusion and passionate political conviction. Burke is evidently as much concerned with the style as with the substance of Auckland's argument. Indeed, he regards them as inseparable. It is at such moments that he makes his most explicit statements about the relationship between politics and language. Denouncing Auckland's tract as a travesty of a once dignified form of address, he exclaims despairingly:

Would that when all our manly sentiments are thus changed, our manly language were changed along with them; and, that the English tongue were not employed to utter what our Ancestors never dreamed could enter into an English heart!   (IX, 83)

Burke believed that the French tongue had already undergone that kind of catastrophic change. In a letter to his 'kinsman', William Burke, who was working on a translation of an address by the Girondist, Jacques-Pierre Brissot, he remarked that 'the very Language of France has sufferd considerable alteration since you were conversant in French books, the way of thinking of the nation and the correspondent Official and publick Style is no longer the same' (*Corr.*, VII, 427). Developing this point in a preface he contributed to the translation, Burke observed of Brissot's work that 'There are some passages ... in which his language requires to be first translated into French, at least into such French as the academy would in former times have tolerated.' Like his predecessor Rousseau, Brissot 'writes with great force and vivacity; but the language, like every thing else in his country, has undergone a revolution' (VII, 327).

This was not an altogether extravagant claim. As Higgonet (1980) has described, the revolutionary upheaval brought with it proposals for the transformation of the French language, both in its relationship with the numerous dialects of France and in its standards of orthography and grammar. Burke was peculiarly sensitive to such changes in language and forms of address. As an aesthetician and man of letters (as well as a statesman) he was quick to spot the currents of a cultural revolution. The French Revolution is perceived in his writings not only as a social and political upheaval but also as a revolution in taste. At the same time he detects a deterioration in the official style of the British state. Implicit in Burke's detailed and critical remarks on various state papers and political pamphlets is a conception of the correct mode of public address. In the recurrent crises of the 1790s, we gather, political writing and action should above all possess grandeur, inspire reverence, and command authority. What is required, as Burke tells us in the third of the *Letters on a Regicide Peace*, is 'the true, unsuborned, unsophisticated language of genuine natural feeling'. In order to illustrate the qualities of this language, so conspicuously missing from the 'declaration' of 1796, Burke alludes to various classes of artistic production and the relation they bear on the passions:

> Never was there a jar or discord, between genuine senti-ment and sound policy. Never, no, never did nature say one thing and wisdom say another. Nor are sentiments of elevation in themselves turgid and unnatural. Nature is never more truly herself, than in her grandest forms. The Apollo of Belvedere (if the universal robber has yet left him at Belvedere) is as much in nature, as any figure from the pencil of Rembrandt, or any clown in the rustick revels of Teniers.   (VIII, 295)

In this passage the Apollo Belvedere is seen to project the grandeur and dignity (if not the terror) which Burke had earlier associated with the sublime. It is a figure capable of inspiring those 'sentiments of elevation' which he considers to be requisite at this juncture for purposes of public address. In his *Discourses on Art* Sir Joshua Reynolds seems to agree with Burke that the Apollo is an example of the 'grand style' of sculpture (1959, pp. 151, 178). Rembrandt, on the other hand, is criticised for his 'narrow conception of nature', for his adherence to a mode of portraiture based on particularities rather than on the 'universal', 'central' forms of the Grand Style (ibid., p. 162). Teniers, though praised for his 'elegance and precision', is a representative of a lesser school of painting, one which chooses to confine its energies to 'low and confined subjects' (ibid., pp. 109, 51). The aesthetic categories of Reynolds and Burke do not always coincide, but in this case their judgments seem compatible.

Reynolds was himself fond of portraying his subjects in grand and epic attitudes. In what has been described as his 'noblest portrait' he depicts a shipwrecked Admiral Keppel, the great naval commander, friend of Burke, and prominent Rockingham Whig, in a pose which 'is roughly that of the Apollo Belvedere, reversed and very slightly modified' (Waterhouse, 1941, pp. 9-10). It is to another of Reynolds's heroic portraits of Keppel that Burke alludes in the closing pages of the *Letter to a Noble Lord*. Concluding his invective against the Duke of Bedford, Burke reflects upon his own retirement from public life and his withdrawal to his estate in Beaconsfield:

> It was but the other day, that on putting in order some things which had been brought here on my taking leave of London for ever, I looked over a number of fine portraits, most of them of persons now dead, but whose society, in my better days, made this a proud and happy place. Amongst these was the picture of Lord Keppel. It was painted by an artist worthy of the subject, the excellent friend of that excellent man from their earliest youth, and a common friend of us both, with whom we lived for many years without a moment of coldness, of peevishness, of jealousy, or of jar, to the day of our final separation. (VIII, 63-4)

Burke introduces the portrait of Keppel almost casually, as he describes the melancholy though not entirely unpleasant task of unpacking his gallery. The passage is written in a style of resigned and reflective intimacy, one to which Burke often resorts in his final works. And yet, in spite of the apparent artlessness of its mode, the passage is as rhetorical as any in Burke. His choice of the portrait of Keppel is purposeful. It was painted in 1779, in celebration of Keppel's acquittal at a famous court martial. On receiving the portrait from the admiral, Burke declared that his son, 'whenever he sees that picture... will remember what Englishmen, and what English seamen were, in the days when name of nation, and when eminence and superiority in that profession were one and the same thing' (*Corr.*, IV, 169). Depicting this military and political hero in his moment of triumph, the portrait is a political symbol rather than a mere item in the inventory of Burke's possessions. The allusion to Reynolds's picture prepares the way for the sustained panegyric on Keppel which will bring the *Letter to a Noble Lord* to a close. The grandson of a Dutchman who had accompanied William of Orange to England in 1688, Keppel is for Burke the perfect representative of a Whig aristocracy based on the Revolution settlement. He is the very embodiment of heroic, Old Whig values. Painted by Sir Joshua Reynolds (an artist with close Whig associations), and owned by Burke, this portrait of the Rockinghamite lord discloses the connections at the heart of political society. In the portrait of Keppel, politics and aesthetics come together in the concrete form of a political work of art.

4

The Triumph of Economy

Looking back over his parliamentary career in the *Letter to a Noble Lord*, Burke took particular pleasure in recalling his achievements in the field of political economy. He felt able to claim that the measures of economical reform which he had planned and introduced in the early 1780s had saved the state from the menace of innovation by redressing the grievances of a discontented people. Burke's feelings of pride were not entirely unjustified. Although he cannot be said to have made a significant contribution to the development of economic theory, he was more aware than perhaps any other statesman of his time of the need to elaborate a form of political argument which could express the interests of men of property in economic terms. In a number of his works it is primarily in the stance of a political economist that he addresses his audience and argues his political case. In so doing he speaks and writes in what is certainly one of his plainer styles. The language of economics is not presented as a language of confrontation or controversy; it is designed to appeal to our common sense rather than to play on our feelings. Perhaps it is for this reason that literary critics have in general found little of substance to say about Burke's economic writing, preferring to highlight his more splendid passages of persuasion, the fruitful ambiguities and marvellous excesses of his more combative prose. This preference is part of a more general tendency to limit the field of Burke's rhetoric to spectacular and theatrical episodes of the kind denounced by Paine in *Rights of Man*. The position I am trying to develop in this study, however, is that the entire body of Burke's writing is rhetorical in the sense that even the very plainest of the languages at his command has a place in his art of persuasion. If this is so, Burke's economic discourse, in its various forms, deserves to be read with the kind of attention usually reserved for set pieces like his celebrated portrait of Marie Antoinette.

It would be misleading to suggest that Burke's writings incorporate a single and self-contained mode of economic discourse. The objects and emphases of two of his major economic pronouncements, the *Speech on Oeconomical Reform* (1780) and the tract entitled *Thoughts and Details on Scarcity* (1795), are quite different, reflecting in part the different political circumstances in which they were conceived. At its broadest, Burke's political economy encompasses the whole range of functions associated with political administration and management. At its narrowest and most specialised, it involves a more abstract and systematic description of the elements of an agrarian capitalist economy. The rhetoric of these different strands of economic discourse will be examined, and their historical significance considered, in the sections which follow.

1. *The Survey of the State of the Nation*

Burke's celebrated rhetorical excursions are often sustained by a quieter mode of economic exposition which provides an empirical basis — a context of economic 'fact' — for the more pointed political argument. By supporting and feeding into the language of statecraft his economic writing contributes directly to a larger rhetorical design. The *Reflections on the Revolution in France* is famous for its fiercely polemical appraisal of the political situation in England, for its denunciation of radical organisations, and, most of all, for its portrait of Marie Antoinette. These celebrated passages occur early in what is, even by eighteenth-century standards, a pamphlet of extraordinary length. They are followed by a less spectacular historical and economic survey of the French state. This second part of the *Reflections* takes the form of an account and comparison of pre-revolutionary and post-revolutionary France, including its civil and religious apparatus, its constitution, its financial condition, and so on. Burke's object, we might say, is the *oeconomy* of the French state — 'oeconomy' here in its widest sense of an arrangement of parts or a disposition of forces. In his *Dictionary* (1755) Samuel Johnson defines 'economy' not only as (1) 'The management of a family' but also as (3) 'Disposition of things; regulation' and (5) 'System of motions; distribution of every thing active or passive to its proper place.' Eighteenth-century physicians could therefore speak of an 'oeconomy' of the body, the articulation of the skeleton and the interaction of the vital organs. The 'oeconomy' of a nation is manifest in its political institutions and in the relations between different social and economic forces.

Properly speaking, then, this 'oeconomy' includes both the political and what we should now call the 'economic' spheres of society. In the *Reflections* Burke's account of the economy (to revert to the modern orthography) of France performs a strategic function in a broadly 'political' argument. An economic survey of the condition of France in 1789 enables him to claim that the revolutionary upheaval was unjustified. 'Was the state of France so wretched and undone,' he asks, 'that no other resource but rapine remained to preserve its existence?' The refutation, together with supporting financial evidence, is to be found in the 'detailed exposition of the state of the French nation' (V, 219) provided by Jacques Necker, one-time French Director General of Finance, whose account Burke proceeds to summarise and extend. Necker's 'exposition', it appears, is not primarily concerned with the moral or political condition of the French people but with national questions of revenue, taxation and public credit — the themes and objects of political economy.

The form of writing which Burke adopts in this part of the *Reflections* might be described as a 'survey of the state of the nation'. It is a mode of economic exposition he practised throughout his career. It appears, for instance, in the title of one of his earliest pamphlets, the *Observations on a Late Publication, intituled, 'The Present State of the Nation'* (1769). Written in reply to William Knox's tract (the 'Late Publication' of the title-page), Burke's pamphlet sets out an alternative account of the state of the nation, one which employs economic criteria in order to demonstrate that the Rockingham administration of 1765 had been of signal service to the realm. While producing answers at odds with those of Knox, in practice Burke asks the same questions, or at least poses them in identical terms. In both cases the major points of reference are trade, excise, taxation, and the like. Burke casts his eye over the revenue and public credit, over accounts of manufactures and the price of provisions — those 'signs of national prosperity' (II, 77) which the political economist, like some financial augur, is required to interpret. For at this stage in its history political economy was an empirical practice, dependent more upon the skill and experience of the observer than upon the rigour of its concepts. The state of the nation is further to be estimated upon a view of its external features, most notable of which are its architecture, its types of cultivation and its manufactures. In the *Reflections* such features are the most powerful evidence Burke can muster of the opulence of pre-revolutionary France. The detailed accounts supplied by Necker are complemented by an economics based on the visual register of manifest signs of wealth. This economic method has a number of set procedures, determined by the character of its objects. It comprises a sequence of activities which provide the structure of the following effusion on the wealth of Bourbon France:

> when I consider the face of the kingdom of France . . .
> when I turn my eyes to the stupendous works of her ports
> and harbours . . . when I bring before my view the number
> of her fortifications . . . when I recollect how very small
> a part of that extensive region is without cultivation . . .
> when I reflect on the excellence of her manufactures and
> fabricks . . . when I contemplate the grand foundations of
> charity, publick and private; when I survey the state of all
> the arts that beautify and polish life; when I reckon the
> men she has bred . . . I behold in all this something which
> awes and commands the imagination. . . .   (V, 240-1)

As a statesman and economist it is Burke's task to scan the physiognomy of the state — 'the face of the kingdom' — to take note of the material evidence of its progress, as well as the minutiae of finance. In so doing he makes repeated use of metaphors of sight and observation: 'consider the face', 'turn my eyes', 'bring before my view', 'contemplate', 'survey', 'behold'. Although in his estimate of the condition of France Burke relies largely on accounts and records, in this passage he chooses to write in the style of a traveller recalling the experiences of a recent tour. There is indeed a close relationship between this form of empirical economic observation and the eighteenth-century genre of travel writing. One of the principal duties of the traveller in such works is to assess the wealth of the nation by describing the cultivation, commerce, population and architecture of its various provinces. Thus Defoe's famous *Tour* is more remarkable for its detailed comments on manufactures and inland trade than for its attention to the landscapes and antiquities of Britain. In the agrarian economics of Arthur Young the tour was the major mode of inquiry. And Samuel Johnson's great *Journey to the Western Islands of Scotland* (1775) is essentially a survey of the Scottish nation, an account of the culture and society of the Highland clans, much of which is presented in broadly economic terms.

Johnson's familiarity with the language, methods and preoccupations of political economy is evident throughout the *Journey* (and indeed in many of his other works). Compare, for instance, the following passages:

> Kelp is a species of sea-weed, which, when burnt, yields an alkaline salt, useful for making glass, soap, and for several other purposes. It grows in several parts of Great Britain, particularly in Scotland, upon such rocks only as lie within the high water mark, which are twice every day covered with the sea, and of which the produce, therefore, was never augmented by human industry. The landlord, however, whose estate is bounded by a kelp shore of this kind, demands a rent for it as much as for his corn fields.

> Their rocks abound with kelp, a sea-plant, of which the ashes are melted into glass. They burn kelp in great quantities, and then send it away in ships, which come regularly to purchase them. This new source of riches has raised the rents of many maritime farms; but the tenants pay, like all other tenants, the additional rent with great unwillingness; because they consider the profits of the kelp as the mere product of personal labour, to which the landlord contributes nothing. However, as any man may be

said to give, what he gives the power of gaining, he has certainly as much right to profit from the price of kelp as of any thing else found or raised upon his ground.

The first passage is from Adam Smith's *Wealth of Nations* (1776), the second from Johnson's *Journey* (Smith, 1976a, I, 161; Johnson, 1971, p. 81). There is no need to propose Johnson's text as a 'source' later developed by Smith, the latter being no doubt equally well acquainted with such features of the Highland economy. The more important point is that the same concerns, posed in broadly similar terms, are encountered in apparently diverse modes of writing, in Smith's *Wealth of Nations*, conventionally described as the founding text of modern economics, and in Johnson's travel book. The similarities of the passages on kelp are not confined to a mere coincidence of subject-matter. Not only do both Johnson and Smith note the growing economic importance of the seaweed, they also understand this as posing the same economic question: is kelp a 'natural' offering of the sea which may be appropriated, irrespective of existing property rights, by anyone willing to expend the necessary labour? Or is it a 'raw material' already subject to social ownership, and which would therefore be assessed in rent?

Economic concerns of this kind are by no means exceptional in Johnson's text. Struck by the primitive mode of cultivation still practised in many parts of the Highlands, and by the feudal social relations still apparent in the remnants of the Highland clans, he utilises economic terminology in order to measure the distance between Scottish and English production. On his arrival at each new village or island his inquiries will not be confined to the state of oral literature or the progress of education in the district, but will also take in local agricultural practices, the spread of money and exchange, the rate of ground rent, and so on. The literary strategy of the *Journey*, it would appear, is to forgo the grand moral statements of *Rasselas* and Johnson's essays — or at least always to ground them in the careful observation of social and economic life. The farm accounts of Col or a register of Highland rents may therefore find a place in the discourse of the travel book. Although these are hardly the weighty maxims or pithy declarations likely to attract the attention of literary criticism, they are central to the *Journey*'s style, objects and theme.

The conventions of sociological observation and economic assessment which I have just described play an important role in the rhetoric of the *Reflections*. In the survey of the French nation which Burke includes in that work substantial use of the procedures of political economy is made on at least four occasions: first, as we have seen, in his development of Necker's 'exposition' of the financial state of France; secondly, in his account of the transfer of church lands, a policy on which Burke offers 'a few thoughts', general reflections on the economic function of rent; thirdly, in his remarks concerning the personnel in charge of the *assignats*, 'the managers and conductors of this circulation'; lastly, in his critique of the French revenue and its administration (V, 219-45, 290-6, 340-50, 402-33). In the third of the *Letters on a Regicide Peace* the survey of the state of the nation appears in a more coherent form. Its function in the bellicose rhetoric of the *Letters* is made quite explicit. Burke provides a detailed and optimistic account of the condition of England in 1796 as evidence that she possesses sufficient resources to continue the war with France. Burke's argument that the wealth of the nation is increasing relies on data extracted from the reports of the finance committee of the House of Commons (VIII, 376-417). It is presented in the form of tables which chart the growing returns in taxation on various commodities and the healthy rate of investment in enclosures and inland navigation. In his concluding remarks Burke summarises the criteria he has used in this estimate of the condition of England:

> If then the real state of this nation is such as I have described ... if no class is lessened in its numbers, or in its stock, or in its conveniences, or even its luxuries ... on what ground are we authorized to say, that a nation, gamboling in an ocean of superfluity, is undone by want?   (VIII, 417-18)

This may not be the most exciting or alluring sequence in the *Letters on a Regicide Peace*, but its appeal to the reader's economic common sense is an essential part of the rhetoric Burke unfolds there.

2. *The Rhetoric of Economical Reform*

The mode of economic exposition I have just discussed underpins many of Burke's more memorable flights of rhetoric. It belongs to what Conor Cruise O'Brien has described, in an analysis of Burke's prose style, as his 'Whig manner: rational, perspicacious, business-like'. O'Brien distinguishes two other styles in Burke: the '"Jacobite": both Gothic and pathetic' and 'a peculiar kind of furious irony'. Of these three styles, only the 'Whig', he argues, is often found in its 'pure state'; in general the others are to some degree fused with it (1968, pp. 42-9). In my view, these different styles do not always coexist harmoniously in Burke's writing. At times they come into conflict and give expression to contradictory ideological forces. Thus when Burke speaks in the 'Whig' voice of a political economist, he may subject a particular literary style or attitude to the indignities of parody. Elsewhere in his work, however, the same manner of writing will be deployed unashamedly for the purposes of rhetorical appeal.

The object of Burke's *Speech on Oeconomical Reform* (1780) was to secure the independence of parliament by eliminating certain sinecures in the gift of the Crown. Burke's stance in the speech is that of a sound financial administrator. He employs the 'modern' idiom of political economy throughout. In its determination to offer the Crown estates for sale, and to abolish all 'medieval' royal offices, the speech is resolutely anti-feudal in tone. At various points in the speech Burke's businesslike exposition of this economic and administrative policy is enlivened by passages of irony and ridicule. In particular, he indulges in frequent parody of the 'Gothic' mode. For the Gothic gives rise to a pseudo-feudal sensibility which is offensive to the modern, rational and reforming spirit of political economy. Burke argues that the feudal division of the realm into semi-autonomous principalities, duchies and palatinates has been retained only in order to justify the creation of superfluous offices and the award of unnecessary pensions. In a recent case, he alleges, the administration of Lord North had granted a pension to one John Probert on the unlikely pretext that he had been appointed to improve the revenues of the obsolete 'principality' of Wales.

In this corrupt ministerial bungling Burke finds all the implausibilities of the most extravagant Gothic romance. John Probert, the instrument of Lord North and the hero of this romance, is likened to 'a knight-errant dubbed by the noble lord in the blue-ribbon, and sent to search for revenues and adventures upon the mountains of Wales'. 'Armed, and accoutred' for his expedition, he is figured ironically as the gallant knight — the *'Preux Chevalier'* — of the administration (III, 259-61).

The abuses to be eliminated by Burke's economical reform are likewise lacking in the conveniences of an age of reason. political economist, much of the expenditure of the royal household is anachronistic and wasteful, 'the cumbrous charge of a Gothick establishment' (III, 278). The royal residences are likewise lacking in the conveniences of an age of reason. Seats of prejudice and superstition, they are like the fortresses in which the absurdities of some hackneyed Gothic adventure are played out:

> Our palaces are vast inhospitable halls. There the bleak winds . . . howling through the vacant lobbies, and clattering the doors of deserted guard-rooms, appal the imagination, and conjure up the grim spectres of departed tyrants — the Saxon, the Norman, and the Dane; the stern Edwards and fierce Henries — who stalk from desolation to desolation, through the dreary vacuity, and melancholy succession of chill and comfortless chambers. (III, 278-9)

I have described how, in the survey of the state of the nation, the function of Burke's economic writing is mostly secondary and supportive. In the *Speech on Oeconomical Reform*, however, he raises this humble instrument of policy from its somewhat subordinate role and offers it a kind of literary tribute. His language becomes highly figurative; political economy becomes the object of metaphor, and almost of myth. In order to demonstrate its value, Burke draws the attention of the House to Necker's recent reform of the French financial system:

> The king's *household* — at the remotest avenues to which all reformation has been hitherto stopped, that household,

which has been the strong hold of prodigality, the virgin fortress which was never before attacked — has been not only not defended, but it has, even in the forms, been surrendered by the king to the oeconomy of his minister. . . . Oeconomy has entered in triumph into the publick splendour of the monarch, into his private amusements, into the appointments of his nearest and highest relations. Oeconomy and publick spirit have made a beneficent and an honest spoil; they have plundered, from extravagance and luxury, for the use of substantial service, a revenue of near four hundred thousand pounds.   (III, 240-1)

While it might appear that in this passage Burke's 'Whig' style has joined hands with his 'Gothic', it would be more accurate to say that the Whig has usurped the Gothic, captured its metaphors, and laid claim to its rhetoric. Burke celebrates the triumphant spirit of Oeconomy. It is personified as a champion who has conquered the feudal excesses of Louis XVI's court. That the passage should be cast in the form of a panegyric, or literary triumph, indicates the extent of Burke's ideological and rhetorical commitment to the cause of political economy.

Speaking as an economist, and exercising his talent for arguing in metaphor, Burke glories in the 'capture' of the royal palace of Louis XVI. But when, a decade later, this figure of speech was to be realised in fact, his literary response was quite different. While in the *Speech on Oeconomical Reform* John Probert is ridiculed along with the whole notion of the 'preux chevalier', in the *Reflections on the Revolution in France* the passing of the 'age of chivalry' is the theme of extended lamentation. The famous eulogy of Marie Antoinette is indeed the most 'Gothic' passage in the whole of Burke. For there it is the downfall of a court and its retinue, the decline of 'a nation of gallant men . . . a nation of men of honour and of cavaliers' (V, 149) that Burke regrets. The 'preux chevalier', the royal household and the remnants of the feudal establishment are now objects of Burke's tender regard rather than items on his agenda of reform. This muchanthologised passage (which is in many ways unrepresentative of the *Reflections*) is quite explicitly set into place as a protest against the tyranny of a rational economics. For according to Burke, the 'age of chivalry' has been displaced by an era of the economic, over which not courtiers but 'sophisters, oeconomists, and calculators' will preside. Commerce, trade and manufactures, the organs of wealth which in Burke's own economic discourse are of the very first importance, can now be described as the fetishes of the irreligious, 'the gods of our oeconomical politicians' (V, 155).

It is not surprising, in view of such pronouncements, that contemporary commentators should often have found the outlook of the *Reflections* to be inconsistent with Burke's earlier thinking. The diarist Nathaniel Wraxall saw the work as a kind of political recantation in which Burke had broken with the ideology of economical reform. Wraxall found himself in sympathy with Burke's later position. He was willing to concede that the sinecures which Burke's measures of reform had suppressed may at the time have appeared 'exceptionable or unnecessary, yet, as carrying us back in imagination to the reigns of the Tudors by whom they were instituted, [they] diffused over the throne itself a Gothic grandeur, calculated to protect and to perpetuate the sanctity of the monarchical office' (Wraxall, 1884, II, 285-6). What Wraxall recognises here, and what he felt Burke's programme of economical reform had put at risk, is the ideological power of images of hierarchy and tradition. In the pronounced Gothicism of the early parts of the *Reflections* Burke harnessed that power to the full. Central to his argument there is the doctrine of prescription: the constitution, he argues, has been handed down from generation to generation in a manner analogous to the inheritance of a family estate. It therefore has the legitimacy both of a 'natural' process and of a legal right. The force of Burke's argument here rests less on its quality as logic than on its appeal as ideology and myth. The antiquity, continuity and authority of the British constitution are not so much demonstrated as evoked — presented not as a set of abstract propositions but in a powerful sequence of metaphors, analogies and Gothic motifs. Thus in asserting that the liberties of the subject are enjoyed by virtue of tradition rather than natural right, Burke adopts the language of a genealogist or herald, thrilled to discover a lineage which runs back unbroken to feudal times:

our liberty . . . carries an imposing and majestick aspect. It
has a pedigree and illustrating ancestors. It has its bearings
and ensigns armorial. It has its gallery of portraits; its
monumental inscriptions; its records, evidences, and titles.

(V, 80)

Turning to the constitution of pre-revolutionary France,
Burke images it as 'a noble and venerable castle' which had
been allowed to fall into disrepair. In the later *Letter to a
Noble Lord* the 'proud Keep of Windsor' — one of those 'vast
and inhospitable halls' he had once derided — is rehabilitated
as the great symbol of monarchical power (VIII, 49).

Burke's problem in his writings of the 1790s was to reconcile this potent imagery of tradition (and the quality of elegy
which it sometimes assumed) with the unsentimental viewpoint of the political economist. Although the threat of
Jacobinism had made this task more urgent, it was not essentially new. In the speech of 1780 Burke was keenly aware of
the delicacy of his position as one burdened with the duty of
severing traditional relations of power. He speaks the language of the political economist, but his manner is at first
cautious and even regretful. The opening passages of the
speech take the form of an apology for political economy in
which Burke issues a plea in mitigation of its ruthless but
necessary procedures. 'I feel,' he admits,

> that I engage in a business, in itself most ungracious. . . .
> I know, that all parsimony is of a quality approaching to
> unkindness. . . . Indeed the whole class of the severe and
> restrictive virtues, are at a market almost too high for hum-
> anity.   (III, 232)

Burke is evidently anxious not to appear an enemy to the arts
of benefaction. He is concerned not to breach that decorum
which constitutes civilised social relations. Yet as a political
economist he is obliged to draw up a plan of retrenchment
which is ungracious, illiberal and indecorous, which by limiting the patronage in the hands of the Crown will break a
chain of political attachments:

> Very few men of great families and extensive connections,
> but will feel the smart of a cutting reform, in some close

relation, some bosom friend, some pleasant acquaintance, some dear protected dependant.   (III, 234)

In this way Burke presents himself as a reluctant champion of frugality who has been appointed to curtail the splendour and profusion of the Court. According to the principles of accountability and good management, the pension fund must be contracted to a fixed sum and the more outrageous sinecures of the Court abolished. For the grants and pensions required to establish dependencies and extend political influence were, in a strictly economic sense, just so much unnecessary profusion. According to Adam Smith,

> The whole, or almost the whole publick revenue, is in most countries employed in maintaining unproductive hands. Such are the people who compose a numerous and splendid court, a great ecclesiastical establishment, great fleets and armies, who in time of peace produce nothing, and in time of war acquire nothing which can compensate the expence of maintaining them, even while the war lasts.
>   (Smith, 1976a, I, 342)

Smith does not go so far as to condemn outright this kind of unproductive labour and its agents in the social retinue. He felt, in any case, that while the profligacy of government might hinder the growth of the national wealth, it would rarely be significant enough to deplete it. Nonetheless such profligacy could not simply be condoned. Political employments may be honourable enough, and even essential for the defence of the realm, but from the point of view of the accumulation of capital they are little more than incumbrances. Smith's irritation becomes evident when he complains that

> It is the highest impertinence and presumption . . . in kings and ministers, to pretend to watch over the oeconomy of private people, and to restrain their expence either by sumptuary laws, or by prohibiting the importation of foreign luxuries. They are themselves always, and without any exception, the greatest spendthrifts in the society.
>   (ibid., p. 346)

Burke's approach in the *Speech on Oeconomical Reform* is

a little more politic and pragmatic than this. He draws the attention of the House to the limited nature of his proposals for reform. Perhaps thinking of his own position as one who in time might welcome the aid of a pension, he is careful to reserve some provision for such grants: 'There is a time,' he concedes, 'when the weather-beaten vessels of the state ought to come into harbour. . . . Many of the persons, who in all times have filled the great offices of state, have been younger brothers, who had originally little, if any fortune.' (III, 311) It is evident in such remarks that Burke, along with other eighteenth-century legislators, regarded political economy as an administrative instrument at the service of the statesman rather than as a set of doctrines to be rigorously applied. Thus Burke recalls in the *Letter to a Noble Lord* that 'Oeconomy in my plans was, as it ought to be, secondary, subordinate, instrumental. I acted on state principles.' (VIII, 18) The retention of the Greek orthography is of some significance here. Etymologically the 'oeconomy' derives from the administration of the *household*. Political economy therefore tends to conceive of the state itself as a vast household in which management will be conducted upon 'domestic' principles.[1]

In this sense 'political oeconomy', the form of economic regulation generally practised by Burke, is to be differentiated from 'classical economics', a science which is usually said to originate in the work of Adam Smith. In the latter the 'economy' is highly theoretical and conceptual in character. Economics of this kind operates at a level of abstraction completely distinct from, and alien to, the practical and administrative measures introduced by Burke. Political economy, which even in the *Wealth of Nations* is no more than 'a branch of the science of a statesman or legislator' (Smith, 1976a, I, 428), has no systematic conception of the economy, but divides the national 'household' into various sectors (commerce, manufactures, public credit, and so on) over which the statesman presides.

The procedures and priorities of Burke's *Speech on Oeconomical Reform* are quite clearly derived from this 'domestic' form of management. For according to Burke, 'the first thing in dignity and charge that attracts our notice, is the *royal household*' (III, 276). It is the task of the statesman to rationalise royal expenditure, to contract services upon the most reasonable terms available, and to establish an accurate and regular system of accounts — just the principles upon which Burke would no doubt have hoped to run his own farm. From the point of view of classical economics, with its complex theoretical categories, Burke's proposals for reform may seem somewhat banal, and unworthy of the grandiose rhetoric in which they are unveiled. But once political economy is understood as a system of 'householding', the offices and expenditure of the Court acquire a more than marginal significance. In this sense Burke may be indulging in only minor hyperbole when he claims that 'The gorging a royal kitchen may stint and famish the negotiations of a kingdom.'

(III, 282)

3. *The Divine Economy*

The *Speech on Oeconomical Reform* was not the only mode of economic discourse in which Burke engaged. In his later tract, *Thoughts and Details on Scarcity* (1795), there is a shift both in the areas of concern and in the presentation of economic affairs. It is not that the pamphlet contravenes Burke's earlier work (though there are some striking differences in tone), but rather that it takes into consideration those sectors — such as production itself — which he regarded as outside the economic purview of the statesman. While the *Speech on Oeconomical Reform* saw political economy in an active, regulative role, the purpose of the *Thoughts* is to designate those areas which are of their nature beyond the competence of the legislator: 'To provide for us in our necessities is not in the power of government. It would be a vain presumption in statesmen to think that they can do it.' (VII, 376) This admonition is directed at those who, in order to alleviate the worst effects of the scarcity of 1795, proposed to regulate agricultural wages and to reorganise the distribution of corn. The immediate occasion of the *Thoughts* was a parliamentary debate on the high price of corn (*PH*, XXXII, 235-42). In opposing the policy of regulation Burke is led to consider its implications for agricultural production itself, the components of which are, in the opening pages of the

Thoughts, discussed at a certain level of generality.

This is not to say that the pamphlet is a work of theoretical abstraction. Its form is that of a practical letter of advice to a statesman (presented, according to the title-page, to William Pitt) in which the limits of economic regulation are stressed. Taken in its entirety, the *Thoughts* comprises a workmanlike manual on various aspects of agrarian capitalist production. For here Burke approaches economic problems not from the point of view of a statesman but from that of a *farmer*: 'so far as my own information and experience extend', 'for the seven-and-twenty years, during which I have been a farmer' (VII, 379, 405). Thus the earlier, more 'abstract' remarks find empirical support in the concluding pages of the tract, where Burke compiles a detailed record of his own harvests of 1794 and 1795.

The mode of writing in which the *Thoughts* is cast, unique among Burke's published works, reflects his changed personal circumstances in the mid-1790s. In 1794 he had resigned his parliamentary seat and retired to his farm in Beaconsfield. Burke, however, was by no means politically inactive. The *Thoughts*, his clearest and most coherent exposition of economic principle, is also an intensely and overtly political work, a deliberate intervention in a debate on agricultural policy. There is, indeed, a clear line of continuity between the economic discourse of the *Thoughts* and the anti-Jacobin rhetoric of the *Letters on a Regicide Peace* which followed it. Several passages in the *Letters* draw more or less directly on ideas presented in the *Thoughts*. Occasionally this general connection is crystallised more particularly in metaphor. In the *Thoughts* Burke had commented in detail on the crop failures and scarcities brought about by the exceptionally severe weather of 1795. The wheat, he recalls, was badly affected. Having survived the rigours of winter, it was struck down as it came into bloom: 'at that most critical time of all, a cold dry east wind, attended with very sharp frosts, longer and stronger than I recollect at that time of year, destroyed the flowers, and withered up, in an astonishing manner, the whole side of the ear next to the wind' (VII, 406). A correspondent to the *Gentleman's Magazine* of 1795 (LXV, 627) suggested a further cause of the blight, an insect 'imagined to come in an East wind', whose worm-like larvae had greedily devoured the pulpy juice contained within the kernels of the wheat, leaving a 'reddish dross' behind. In the first of the *Letters on a Regicide Peace* (1796) Burke combines these recent memories of agricultural distress with a more traditional imagery of plague. The result is a metaphor which depicts the ideology of Jacobinism as a natural disaster in the state:

> They who bow to the enemy abroad will not be of power to subdue the conspirator at home. . . . In proportion as we are attracted towards the focus of illegality, irreligion, and desperate enterprise, all the venomous and blighting insects of the state are awakened into life. The promise of the year is blasted, and shrivelled, and burned up before them. Our most salutary and most beautiful institutions yield nothing but dust and smut: the harvest of our law is no more than stubble. (VIII, 96-7)

In one of those 'organic' metaphors with which Burke's political writings abound, the state, its institutions and laws are figured as elements of a natural process, a seasonal cycle, which is threatened by the disease of Jacobinism. As is often the case in Burke, the origins and applications of the metaphor are local and specific. It is the process of agrarian production, analysed in detail in the scarcity tract, that Burke has in mind here. Just as the blight of 1795 had interrupted the natural processes of growth and harvest, so Jacobinism subverts the 'natural' order of the state. Burke frequently turns to metaphors of this kind in his political and economic writings of the 1790s. As Macpherson (1980, pp. 51-70) has shown, he insists that a self-regulating economy is both 'natural' and just. In urging this his style becomes increasingly figurative and even excitable. It reads more like the language of a votary than the discourse of a practical Whig man of business. In a passage which has become notorious he declares that

> We, the people, ought to be made sensible, that it is not in breaking the laws of commerce, which are the laws of nature, and consequently the laws of God, that we are to place our hope of softening the Divine displeasure to

remove any calamity under which we suffer, or which hangs
over us.   (VII, 404)

This can be read as an excessively cynical piece of rhetoric.
'We, the people, ought to be made sensible,' preaches Burke,
hand on heart, as if he were not himself a farmer, an employer, and a defender of privilege. But it would be wrong to
dismiss this deification of the economic order simply as an
act of conscious manipulation. Burke's fears for the safety of
this natural, moral and divine economy are as deeply rooted
as his fears for the safety of the state.

These fears manifest themselves in various ways. In the
Speech on the Nabob of Arcot's Debts (1785) the financial
corruption associated with the rule of the East India Company
provokes an excited (some would say an exaggerated) response
from Burke. Despite its apparently unpromising title and
mundane theme, the speech reveals Burke at his most impassioned. The debt itself is a central motif. Winding its way
through the speech, and defying every attempt to grasp its
origin, it is the hidden cause of imperial corruption, the dark
secret buried deep in the body politic of India:

That debt to the company is the pretext under which all
the other debts lurk and cover themselves. That debt forms
the foul putrid mucus, in which are engendered the whole
brood of creeping ascarides, all the endless involutions, the
eternal knot, added to a knot of those inexpugnable tape-
worms which devour the nutriment, and eat up the bowels
of India.   (IV, 282)

If Burke's disgust, expressed in an imagery which is little short
of scatalogical, seems excessive in relation to his theme, that
is an indication of his commitment to the principles of economy and financial probity which the debt has contravened.
His rhetoric begins to slip out of control. His Whig confidence
breaks down into something closer to panic.

It is the kind of alarm one might expect from a man who
fears that throne and altar are in danger. It is a feature of
Burke's writings of the 1790s that the economy should be
regarded as an object worthy of equal veneration. Like other
economists of his time, he stresses that the self-regulation of

certain economic categories (wages, prices, rents, and so on) is a process fully sanctioned by the laws of nature and God (see Copley, 1982). His economic writing itself draws on the language and imagery of morality and religion. As a political writer he was no doubt aware of the rhetorical possibilities inherent in such an approach. Macpherson (1980) has shown how it enabled him to celebrate and defend 'a specifically capitalist' economy as if it were traditional, inevitable and just. Burke's strategy becomes clearer when one looks in detail at the imagery of the *Wealth of Nations*, the author of which was not only a celebrated economist but also a close associate of Burke's. Smith's use of quasi-religious formulae such as 'the sacred rights of private property' is well known and has sometimes been ridiculed. Although in Smith's case it may represent something more than a rhetorical sleight of hand, it is nonetheless true to say that there are occasions in the *Wealth of Nations* when he seems to call upon the authority of religion primarily to confer a kind of moral legitimacy on his argument. In his discussion of the accumulation of capital, for instance, Smith argues that the habit of parsimony is preferable to the luxury of profusion. He images capital as a sacred fund set aside for the employment of productive hands. Profligacy is not only the road to ruin as far as the individual spendthrift is concerned, it is also a form of social and economic sacrilege. The prodigal, 'like him who perverts the revenues of some pious foundation to profane purposes . . . pays the wages of idleness with those funds which the frugality of his forefathers had, as it were, consecrated to the maintenance of industry' (Smith, 1976a, I, 339). Though the *Wealth of Nations* is often praised for having established a science, Smith is not above appealing to our sense of sin.

But it is not enough that capital, the awesome force that sets the employment of hands into motion, should be sanctified. The manner of its circulation, and the workings of the market, must also be demonstrably just. In the *Wealth of Nations* acts of individual advantage lead, by strange but purposeful indirection, to social improvement. It is just at those moments when Smith refers to this righteous self-regulation of the economy that his language is at its most imprecise. A sort of allusive, incorporeal imagery, which is more than simply illustrative, finds a place in the language of economics. There is, for instance, the famous image of the 'invisible hand'. The individual, Smith tells us,

> By preferring the support of domestick to that of foreign industry . . . intends only his own security; and by directing that industry in such a manner as its produce may be of the greatest value, he intends only his own gain, and he is in this, as in many other cases, led by an invisible hand to promote an end which was no part of his intention.
>
> (ibid., p. 456)

Smith's metaphors in the *Wealth of Nations* are generally practical, explicatory and businesslike. The image of the 'invisible hand' is exceptional in its allusion to the otherworldly force which is overseeing economic affairs. Unusually for Smith, it is an image which seems to stand in place of — rather than illustrate — an economic concept. It is introduced in order to represent a mysterious act of divine intervention. It is in a similar sense that it appears in Smith's earlier *Theory of Moral Sentiments* (1976b, pp. 184-5) and, indeed, in the work of other eighteenth-century writers. In *Moll Flanders* Defoe, like Smith, describes the movement of economic forces in quasi-religious terms. One of Moll's more respectable husbands, the 'quiet, sensible, sober' bank clerk, is lured into some ruinous business deals. This financial catastrophe is likened to 'a sudden Blow from an almost invisible Hand', a visitation which, Moll complains, 'blasted all my Happiness, and turn'd me out into the World in a Condition the reverse of all that had been before it' (Defoe, 1971, p. 189). Here — and perhaps a sense of this lingers in Smith's work — the economy is regarded as divine in its regulation, its vicissitudes (traversed in the passage from plenty to scarcity, from profit to loss) representing the commands of Providence rather than the caprices of chance.

The religious associations of the metaphor of the 'invisible hand' are made explicit in the closing paragraphs of *A Journal of the Plague Year*, where Defoe attributes the sudden disappearance of the plague to 'the secret invisible Hand of him, that had at first sent this Disease as a Judgment upon us' (1969, p. 246). Traces of this evidently religious sensibility remain in the economic discourse of the *Wealth of Nations*. They lie behind Smith's belief, apparent in many parts of the work, that the natural economic order, instituted by God, is fundamentally just. This conviction is implicit in his critique of the mercantile system. For in his view the regulations which a state enforces in order to secure itself an exclusive colonial trade, and which thereby inhibit the natural movement of stock, are offences which will ultimately revisit the transgressor. Like a poisoned chalice returned to one's own lips, 'The unjust oppression of the industry of other countries falls back . . . upon the heads of the oppressors, and crushes their industry more than it does that of those other countries.' (Smith, 1976a, II, 627-8) Burke, who also saw the economy as an agent of justice, felt that indiscreet tampering with the domestic economy would prove equally perilous. In the *Thoughts and Details on Scarcity* he warns that if, during a period of low wages, an effort is made 'unnaturally' and injudiciously to raise the price of labour, the market itself will mete out the appropriate punishment. In such cases, he observes, 'the wheel turns round, and the evil complained of falls with aggravated weight on the complainant' (VII, 387).

This image of the wheel lacks the otherworldly associations of Smith's 'invisible hand'. It both illustrates and arises from Burke's conception that the economy is a mechanism regulated by natural laws of motion. In his view, it would be mischievous for statesmen to meddle with this great machine and its distribution of the products of labour. In the *Reflections on the Revolution in France* the image had appeared in a slightly different context as 'the great wheel of circulation'. In an attack on the confiscation and sale of church lands decreed by the National Assembly in the final months of 1789 Burke argues that the monastic orders of France

are as usefully employed as if they worked from dawn to dark in the innumerable servile, degrading, unseemly, unmanly and often most unwholesome and pestiferous occupations, to which by the social oeconomy so many wretches are inevitably doomed. If it were not generally pernicious to disturb the natural course of things, and to impede, in any degree, the great wheel of circulation which is turned by the strangely-directed labour of these unhappy people, I should be infinitely more inclined forcibly to rescue them from their miserable industry, than violently to disturb the tranquil repose of monastick quietude.(V, 291)

In this case Burke is not entirely confident that the economy can be presented as equitable at the level of its own operations and exchanges. He will even admit that his humanity leads him to regret the sufferings borne by the unhappy children of toil. And yet as an economist he cannot permit his feelings of sympathy to interfere with the course of nature, represented in this case by 'the great wheel of circulation'. It is a grandiose but still essentially mechanical figure of speech. What makes the passage in some ways comparable to Smith's evocation of the 'invisible hand' is the combination of the image of the wheel with the phrase 'strangely-directed labour'. The suggestion, once again, is that some unknown providence is at work. The language of the Whig man of business is enlivened by this hint of the sublime and the mysterious. The economy, that most mundane and prosaic of things (in which, nevertheless, everyone takes an interest) becomes an object of awe and almost of veneration. Burke's achievement in such passages is primarily a rhetorical one. He offers us no real knowledge of the economy, nor any insight into its workings. More importantly, given the context of social and political crisis in which he wrote, he provides it with an authoritative language and an almost unbounded prerogative.

5

Patronage, Deference and the Language of Dissent

Wit, my Lords, is a sort of property: it is the property of those
that have it, and too often the only property they have to
depend on. It is, indeed, but a precarious dependence. Thank
God! we, my Lords, have a dependence of another kind. . . .
Lord Chesterfield on the Stage Licensing Bill,
20 May 1737

The idioms in which Burke conducts political argument are
by no means ideologically neutral. They embody the wider
social and cultural assumptions which underpin his stance on
any particular issue. Like any successful political writer, Burke
communicates in terms which will be felt and understood
beyond the confines of the established political world. He
canvasses support by appealing to the reader's taste, sense
of legal right and understanding of proper economic relations.
It is not, however, in the terminologies of economics, aesthetics
and law that Burke's values are made most explicit. In the
literary forms and conventions — as well as the arguments —
of public letters like *A Letter to a Noble Lord* his social role
and values as a writer are directly presented. It is this aspect
of Burke's writing that I now intend to examine. My primary
concern will be with the way in which Burke's experience
of a particular kind of social relationship — patronage — shapes
the literary form of *A Letter to a Noble Lord*.

J. T. Boulton has identified the *Letter* as belonging to an
'eighteenth-century "genre"' which was 'associated both with
the defence of the writer's reputation and the denunciation
of his enemies'. It was the vehicle of 'men whose reputation
derived not from hereditary rank but solely from personal
talents' (1966b, pp. 77, 73). It is in this immediately social
context that the rhetorical strategy and conventions of the

Letter should be examined. Before coming to a detailed consideration of the *Letter* I shall therefore look briefly at some other responses to patronage in the writings of Burke and his contemporaries. For the *Letter*, one of Burke's richest and, for reasons which I hope will become clear, most contradictory pieces of work, seems to draw upon a number of eighteenth-century precedents. These had, in effect, established the terms in which a writer could indicate a measure of dissent from the sometimes excessive demands of patronage without repudiating the social relationship of which it was a particular instance.

In his well-known survey of English class relations since the Civil War, Perry Anderson argues that 'There was . . . from the start no fundamental, antagonistic contradiction between the old aristocracy and the new bourgeoisie. English capitalism embraced and included both. The most important single key to modern English history lies in this fact.' (1964, p. 31) In so far as they concern themselves with social relationships, the works of the great eighteenth-century writers tend to confirm this view. For the most part the alliance between the aristocracy and its junior partner is accepted as a social and political necessity. It was not, however, without its moments of discord, tension and even occasional revolt. The career of Samuel Johnson is a case in point. In the celebrated definitions of 'patronage' and 'pension' listed in his *Dictionary* (1755) Johnson crystallised the feelings of the writer in dissent. Anxious to assert his independence of the aristocracy, he defined a *patron* as 'One who countenances, supports or protects. Commonly a wretch who supports with insolence, and is paid with flattery.' As one proud to be regarded as a literary wage-labourer, he lampooned the *pensioner* as 'A slave of state hired by a stipend to obey his master.' No less acrimonious was Johnson's definition of a *pension*: 'An allowance made to any one without an equivalent. In England it is generally understood to mean pay given to a state hireling for treason to his country.'

The antipathy Johnson felt towards patronage and the individual patron had its immediate source in the experience of compiling the *Dictionary*. Although the costs of production were to be met by a consortium of publishers, Johnson dedicated the *Plan* to Lord Chesterfield, indicating at least a residual dependence upon the system of patronage. The dedications and titles which preface a great many eighteenth-century works (as in the formula 'A Letter to a Noble Lord') suggest that although patronage may have declined as a mode of literary production, it yet retained considerable cultural and rhetorical prestige. Johnson found that while patronage demanded a measure of deference on the writer's part, it brought with it little material reward. The celebrated letter to Chesterfield, gathering together a whole set of responses to the problems of patronage, is like a paradigm of relations between bourgeois and aristocrat in eighteenth-century England. Accusatory yet restrained, the letter established the terms by which self-justification might be conducted with decorum:

> Seven years, my Lord, have now past, since I waited in your outward rooms, or was repulsed from your door; during which time I have been pushing on my work through difficulties, of which it is useless to complain, and have brought it, at last, to the verge of publication, without one act of assistance, one word of encouragement, or one smile of favour. Such treatment I did not expect, for I never had a Patron before.   (Boswell, 1934-50, I, 261-2)

The image of the writer who is suffered to wait in the ante-chamber of his lord, to attend at his patron's pleasure, the contrast between bourgeois exertion and courtly indolence — such are the stereotypes to which many eighteenth-century writers turned when they wished to give shape to their social experience or give vent to their social discontents.

In Henry Fielding's *Amelia* (1751) Mrs Bennet describes her husband's visit to an aristocratic acquaintance 'who had received from him many Civilities and Assistances in his Learning at the University, and had promised to return them fourfold hereafter'. His reception, like Johnson's, is not altogether cordial:

> It was not without some Difficulty that Mr. *Bennet* got into the Antichamber. Here he waited, or, as the Phrase is, cooled his Heels for above an Hour, before he saw his Lordship; nor had he seen him then, but by an Accident:

For my Lord was going out, when he casually intercepted
him in his Passage to his Chariot. He approached to salute
him with some Familiarity, tho' with Respect, depending
on his former Intimacy, when my Lord stepping short very
gravely told him, he had not the Pleasure of knowing him.

(Fielding, 1983, p. 287)

Social antagonism of the same kind, and expressed in similar
terms, occasionally troubled relations between the two Houses
of Parliament. 'Had gentlemen any feeling for the honour of
the House,' protested Burke in the Commons in June 1772,
'would they submit to the disgrace of waiting three hours
in the lobby of the House of Lords, among their lordships'
footmen? Sir, this has been my fate, when ordered by the
House to carry their Bills to the Lords.' (*PH*, XVII, 514) In
these extracts Johnson, Fielding and Burke share a kind of
vocabulary of dissent. It was one upon which Burke was to
draw again, more than twenty years later, in the *Letter to a
Noble Lord*.

Eighteenth-century literary criticism, concerned, as it
often is, with the biography of the writer, offers a detailed,
dramatic and sometimes highly critical commentary on the
conduct of the alliance between the aristocratic patron and
the bourgeois intellectual. In view of Johnson's arduous and
courageous progress through the ranks of the literary profession, it is not surprising that his critical biographies should
never lose sight of the conditions under which works were
produced. The economic and social struggles of literary life
are one of his major concerns. Thus we are told in the *Lives
of the Poets* (1779-81) that Collins, the poetic counterpart
of Defoe's metropolitan entrepreneurs, 'came to London a
literary adventurer, with many projects in his head, and very
little money in his pocket', very much as Johnson himself
had done in 1737 (Johnson, 1905, III, 335). The turning-
point of Johnson's *Life of Pope* can then be seen as economic
in character — the financial success of Pope's translation of
the *Iliad*. Launched by subscription, a means of securing a
limited but certain market, and hence poised somewhere
between patronage and full commodity production, it earned
Pope sufficient means to remain gloriously independent of
both social and political obligation.

Some of Johnson's most significant remarks on the position of the writer are to be found in the early and elegiac *Life of Savage* (originally published in 1744), a history of financial disaster, of connections sought and broken off, of projects floated and foundered. Savage is a poet forever out of place, resenting the deference required by the patron, yet unable to reconcile himself to the burdens and expectations of the market. The secret of Savage's birth determines the course of his career, making his social position and economic function equally uncertain:

> Born with a legal claim to honour and to affluence he was in two months illegitimated by the parliament and disowned by his mother, doomed to poverty and obscurity, and launched upon the ocean of life only that he might be swallowed by its quicksands or dashed upon its rocks.
> (Johnson, 1905, II, 324)

Savage, the aristocrat denied his proper rank, is obliged, by a humiliating reversal, to seek a patron. No wonder, then, that he was often ready 'to lament the misery of living at the tables of other men, which was his fate from the beginning to the end of his life' (ibid., p. 364). The rupture with his patron, Lord Tyrconnel, is one of the central incidents of Savage's chequered career. From Johnson's account there emerges a pattern which will be repeated in later instances of the relationship between the writer and patron, a liaison marked by successive moments of concord, tension and severance. Savage, for instance, voiced exactly the kind of complaint that led, in turn, to the break between Burke and his first patron, William Gerard Hamilton. Objecting to the demands Tyrconnel made on his time, Savage — like Burke — was 'inclined to resent such expectations as tending to infringe his liberty, of which he was very jealous when it was necessary to the gratification of his passions' (ibid., p. 369). On failing to find a secure place under a patron, Savage resolved to offer himself to a wider market, to 'live upon the profits of his own labour', but he was unable to cast off the aristocratic values of his birth and to practise the parsimony demanded of wage-labour. As a final paradox, the coterie of fellow-writers organised by Pope to relieve Savage in his indigence merely served as a reminder that coercion was not the monopoly of the aristocratic patron. 'Those by whom he was to be supported', comments Johnson, 'began to prescribe to him with an air of authority, which he knew not how decently to resent nor patiently to bear.' (ibid., p. 411)

In the lives of Savage and Burke there is evidence of an understandable need for the pensioner both to acknowledge and disavow his sense of obligation. Johnson was also to experience this tense and contradictory pattern of feeling. In 1762 he accepted the grant of a royal pension worth £300 per annum, even though, as we have seen, he had earlier defined a pensioner as a 'slave of state'. Like Savage and many other writers whose biographies are included in the *Lives of the Poets*, he was obliged to live out such apparent contradictions. It is worth looking at Johnson's manner of handling them, if only because some of Burke's most impressive writings were conceived under similar pressures.

In a formal letter of acceptance to the Earl of Bute (through whose good offices the pension had been obtained) Johnson remarked upon that statesman's patrician regard for matters of decorum and good taste. Masking the vulgar cash nexus established by the pension, this courtly etiquette, this art of giving, had the effect of raising donation to the level of ritual:

> Bounty always receives part of its value from the manner in which it is bestowed; your Lordship's kindness includes every circumstance that can gratify delicacy, or enforce obligation. You have conferred your favours on a man who has neither alliance nor interest, who has not merited them by services, nor courted them by officiousness; you have spared him the shame of solicitation, and the anxiety of suspense.
>
> What has been thus elegantly given, will, I hope, not be reproachfully enjoyed. . . .   (Boswell, 1934-50, I, 376-7)

Reading this letter, it is difficult not to feel that the elegance was Johnson's rather than Bute's. Yet beneath the gracefully deferential address there may be at least a hint of self-assertion. Certainly he admits, in conventional style, that he has not 'merited' Bute's favours, but neither, he quietly reminds the noble lord, had he 'courted them by officiousness', a claim which is perhaps to be construed as a polite declaration of independence. Johnson clung to his belief that the pension had been granted as a reward for literary services already rendered. If the gift had established obligations on his part, they were to be understood as social rather than political in character. To Johnson's alarm, however, there were others who seemed to regard the pension as having sealed an unspoken but binding contract. Boswell (1934-50, II, 317) reports that during the struggles with the American colonies Johnson complained that ministers were exerting pressure on him to write pamphlets on their behalf.

A year after Johnson had received his favours from Bute, Burke was himself granted a pension of £300 per annum, secured on the Irish establishment by his employer, William Gerard Hamilton. Within two years the relationship between the two men had broken down irretrievably. The drama of Hamilton, the patron, and Burke, his talented but excitable secretary, unfolds in a series of letters written between 1763 and 1765. In a searching discussion of this correspondence Isaac Kramnick has recently remarked on 'the tension between the contradictory forces of Burke's ambition to make his own mark and the necessity of dependence and service to his superior' (1977, p. 101). In literary terms this tension finds release in a kind of reluctant irascibility, in an uneasy juxtaposition of the attitudes of deference and dissent which anticipates the discrepancies of the *Letter to a Noble Lord*. Burke's initial response to the grant of his pension was one of cautious gratitude. In March 1763 he wrote a letter of acceptance to Hamilton, expressing his appreciation but also betraying his anxiety:

> I should think myself inexcusable in receiving this pension, and loading your interest with so heavy a charge, without apprizing you of those conditions on which alone I am able to take it; because, when I have taken it, I ought no longer to consider myself as possessed of my former freedom and independence. (*Corr.*, I, 164)

Burke's proviso was that he should be allowed to cultivate his 'literary reputation', an ambition independent of, though entirely secondary to his efforts to further Hamilton's political career. Already, then, the extent of obligation is uncertain: Hamilton was later to argue – and Burke was as vehemently to refute – that this letter represented a legal and binding contract, a kind of charter of service, by which Burke had signed away his right to self-determination.

The same letter to Hamilton is marked by a kind of nervous attention to protocol and form, a guarded correctness of address. Struggling to concede obligation and yet also to assert his independence, Burke composes a letter which is admirably clear in its sentiments but which is at the same time a curiously stiff and formal communication to send to such a close acquaintance. He admits to Hamilton that

> I have often wished to explain myself fully to you on this point. It is against my general notions to trust to writing, where it is in one's power to confer otherwise. But neither do you hear, nor do I speak, on this subject, with the same ease with which we converse on others.   (*Corr.*, I, 164)

The delicate 'subject' to which Burke refers here concerns the matter of his pension and the more general conditions of his service to Hamilton. Speech and conference, the proper vehicles of political negotiation, are paradoxically deemed inappropriate for the conduct of private business between a patron and his secretary. In this sense we might see the very formality observed by the letter as an effort to smooth over the antagonisms aroused by an unequal alliance and to repress Burke's feelings of disquiet. But even that formality can be disturbed – as it is, much later, in the *Letter to a Noble Lord* – by a moment of self-assertion. As deferential address gives way to an insistence on his own merit, Burke's letter, urged on by hints of accusation and resentment at neglect, becomes increasingly indiscreet. Perhaps against his better judgment, Burke breaks into a language which at times sounds almost insubordinate:

> I protest to God I have applied to whatever you have thought proper to set me, with a vigour and alacrity and even an eagerness that I never felt in any affair of my own whatsoever. If you have not observed this, you have not I think observd with your usual sagacity. (*Corr.*, I, 165)

By 1765 the tensions evident in Burke's earlier letters had culminated in complete rupture. In the correspondence which effects this break the terms of the dispute are manifestly those of class antagonism. Again and again Burke writes as if his patron were bent on reducing him to the status of a servant. He cannot accept the indignities of a 'domestick situation'; his position is worse than that of a 'footman' or even a 'felon'. In May 1765 he wrote to John Hely Hutchinson complaining that Hamilton

> would fain have had a *Slave*, which, as it is a being of no dignity, so it can be of very little real utility to its owner; and he refused to have a faithful *friend*, which is a creature of some rank. . . .   (*Corr.*, I, 199)

Burke's opinion of the inutility of slavery was to become a favourite theme of classical political economy. Adam Smith, for instance, was to contrast the moral and economic indigence of serfdom with the productive capacity and humanising potential of 'free' wage-labour. A renegade against what he regards as Hamilton's imperious regime, Burke puts aside the deferential gestures of patronage in favour of the more combative terminology of political economy. He protests that his relation to Hamilton is not social at all, but a mere relation of property or right of possession. 'How faithful, how attached, and how Zealous I have been to him, you were yourself in part a Witness', he reminds Hely Hutchinson, adding that

> though you could be so only in part, yet this was enough I flatter myself to let you see that, I deserved to be considerd in another manner than as one of Mr H's Cattle, or as a piece of his Houshold stuff.   (*Corr.*, I, 199-200)

As Goldsmith was wryly to remark in 'Retaliation' (1774), Burke was too 'disobedient' to succeed as 'a drudge'.

Burke's quarrel with Hamilton was a highly acrimonious but not altogether exceptional affair. For although as a system patronage was in general remarkably effective, in individual cases it was always likely to be torn by a conflict of interests. A few months after the break with Hamilton, Burke entered into a more profitable engagement as private secretary to the Marquis of Rockingham, the great Whig land-owner who became First Lord of the Treasury in the new administration of July 1765. In a letter written at this time Burke described his new patron as one 'who has the reputation of a man of honour and integrity; and with whom, they say, it is not difficult to live' (*Corr.*, I, 211) – no doubt recalling, in this final phrase, his recent difficulties with Hamilton. Burke's information seems to have been substantially correct. The connection with Rockingham, which made his political career possible, appears to have been largely untroubled. There is little evidence of discord in their surviving correspondence. A letter written by William Burke (Edmund's long-time companion, adviser and confidant) is an interesting exception. It suggests that even the relationship with Rockingham, generally a model of continuity and ease, could arouse powerful feelings of discontent.

In 1780 Burke's career had entered a critical phase. In the election of that year he lost his highly prized seat at Bristol, and his political future seemed in doubt. He even talked of retiring altogether from public affairs. At this troubled time William Burke wrote to the Duke of Portland, a prominent member of the Rockingham Whigs, advising him of their friend's difficulties. In this unusually critical letter Rockingham is accused of failing to inform Burke of the provision which has been made for his future. Rockingham wished to set aside for his secretary's use one of the seats at his disposal, but had yet, according to William, kept Burke in the dark. Although the opening phrase of the following extract from William's letter ('with great deference') observes the protocols of patronage, it gives way almost at once to a list of complaints and a tone of barely suppressed indignation:

> with great deference, I should doubt whether this sort of concealed friendliness, this kind of covered, masked attention to a friends Concerns, this mental regard, could just at this Crisis altogether suit our friend Burke's Situation. Times and Seasons and Circumstances give the Colour to human actions. The handsomest Conduct in the world towards one man, may therefore not be well advised towards another. – Our Servants do not ask what is for

supper, they are to suppose that wholesome food, and fit for Christians, will be provided for them, but it is the manner of the invitation that brings the Guest to the Table. . . . To treat any Man with . . . reserve, is at best to treat him like a Child. (*Corr.*, IV, 288-9)

Hamilton had treated Edmund like a slave rather than as a friend; now, William complains, Rockingham behaves as if he were a servant or a child rather than an honoured guest. He asks that the connection between classes be maintained with a certain delicacy and good taste. If Johnson had been able to commend Bute for his aristocratic observance of the arts of giving, William Burke feels obliged to rebuke Rockingham for his neglect of such rites. It is not only the pension, but the manner of its giving, not only the feast, but 'the manner of the invitation', that matter. Rockingham has failed to keep this decorum. Whether or not William Burke was justified in making this criticism is not at issue here. It is enough to observe the manner in which dissent is displayed, once offence has been taken. It is by ridiculing the literary trappings of patronage that William Burke makes known his displeasure:

That Superior designation of what is good for a man without any heed to, or any care of knowing his own Sentiments, may be munificent and magnificent, and benevolent, and generous, it may be the quintessence (if they please) of all the pompous Virtues that ever swelled a Dedication, but my dear Lord — It is not kind. (*Corr.*, IV, 289)

Burlesque half-rhymes ('munificent and magnificent') and shafts of satire combine to mock the conventional language of compliment. Rockingham's conduct as a patron, it is implied, is in this case as thoughtless as the panegyrics a man of his rank will naturally receive.

It was apparent in Johnson's letter to Chesterfield that this form of protestation carried with it a deeply felt pride in the writer's expenditure of labour power. Burke himself is always willing, in the formality of discourse, to defer to the superior talents, intelligence and even usefulness of his contemporaries, but he is reluctant to concede that they are more industrious. 'I value myself upon nothing but my industry,' he asserted in the House of Commons in June 1773 (Eg. MS. 250, pp. 219-20). Reviewing his parliamentary career more than twenty years later, he declared to William Windham that 'I have Labourd I have strong reason to be persuaded far more combining time and quantity together than any Member, that ever sat in that House.' (*Corr.*, VIII, 340) In publicly pressing such claims Burke is faced with delicate problems of style and etiquette. His need to proclaim the value of his own efforts sometimes comes into conflict with the more deferential attitudes expected of one of his class. Johnson's letter to Chesterfield had demonstrated how a rhetoric of self-justification might be deployed without undermining distinctions of rank. The desire both to register one's dissent and at the same time to negotiate the difficulties of patronage seems to establish a definite form of address.

As if anxious that he should not fly in the face of such forms, Burke apologised to Hamilton in one of their final exchanges for a momentary lapse from decorum:

> If I have spoken too strongly, you will be so good to pardon a man on his defence, in one of the nicest questions to a mind that has any feeling. I meant to speak fully not to offend. I am not used to defend my conduct, nor do I intend for the future to fall into so bad a habit.
>
> (*Corr.*, I, 180)

Yet there were to be many occasions in his subsequent career when Burke would find it necessary to defend himself in print or on the platform. Feeling himself to be an outsider in an English political establishment which remained primarily aristocratic in character, he was peculiarly sensitive about his own position. Among his most celebrated works of justification and defence were those relating to the American war (the *Letter to the Sheriffs of Bristol*, 1777, and the *Speech at Bristol, previous to the Election*, 1780). A decade later came Burke's quasi-juridical defence of his break with the Foxite Whigs (the *Appeal from the New to the Old Whigs*, 1791). Lastly, justifying the grant of his civil list pension, Burke made an impassioned defence of his entire political career in the *Letter to a Noble Lord* (1796).

This final act of self-defence was provoked by an attack on the pension Burke had received on his retirement from parliamentary politics. It was not long before the propriety of this award was to be questioned. In November 1795 Burke was attacked by the Earl of Lauderdale and the Duke of Bedford, who, in a debate in the House of Lords, delivered a broadside against the alleged corruption of ministers. Bedford condemned the grant of 'pensions of almost unparalleled profusion' which, he claimed, had been 'lavished upon the avowed advocates of economy; nay upon the very man who distinguished himself at one time as the advocate of rigid economy' (*PH*, XXXII, 260-1). Bedford, in other words, accused Burke of apostasy: in accepting a civil list pension he had broken faith with his earlier efforts, enshrined in the celebrated *Speech on Oeconomical Reform* (1780), to check improper ministerial influence.

The place of this attack (the House of Lords) and the status of Burke's assailants (both of whom belonged to the class of patrons) introduce an element of instability into the rhetoric and argument of the *Letter to a Noble Lord*. The tensions and discrepancies which had marked Burke's correspondence with Hamilton re-emerge as his discontent begins to propel the argument beyond the limits of simple vindication. Faced by the abuse of a class whose interests he had long and loyally served, Burke at first retaliates by resorting to parody, the literary form used to indicate an amused, assured and intimate dissent. From the outset Burke's letter, addressed without irony to one noble lord (usually identified as Lord Grenville), proceeds, in its reply to another, to contort and parody the language of deference. Thus in his opening address Burke plays on and gently mocks the conventions of polite society:

> I could hardly flatter myself with the hope, that so very early in the season I should have to acknowledge obligations to the duke of Bedford and to the earl of Lauderdale. These noble persons have lost no time in conferring upon me, that sort of honour, which it is alone within their competence, and which it is certainly most congenial to their nature and their manners to bestow. (VIII, 3)

The Whig lords had made their attack on Burke in the opening weeks of the new parliamentary session — 'early in the
season', as Burke puts it. It is 'season' rather than 'session'
because then a strictly parliamentary incident can be transferred to an ironic social context. Quietly sarcastic, Burke
introduces his reply as if he were a grateful client come to
pay his respects at the levee of a lord.

The *Letter to a Noble Lord* does not continue long in this
mode. For parody of that sort requires a control — the control, say, of Johnson's letter to Chesterfield — which Burke
is in the end unable or unwilling to sustain. For as Burke sees
it, the clash with Bedford is more than a slight disturbance
within a generally secure and harmonious social system. It
comes at the crisis of the French Revolution, with aristocrats
like Bedford and Lauderdale celebrating the overthrow of
the *ancien régime*, apparently in defiance of their own class
interests. The political situation in Europe, and Burke's
personal position, harried and derided by the Foxite Whigs,
demand a mode of writing which is more combative and
direct than parody. In his reply to Bedford Burke moves
from parody to ridicule, and from ridicule to darker and
more desperate ironies. As J. T. Boulton has pointed out, the
Letter is itself based upon an irony of situation which fas-
cinated Burke: 'the commoner Burke had diligently defended
the aristocratic system against republicanism while Bedford
had been his traducer' (1966b, p. 78). Thus Burke expresses
the meaning of his political career in the form of a paradox:
'I have strained every nerve to keep the duke of Bedford in
that situation, which alone makes him my superiour.' (VIII,
32) That 'alone' is emphatic. The paradox is one which neatly
sets out the contradictions in Burke's role, but which cannot
contain or resolve them. His social discontents remain un-
assuaged.

What confronts Burke in the *Letter to a Noble Lord* is
therefore not only a problem of political strategy (how to
check the influence of the Foxite Whigs) but also a related
and equally urgent rhetorical dilemma. It is the dilemma he
had already faced in his correspondence with Hamilton when
he had sought to set forth his own merits and demand his
independence while yet observing the requirements of social

propriety and good taste. In his *Appeal from the New to the Old Whigs* Burke had devised one solution to this problem. We have already seen how this pamphlet, a quasi-legal justification of the rupture with Fox, cites the testimony of Burke's ideological ancestors as evidence of his fidelity to the true principles of Whiggism. But formally speaking he is not responsible for his own defence. Burke writes in the guise of an advocate who may speak on his behalf before a tribunal of readers:

> It is certainly well for Mr. Burke that there are impartial men in the world. To them I address myself, pending the appeal which on his part is made from the living to the dead, from the modern Whigs to the antient. (VI, 75-6)

In this way Burke discovers in the *Appeal* a mode of speaking for himself without ever having to admit that it is indeed himself speaking.

But the uses of a device of this kind — a political argument in the third person — are strictly limited. Burke contrives less unwieldy forms of protestation and defence in the *Letter to a Noble Lord*. Again he is sensitive to matters of decorum. He figures his argument with the Duke of Bedford as nothing more than a formal device, as merely a literary rite of passage into a public debate on the French Revolution. Eager to demonstrate that the *Letter* is more than a product of wounded pride, Burke is at pains to explain that nothing personal is at stake:

> The awful state of the time, and not myself or my own justification, is my true object in what I now write; or in what I shall ever write or say. It little signifies to the world what becomes of such things as me, or even as the duke of Bedford. What I say about either of us is nothing more than a vehicle, as you, my lord, will easily perceive, to convey my sentiments on matters far more worthy of your attention. (VIII, 34)

'Nothing more than a vehicle,' claims Burke, and yet the reputation of the *Letter* rests upon its status as an impassioned apologia. It is the most directly autobiographical piece Burke ever published.

It is not, of course, that Burke has no time for the great public issues of the day; rather that in the *Letter* he anchors them in immediately personal concerns. Sometimes the link between the two is direct and obvious. More often it is made obliquely, through metaphor. One of the central and organising metaphors of the *Letter* is the image of the storm. Ronald Paulson (1983, pp. 43-7) has recently shown how the French Revolution was often portrayed through such images of natural upheaval. Burke introduces a sublime imagery of this kind into the rhetoric of the *Letter*. He warns Bedford, whom he has just ridiculed as 'the leviathan among all the creatures of the crown', that 'If a great storm blow on our coast, it will cast the whales on the strand as well as the periwinkles.' (VIII, 50) A little later, and in similar terms, he laments the fate of the aristocrats of France: 'security was their ruin. They are dashed to pieces in the storm, and our shores are covered with the wrecks.' (VIII, 54-5) On occasion it is evident that Burke finds himself involved in this tempest:

> The storm has gone over me; and I lie like one of those old oaks which the late hurricane has scattered about me. I am stripped of all my honours; I am torn up by the roots, and lie prostrate on the earth!   (VIII, 46)

In this instance the primary reference is not to the revolutionary storm but to a more personal cataclysm, the death of Burke's beloved and only child, Richard. Though the emphasis is different, the continuity of metaphor is significant. The revolution is figured as a natural phenomenon, a storm sweeping the shores of the western world, and catching the ailing, isolated, derided and grief-stricken Burke in its wake.

The storm is therefore an image which incorporates both the public and personal crises which exercise Burke in the *Letter*. It may well be that it is an archetypal image of revolution. But Burke, always alert to the claims of circumstance, is concerned to show that it has a more immediate source. For when he refers to 'the late hurricane', it is more than a figure of speech. The gales of 6 November 1795 were, according to the *Gentleman's Magazine* of that year (LXV, 960-4), the most violent the country had known since the great storm of 1703. On 19 November there was a further storm at sea. The *Annual Register* (XXXVII, 44-6) records how several ships, surprised by the storm, 'were lost by striking on a bank of pebbles extending from Portland nearly to Bridport'. Bedford's attack on Burke had been made on 13 November, midway between these more natural disturbances. Burke seems to have embarked on his reply almost at once. In a manner which is highly characteristic of his political writing, and with these events and reports — parliamentary and meteorological — fresh in mind, Burke binds together his private grief and anger and the agony of old Europe within a sequence of images of storm.

In so doing he produces some of the most memorable passages in the *Letter to a Noble Lord*, and at the same time conducts an argument which is rhetorically astute, for it allows him to speak of his own sufferings, without impertinence, as part of his vision of 'the awful state of the time'. But much of the argument of the *Letter* is pitched in quite different and certainly less sublime terms. In order to refute Bedford, Burke needs to assert his worth as well as demonstrate his suffering. The images of natural disaster give way to a more combative language which is social and economic in character, and in which the tensions of his position are made manifest. Though contemptuous of the Duke of Bedford, Burke wishes to make plain his respect for the class of patrons. Anxious to justify his own conduct, he nevertheless desires to reply in a style which is 'correct', both in the social and literary sense: 'Even in the utmost latitude of defensive liberty, I wish to preserve all possible decorum.' (VIII, 9) In this statement Burke certainly expresses his intentions with poise, as if his rights as an individual and his social duties were fully compatible, accommodated in a perfect Whig balance of liberty and restraint. But the division of the line may also denote a place of struggle, a point at which Burke strives both to acknowledge and disavow the relations of patronage (the relations confirmed by the grant of his pension). Indeed, this sensitive issue opens up a kind of division in the argument. It provokes a shift from deference to dissent:

When I say I have not received more than I deserve, is this the language I hold to majesty? No! Far, very far, from it! Before that presence, I claim no merit at all. Every thing towards me is favour, and bounty. One style to a gracious benefactor; another to a proud and insulting foe.

(VIII, 10-11)

This discrepancy between styles is apparent both in the presentation of Burke's argument in the *Letter* and in the forms of address it takes. Addressed with all due deference to one noble lord, the letter, in taking issue with the Duke of Bedford, challenges the authority of another. A kind of conflict of interests is already suggested. It is true that Burke never addresses Bedford directly, but neither is Grenville himself often afforded that courtesy. The consequence is that in the act of reading the *Letter* one's sense of its addressee becomes confused. Is he, according to epistolary convention, Lord Grenville, the unnamed 'noble lord' of the title-page? Or is he, according to the logic of the argument, and the expectations it raises, the Duke of Bedford himself?

This kind of discrepancy, deeply rooted in the writing of the *Letter*, is one which Burke himself recognises and seeks to justify: 'One style to a gracious benefactor; another to a proud and insulting foe.' In his speech in the House of Lords that 'foe', the Duke of Bedford, had drawn attention to Burke's record as a political economist. The man who had once distinguished himself as 'the advocate of rigid economy' was now prepared to accept the patronage of the Crown. Appropriately, it is in the style of an economist that Burke chooses to reply. His right to the pension having been challenged, he contrasts the value to the public of his own labours with the negligible contributions of the inexperienced duke. He draws up a balance sheet of their respective merits, emphasising that the privileges enjoyed by Bedford are, unlike his own, inherited and unearned. Burke, in other words, writes as an experienced economist and self-made man who is entitled to calculate the recompense due to his expenditure of labour. His argument takes the form of a casting of accounts: 'Thus stands the account of the comparative merits of the crown grants which compose the duke of Bedord's fortune as balanced against mine.' (VIII, 43)

This is the assertive and irreverent stance of the bourgeois political economist. It is Burke's dominant voice in the *Letter*. Yet as one who is subject to the patronage of the Crown, he is obliged to declare his allegiance to a different system of values. It is the language of deference which leads him to admit that he is no more than a humble and undeserving beneficiary of 'the justice, the bounty, or . . . the charity of the crown' (VIII, 32). Throughout the *Letter*, one senses that Burke is bringing together two sets of terms which belong to quite different forms of social relationship. On one hand, there are the terms appropriate to a relation of subordination and service — 'obligation', 'bounty', 'gratitude', 'favour'. On another, there is the language of free competition and the market economy — 'labour', 'earn', 'pay', 'merit'. The tension which exists between these two idioms makes *A Letter to a Noble Lord* Burke's richest and most revealing work. He may not, after all, even in the 1790s, have been an altogether reliable spokesman for the old order. In one breath, and in his most reverential style, he will speak of 'the sacred rules of prescription', 'the great stable laws of property', and the rights consequent upon 'an immemorial possession'. In another, he will trace the Duke of Bedford's titles back to their relatively recent and corrupt historical origins. He becomes a half-reluctant critic of hereditary privilege.

Coleridge was among the first to recognise this incongruity when, in an early review of the *Letter*, he observed that Burke 'lays down propositions, from which his adversaries are entitled to draw strange corollaries. The egg is his: Paine and Barlow *hatch* it.' (1970, p. 36) Many later critics have remarked on the instability of Burke's position, both in the *Letter* and in his other counter-revolutionary works. Conor Cruise O'Brien (1968, p. 76) has suggested that there is 'a suppressed sympathy with revolution' in Burke's writings, a hidden capacity for revolt which can in large part be explained by his Irish birth and experience. It is a persuasive argument, but it can be seen from the account O'Brien himself provides that the forces of disruption in Burke's life were as much social as national or religious in character. The strongest evidence we have of this is, as I have suggested,

A Letter to a Noble Lord, the work in which the social contradictions Burke experienced find their most urgent and eloquent expression.

PART TWO
Parliamentary Discourse

6

The Conditions of Performance

'We shape our buildings and afterwards our buildings shape us.' So said Winston Churchill in October 1943, opening a debate on the rebuilding of the House of Commons.[1] Two years earlier the chamber in which the Commons had been accustomed to assemble for almost a century had been destroyed in an air-raid. In his speech Churchill drew attention to the influence which the physical structure and layout of the chamber had had on parliamentary customs and conventions. In so doing he gave voice to a quite widespread desire that the new chamber should retain all the 'essential features' of the old. The latter, a Victorian structure, had itself been modelled on an earlier chamber, St Stephen's Chapel, in which Burke had himself spoken, and in which the Commons had met until the building was gutted in the great fire of 1834. In the teeth of such disasters the main characteristics of the House had been lovingly preserved. It was a record of continuity which Churchill, and other members gathered for the debate, greatly valued and wished to extend.

Churchill's attachment to the traditional forms of parliament was such that one suspects he would have regarded any innovation in its architecture as virtually unconstitutional. In characteristic style he remarked that

> Logic is a poor guide compared with custom. Logic which has created in so many countries semi-circular assemblies which have buildings which give to every Member, not only a seat to sit in but often a desk to write at, with a lid to bang, has proved fatal to Parliamentary Government as we know it here in its home and in the land of its birth.

It is 'Parliamentary Government' rather than parliamentary

democracy that Churchill extols. For the customs he wishes to preserve were, in many cases, established before the era of reform. Parliamentary procedure and oratorical styles have certainly changed considerably since the time of Burke. But it has been a pattern of change underpinned by continuity, a pattern of which Churchill spoke fondly, and of which even Burke might have been able to approve.

It is, moreover, a pattern which persists. One of the lessons of the Falklands crisis of 1982 was that the customs and idioms of parliament, however 'archaic' they might sometimes appear, have retained their influence on British political life. Listening to the debates of April and May 1982 (shrewdly examined in Anthony Barnett's fine polemic, *Iron Britannia*), one noted the tendency for the Commons, in times of national 'emergency', to seek refuge in its history and to cling to its ancient customs and privileges. At such moments the exclusiveness of the institution is asserted in certain peculiarities of its discourse. Constituents who seek admission to its galleries may be reminded (as they often were in Burke's day) that they are 'strangers' – a curiously alienating usage for a supposedly modern and democratic assembly to retain. More is at stake here than a mere form of words. The retention of such usages raises important political questions: can parliament be said to have an 'audience'? If so, how is it defined and addressed? These were matters of genuine controversy in the period of Burke's political career. Under the pressure of increasing extra-parliamentary agitation, the reporting of the proceedings of parliament to the political nation outside made significant advances in the 1760s and 1770s. Recent debates concerning the broadcasting of parliament suggest that the issue has yet to be resolved. In different historical circumstances – and under the impact of different technologies – the argument again turns on the principles of access and accountability. Elected under a system of universal suffrage, the House of Commons, like other institutions of the modern British state, remains notably reluctant to throw open its doors to the public and adapt to changing conditions.

Parliamentary discourse – by any reckoning one of the central elements of British political culture – has never been systematically surveyed. Most studies of British political history make extensive reference to parliamentary debates, without paying much attention to their formal and rhetorical qualities. The main currents of British literary criticism have been almost equally reluctant to engage in the analysis of performance and speech, even in such 'high' forms as the parliamentary oration. As a result, the functions and processes of the speech, historically one of the most important forms of political communication, have, in Britain at least, suffered serious neglect. It is not just that an opportunity for an interesting exercise in stylistics has been overlooked. A study of the conventions of the parliamentary speech, including the conditions of its composition, delivery and dissemination, is in effect an inquiry into the developing relationship between parliament and its 'audience' — an inquiry, that is to say, into the changing relations of political power.

The closing decades of the eighteenth century marked a high point in the history of British parliamentary oratory. Contemporary commentators had no doubt that the parliamentary speech, as practised by distinguished orators like Chatham, Fox, Sheridan and Burke, could be regarded as an authentic literary form. Considered in this light, it presents quite specific problems of interpretation and analysis. These problems have not always been recognised in studies of Burke. His works, whether they were issued in the form of pamphlets, letters or speeches, tend to be read at a common level, as if they combined to form an unbroken tract of writing. It is my purpose here, however, to define the special properties and functions which distinguish the parliamentary speech from other modes of political discourse. These formal qualities shape the character and determine the capacities of the speech as an instrument of persuasion. They give it a unique role in the political culture. Unlike the pamphlet, for instance, the speech must be understood as a performance as well as studied as a text. For in effect parliamentary debate is a form of dramatic action. Like the theatre, the House of Commons comprises both a physical locality and a set of procedures which together determine the style and meaning of the drama. Both the speech and the play, unlike most other literary genres, have a significance outside their existence as texts.

They operate as powerfully, and indeed develop their full potential, in the process of performance. While the novel and the poem live only for the moment of their acquaintance with an individual reader, drama and oratory address themselves to a collective audience.

It is primarily in the process of performance, then, that the parliamentary speech is effective as a political act. It may indeed be preserved and transmitted in a written form, but even where a verbatim record exists certain important details of the performance — intonation, delivery, gesture, reception, and so on — will inevitably be lost. What I am suggesting here is that the mode of literary analysis most nearly applicable to the parliamentary speech is that of dramatic criticism, in which one would take into account not only the character of the dramatic text but also more general conditions and conventions, including stage design, audience expectations, acting styles, and so on. In *Drama in Performance* Raymond Williams proposes that 'the relation between a dramatic text and a dramatic performance . . . is the fundamental question in dramatic theory' (1972, p. 2). Seeking to conceive of that relationship as a unity, and thus to close the traditional division between dramatic theory and practice, Williams provides a summary of the 'general conditions of performance' prevailing at different periods of dramatic history, before analysing particular performances in detail. It is along these general lines of inquiry that I intend to consider some of Burke's speeches. For it seems to me that the relation between the speech as a 'performance' and the speech as a published text might be of crucial significance in deciding how the latter ought to be read.

But first some further thought should be given to the analogy between parliamentary debate and the dramatic performance. For if, in the reign of George III, the House of Commons comprised a kind of theatre of oratory, it was yet a theatre only in the most exceptional sense. We might note from the outset that the relationship between the text and performance of Burke's speeches is unlike that of most known forms of drama. For in the conditions of parliamentary debate this 'text' could only rarely be composed in advance of its performance. Although preliminary drafts were an essential aid to parliamentary speaking, the orator would also have to rely upon his talent for improvisation. In most cases, then, the 'text' came into being only during the process of its delivery. In the second place, we should remember that parliament was a theatre in which actors and audience comprised the same personnel. The 'audience' was made up of the members themselves, who not only spoke in debate but also watched and listened to those speakers who sought their votes. 'Still dumb: but see hear, laugh sometimes, am oftener serious but upon the whole very well amused,' wrote Edward Gibbon (an MP from 1774 to 1784 but a non-combatant in debate), as if his role were that of a spectator at a parliamentary performance (1956, II, 62). In theory, it is true, orators addressed a wider audience, but it was one whose presence was frequently discouraged. During some of the most important debates of the century the House of Commons vigorously enforced its right to exclude all 'strangers' from its galleries. Those members who remained to speak, or simply to cast their votes, might then be left as sole witnesses to the drama.

In spite of these important qualifications, it seems to me that the analogy between the parliamentary and the dramatic text is ultimately a productive one. For the model of the drama bestows a kind of formality upon proceedings, enables us to think of the work of parliament not as the chance confrontation of individual politicians, but as a mode of discourse, possessed of its own internal relations, forms of organisation, patterns of regulation, and so on. And yet the dramatic model is more than an heuristic device. It was also the literary analogue most commonly used in the eighteenth century to characterise parliamentary debate and its participants. No biography of Fox, Pitt, Sheridan or Burke was complete without a critical analysis of their oratorical performances, their manner of delivery and their parliamentary style. Orators such as these were viewed not only as political but also as theatrical figures. As Harding (1944) demonstrates, the parliamentary speech, no longer a mere element in the political process, had become a performance in its own right. In his well-known journal of 1782 Carl Moritz considered a visit to the House of Commons to be one of the more splendid forms of entertainment to be enjoyed in London. The prospect of an important debate could arouse considerable public expectation. Of the proceedings which followed the fall of the Rockingham administration in July 1782, Moritz observed that 'At eleven in the morning the gallery was so full that not another seat was to be had, yet the debates do not start until three in the afternoon.' (1965, p. 183)

On a celebrated occasion Burke himself developed the analogy between parliamentary proceedings and the dramatic arts. When a motion was proposed to exclude the actor Garrick, along with other 'strangers', from the galleries of the House of Commons, Burke demurred on the grounds that Garrick was

> a man to whom they were all obliged; one who was the great master of eloquence; in whose school they had all imbibed the art of speaking, and been taught the elements of rhetoric. For his part, he owned that he had been greatly indebted to his instructions.   (Davies, 1781, II, 343)

In order to remind ourselves of the melodramatic possibilities of the parliamentary theatre, we have only to recall the famous 'dagger scene' enacted by Burke during a debate on the Aliens Bill in December 1792. The *Parliamentary History* gives the following account of this incident:

> (Here Mr. Burke drew out a dagger which he had kept concealed, and with much vehemence of action threw it on the floor.) This, said he, pointing to the dagger, is what you are to gain by an alliance with France. . . . He then held the dagger up to public view. . . . It is my object, said he, to keep the French infection from this country; their principles from our minds, and their daggers from our hearts.   (*PH*, XXX, 189)

Passages such as this suggest that the transactions of parliament, as recorded in Burke's speeches, might be susceptible to a kind of dramatic criticism, to a detailed comparison of 'performance' and 'text'. But in order to push this concept beyond the limits of simple analogy we must first define more precisely the conditions in which the parliamentary oration was delivered. The rest of this chapter will therefore be devoted to a brief reconstruction of those conditions and to a consideration of the general manner in which the texts of eighteenth-century speeches were established.[2]

I suggested earlier that the Georgian House of Commons was theatrical in the sense that it comprised both a physical locality and a set of conventions. Like the theatre of classical Greece, the House in which Burke spoke owed its topography to the ceremonies and rituals of religion. We should recall that until 1834, when the building was destroyed by fire, the House of Commons was situated in St Stephen's Chapel, an integral part of the Palace of Westminster. In spite of considerable alterations to the interior of the chapel, the architecture of worship left its mark on parliamentary procedure. The Speaker's chair, for instance, took the place of the altar, the choir-stalls on either side became the members' benches, while the ante-chapel was converted into the lobby of the House of Commons.

This arrangement, however, was not entirely suited to the requirements of a parliamentary assembly. It led to a physical proximity of debate and, in consequence, to the tumult and disarray so often noted in contemporary reports. But the promotion of disorder was only one effect of his design. At the same time it contained within it the possibility of an internal regulation of debate. The conventions of parliament were not only determined by the constraints inherent in location, but also developed in order to overcome them. 'Procedure', that is to say, the means of defining formal parliamentary functions, was often closely linked to the layout of the House. Thus administration and minority began to organise themselves according to the physical divisions of the former chapel. Political affiliation could then be signified by the occupation of benches on one side or other of the House of Commons. In a similar way the central position afforded to the Speaker was transformed into a formal role, a device for preserving the order and continuity of debate. Once primarily the spokesman for the Commons, he had become its arbiter (though not one whose impartiality was invariably accepted without question). The Speaker's function was to decide upon issues of procedure and to provide a focus for debate.

It was to the Speaker that members, forbidden to harangue one another directly, were obliged to address their remarks.

This, a device aimed at preserving parliamentary decorum, was one of many such conventions to be embodied in Burke's published speeches. That these texts should be patterned according to procedures unlike those which characterise other literary genres seems to me a point of considerable significance. To turn for a moment to another aspect of procedure, we might note that participants in debate were not permitted to allude to one another by name. Like the formal address to the Speaker, this convention had an authoritative function: to maintain the public status of parliamentary discourse by denying access to private rancour. Today members of parliament identify one another by naming the places they represent (as in the formula 'the Honourable Member for Sheffield Brightside'); but the multi-member character of eighteenth-century constituencies more or less ruled out this device. Members, rather, were designated according to their position in the House ('the honourable gentleman under the gallery' or 'the learned gentleman over against me'), by their place in the order of debate ('the honourable gentleman, who spoke last but one'), or by any other distinguishing mark (after his award of the Garter in 1772 Lord North often appears in Burke's speeches as 'the noble Lord in the blue ribband').

Formal devices of this kind are not, I would contend, incidental to the speech's status as a literary object. They lend it a quite distinct and public character which makes it almost unique among literary forms. We might view this convention of address not simply as a regulation which promotes discourse but also as a prohibition which may provoke resistance. It poses, for instance, a problem about the naming of individuals, a problem central to the ethics of eighteenth-century satire, and one which arises in many of Burke's writings. We have already seen how the denial of the 'personal' fractures the rhetorical coherence of Burke's *Letter to a Noble Lord*. Parliamentary discourse, produced between the conflicting claims of political confrontation and the regulations of procedure, may be fissured in a similar way. In this sense Burke's notorious violence in debate may be seen as more than the psychological aberration of a wayward individual. It may also represent the realisation in discourse of a formal parliamentary tension.

Parliamentary procedure comprised a quasi-juridical and definitely enforceable set of regulations. The manner in which a motion should be proposed or a petition presented, the way in which a question might be put to the vote, the frequency with which a member could speak in committee or in formal debate — instructions on all these matters were inscribed in the standing orders of the House. In this sense they comprise the general conditions for the delivery of Burke's speeches. The conventions which governed oratory at a level of its composition, however, seem to have been less specific. The general view, but one which may need a good deal of qualification, is that in practice speeches were composed in a largely extemporaneous manner. According to Thomas, orators were not permitted to read their speeches from manuscript, while even undue reliance on notes came to be regarded as unparliamentary (1971, pp. 203-4). Although speeches might be fully drafted in advance and delivered from memory, 'set speeches' of this kind proved to be of decreasing utility and were correspondingly rare.

This view receives some support from Lord Erskine's prefatory letter to the 1815 edition of Fox's *Speeches*. Erskine claimed that the superiority of modern over classical oratory lay exactly in its extemporaneous character. This improvement, however, was determined by political necessity rather than literary predilection, since 'The great affairs of a free government like that of England, could not be usefully discussed in public, by men coming forth from their closets with written discourses, however sublime or beautiful.' (Fox, 1815, I, viii) Thus in Erskine's account the demands of debate and the dramatic interplay of opposing points of view confer a degree of spontaneity on the production of parliamentary discourse. Indeed, contemporary reports will often give the impression that Burke's speeches were delivered absolutely impromptu. Horace Walpole even asserted that Burke's debating skill was developed to such an extent that when he 'replied extempore, his very answers, that sprang from what had been said by others, were so painted and artfully arranged,

that they wore the appearance of study and preparation'
(1894, II, 195).

From accounts such as these it is easy to conceive of parliamentary debate as improvised almost in its entirety. And
yet fluent speaking may have been far more the result of
premeditation than Walpole suspected. In one of the few
surviving treatises on contemporary parliamentary procedure
William Gerard Hamilton is at pains to stress that spontaneity
is itself an *effect* which the orator may prepare in advance.
His somewhat cyncial primer, *Parliamentary Logick*, continually recommends the virtues of study and strategic planning
for the delivery of a speech. Thus Hamilton urges the young
orator to

> Preconsider what you mean should be the finest part of
> your speech, and in speaking connect it with what has in-
> cidentally fallen in debate; and, when you come to that
> premeditated and finest part, hesitate and appear to
> boggle; — catch at some expression that shall fall short of
> your idea, and then seem at last to hit upon the true thing.
> This has always an extraordinary effect, and gives the air
> of extempore genius to what you say.   (1808, p. 43)

Parliamentary Logick is a work of considerable interest,
but Hamilton, though an experienced parliamentarian, is by
no means an unimpeachable authority. His celebrated 'single
speech', from which he received the nickname by which he
was popularly known, was in fact an old-fashioned set speech.
His remarks on the art of speaking, like those of Erskine and
Walpole, are of limited value for an assessment of the conditions of parliamentary debate. In the two following chapters
I hope to reach some more specific conclusions about Burke's
own methods of composition. This inquiry will take the form
of an analysis of the speech at the three stages of its existence:
the preliminary draft, the speech in performance, and the
published text. But it will first be necessary to make some
preliminary observations on the state of parliamentary reporting in the eighteenth century. For this activity, in its
provision of a more or less detailed record of performance,
comprises one of the general conditions determining the publication of Burke's speeches.

The development of parliamentary reporting belongs to a much larger history of the processes of utterance and transcription. In the literature of the eighteenth century an extraordinary prestige is afforded to the spoken word. Conversation, the verbal retort, sallies of wit, and, in a more formal sense, the sermon and the speech, seem at times to achieve a virtual hegemony over writing. The figures who participate in this oral history assume roles according to a division of labour which distinguishes speakers and transcribers, separates orators from reporters. Between the two a definite relation of power exists: the inspired speaker served by his faithful scribe, a relationship given classic form by the ascendancy of Samuel Johnson over Boswell, his amanuensis. A veritable hymn to the majesty of the spoken word, the *Life of Johnson* stands supreme among the volumes of eighteenth-century table-talk. Obliged to lament the evanescent character of speech, Boswell is content to occupy the dignified, though admittedly inferior, role of the scribe. His subservience is demonstrated most dramatically when Johnson expatiates on the four essential requisites of good conversation (knowledge and materials, command of words, imagination, presence of mind and resolution). Overawed by Johnson's eloquence, and unable to make any semblance of a reply, Boswell can only regret the inadequacy of the existing means of transcription: 'While he went on talking triumphantly, I was fixed in admiration, and said to Mrs. Thrale, "O, for short-hand to take this down!"' (1934-50, IV, 166)

Boswell's attempt to preserve Johnson's eloquence for posterity was just one of many such efforts of transcription. At the same time there was, as Thomas (1959a) has shown, an increasing concern to record the performance of the more accomplished parliamentary orators. Nevertheless, in the eighteenth century parliamentary reporting had yet to achieve any official status. The publication of debates was indeed long condemned as a breach of privilege. In 1768, however, soon after Burke's entry into the House of Commons, John Almon systematically began to defy such restrictions and to compile regular reports of proceedings for the *London Evening Post*. After 1771 there was no attempt, by means of prosecution for libel, to enforce prohibition at the point of publication. Instead the House of Commons periodically exercised its right to clear its galleries of 'strangers', in which case the only surviving reports would be those made by members themselves. In adverse conditions such as these the standard of reporting was inevitably low. Forbidden even to take notes until 1783, reporters were obliged to rely upon memory or on information supplied by members. They were consequently often credited with almost superhuman powers of recall. The biographer of Hugh Boyd claimed that

> He never took any notes of the speeches he had heard; but after attending a long debate in parliament, he would sup at a tavern with some friends, return home at two or three in the morning, go to bed directly, rise about seven, and write down such speeches as he had most admired in the course of the debate, without once looking at any of the newspaper reports, to facilitate his recollection.
>
> (Campbell, 1800, I, 197)

In view of the somewhat extravagant nature of these claims, it is worth recalling that Boyd is said to have furnished material for the published version of Burke's *Speech on Oeconomical Reform* (see *Corr.*, IV, 212). Debates printed in later collections, such as Cobbett's *Parliamentary History*, or, indeed, the 1816 edition of Burke's *Speeches*, were generally purloined from newspaper or periodical accounts and consequently share their inaccuracies. Although the reports published during Burke's parliamentary career were no longer, as Samuel Johnson's had been, largely fabrications, they no doubt often remained almost as much the product of the reporter as of the orator.

Against this general background of suspect, fragmentary and inaccurate texts, Burke's published speeches stand out as an exceptional case. Prepared for the press by Burke himself, they have been incorporated into the literary history of the eighteenth century, selected as the authentic productions of an identifiable author. But when the texts are read in terms of the general conditions in which parliamentary speeches were prepared, delivered and reported, their status becomes somewhat problematic. In what manner did Burke prepare his speeches before delivery? Upon what kind of report did he base the published text? What relation, then, does the printed speech bear to the parliamentary drama from which it issued? It is now time to consider these questions in a little more detail.

Preparation and Delivery

While Burke's writings have long been subject to literary interpretation, it has been according to political and historical
criteria that his career has generally been discussed and
understood. Even literary critics tend to classify his works
in terms of the manifest political concern of their subject-
matter: Burke and America, Burke and India, Burke and
France, and so on. But linked to this significant political progress is a less obvious history of literary form. The changing
circumstances of Burke's career in its various phases occasioned
particular forms of argument and address. Thus, in succession,
the political pamphlet, the parliamentary speech and the
printed letter became Burke's favoured mode of political
discourse. My concern here is with the central period of this
literary history. From 1775 to 1790 the texts published on
Burke's own authority were predominantly oratorical in form.

The work which inaugurated this central period, the *Speech
on American Taxation* (1775), is uncommonly informative
about its mode of transmission. Its editor (probably Burke
himself) offers some interesting prefatory remarks:

> The following speech has been much the subject of con-
> versation; and the desire of having it printed was last
> summer very general. The means of gratifying the publick
> curiosity were obligingly furnished from the notes of some
> gentlemen, members of the last parliament.   (II, 347)

This somewhat offhand remark opens up the possibility of re-
constructing the process by which the texts of Burke's
speeches were established. It would seem to enable us to
formulate a genuine relationship between performance and
text. However, within the framework of this theoretical task

(determining the status of Burke's printed speeches) lie a number of empirical difficulties. The material upon which such a reconstruction might be based is often scanty, unreliable and relatively obscure.

In this chapter and the one which follows it some preliminary approaches to this task will be explored.[1] My analysis will be based on two manuscript sources for the parliamentary oratory of the period. The surviving Burke papers, usually known as the Fitzwilliam manuscripts, contain a large body of Burke's correspondence, together with many scattered notes and drafts on various political affairs. Since 1948, when these papers first became generally available for consultation, they have been the object of much scholarly attention, an endeavour now embodied in the ten-volume edition of Burke's *Correspondence*. The notes and drafts of Burke's speeches, however, have until recently suffered a relative neglect.[2] It is upon these disordered, fragmentary, and sometimes almost indecipherable papers that many of the following remarks will be based.

A second and equally valuable source for Burke's speeches is the parliamentary diary of Sir Henry Cavendish.[3] While the inaccuracy of most other reports renders them virtually useless for formal literary analysis, Cavendish's diary has a double value. In the first place, it represents the most sustained and successful attempt to produce a verbatim record of parliamentary proceedings in the eighteenth century. Cavendish, for six years the member for Lostwithiel, and therefore exempt from any orders for exclusion, employed the Gurney system of shorthand to transcribe the details of almost every debate he attended. Although the diary is confined to the years 1768-74, this was a period marked by some of Burke's most important speeches, many of which are unrecorded elsewhere. While the 1816 edition of Burke's *Speeches* includes only thirty fragmentary accounts for the parliament of 1768-74, Cavendish provides over two hundred relatively complete reports.

As Bryant (1952) has shown, Cavendish's detailed record of performance can be compared with Burke's drafts of the period: the speech may then be traced in its progress from preparation to delivery. But, as I intimated above, the diary is valuable in a second sense. Precisely because it comprised the most complete and reliable account of parliamentary proceedings, it was selected by contemporary orators as a source for speeches they might wish to publish. Burke's own *Speech on American Taxation* and George Grenville's *Speech on the Motion for Expelling Mr. Wilkes* were, as we shall see, certainly based on Cavendish's journal. In some cases, then, we are able to extend our analysis and to compare a speech revised by Burke directly with its manuscript source.

It is important, however, to stress the limitations of the available material. Cavendish's reports, copious though they may be by eighteenth-century standards, are yet by no means comparable to *Hansard* in their accuracy. When John Wright published part of the diary in the 1840s, he frequently had to resort to editorial intrusion and speculation in order to make sense of its entries. In the manuscript diary there are gaps in most speeches, but Burke's are perhaps the most fragmentary of all. In a draft preface Cavendish confesses that 'Several speeches of some of the most able Members, are very imperfect. Many sublime, and beautiful passages, are lost, lost I fear, forever . . . the only comfort I have left is, that I believe I have preserved more, than the memory of any individual has.' (Eg. MS. 263, ff. 5-6) Although by this time the phrase 'sublime and beautiful' had no doubt entered common parlance, in this context it may well contain an allusion to Burke, author of the *Philosophical Enquiry* and one of the most able of parliamentary orators. Burke was a notoriously rapid speaker, and his pronounced Irish accent continued to perplex audience and transcribers alike. Frequently marred by lacunae, Cavendish's diary cannot be regarded as a completely verbatim record of performance. This tends to make work on Burke's draft speeches problematical, there being no absolutely reliable parliamentary account against which they can be placed. But by the same token, the analysis of his printed speeches becomes more rewarding: for in the light of Cavendish's notes it appears that these publications may represent more than a minor revision of their source material — that on the contrary, they may have entailed a considerable literary effort, the processes, tactics and transformations of which we can attempt to reconstruct.

More disabling are those occasions when neither the Burke papers nor the Cavendish diary provide information sufficient for us to comment upon important speeches in detail. Such deficiencies apply in some of the potentially most interesting cases. We shall find, for example, that little manuscript record survives of Burke's *Speech on American Taxation*. But even in such an extreme instance, there is sufficient material of a secondary nature for us to reach some provisional conclusions concerning the genesis of the oration and the transmission of the text.

In the preceding chapter I spoke of the three-stage evolution of the printed speech. My initial objective here will be to establish a correspondence between the first two of these stages, the preliminary draft and the speech in performance, by selecting related material from the sources I have described. The extent to which Burke's speeches might be prepared in advance would necessarily depend both upon the nature of the parliamentary occasion and upon his own role in the proceedings. If Burke were no more than a participant in the debate, previous notification of its subject-matter would nevertheless have enabled him to undertake a certain amount of preparation. Even so, a good deal of improvisation would be necessary in order to deploy general lines of argument in the particular context presented by the debate. The *Speech on American Taxation*, in which Burke states the colonial policy of the Rockingham Whigs in the form of a reply to a previous speaker (Charles Cornwall), is an oration of this type. If, on the other hand, Burke were himself moving a motion, or formally proposing resolutions, more elaborate preparation might be possible. Most of Burke's published speeches are of this second kind, a fact which becomes apparent when we refer to their formal parliamentary titles. Thus Burke's famous speech on *Conciliation* is, more properly, *Mr. Burke's Speech on Moving his Resolutions for Conciliation with the Colonies*.

An unpublished speech of a similar kind, and upon a similar theme, was delivered by Burke in the House of Commons on 9 May 1770. Among the Burke papers there are three manuscripts which, although they remain unendorsed, are recognisably the drafts of this speech.[4] Because Burke made a relatively large number of speeches on American affairs, and because his papers are disorganised and sometimes nearly illegible, it is often difficult to make such a positive identification. But in this case Burke's opening address, alluding directly to the time of composition, is itself helpful: 'The Summer is coming on fast upon but I hope the Session is yet far from being spent. . . .' Elsewhere in the draft Burke refers to certain 'motions' that he will lay before the judgment of the House. These papers have recently been published (*Writings and Speeches*, II, 323-34) and identified by Paul Langford as the drafts of Burke's speech on moving his *Resolutions relating to the Disorders in North America*. The speech was one of the final items of business in the session formally closed on 19 May 1770. Cavendish's report establishes the correspondence more definitely.[5] It preserves from the draft not only the general heads of its argument, but also, in places, the precise configurations of its phraseology. The relationship between draft and performance may be judged from a parallel reading of a passage which, in either case, follows immediately on Burke's preamble:

Burke's Draft[6] (A. xxvii. 67)	*Cavendish's Report* (Eg. MS. 222, pp. B 92-4)
The Summer is coming on fast upon but I hope the Session is yet far from being spent; because I trust, that the period of your sitting, (& I wish I could add the diligence of your attendance while you sit) that it will not depend upon the length or the shortness of days, but upon the pressure & importance of the business that waits for you. Sir you sate late yesterday I felt very sensibly, how disagreeable it is to bring on business at this time; & when every circumstance draws your attention to your private affairs, & to your Natural relaxations. But it is from the completion of your Business that you derive your Title to repose. [Your sitting] will be regulated by your Duty & not by the Almanack.	I really am sorry for the trouble I have been obliged to give the House the great trouble & the great delay that I shall give them in commenting upon these papers. I feel this as much as anybody both for myself & others. At a time when the session is almost spent, at a time when Gentlemen wish to retire to their recreation, something overrules this, it makes me wish to try the patience of the House a little longer. Your diligence will not be regulated by the almanack, but by your duty. But we should think that nothing but the accomplishment of our business gives us a title to our repose, so long as the happiness of this country, the dignity of government is concerned, no cir-

I am going to bring before you the affairs of *America*.

If the House does not find at this time in the very sound of that word every argument for your anxious & diligent attention nothing that I can say I (. . .) will ever be able to enforce it.

cumstances of toil or trouble, or of pleasure or repose that will call our minds one moment so arduous in their nature so pressing in point of time. I am now going to bring before you the affairs of America. If you don't find in these words, a motive to give your diligent attention nothing that I can say will induce you.

Although Cavendish's account may be somewhat garbled at points, it would appear from the comparison presented above that in the process of delivery Burke combined elements from the first two paragraphs he had prepared in his draft. Many expressions are repeated virtually verbatim, but the draft material is also reorganised and embellished. While this remains the pattern throughout the speech, in the second half of Cavendish's transcription there is an increasing deviation from the draft, as if reliance on memory had gradually given way to the desire — or to the need — to improvise. But even at an early stage in the performance Burke modifies and revises the words and phrases he had rehearsed. In the following passage he appeals to Speaker Norton to bear witness to his consistency in colonial affairs:

Burke's Draft
(A. xxvii. 67)

My Principles upon this Subject such as they are have ever been uniform. You who have a memory good enough to remember were my Sentiments. I know that America cannot be regulated here — I know that the detail of Government cannot be settled in an house of Parliament. I am deeply sensible that the maturest and safest deliberations of Cabinet Wisdom, would become folly and peril if blown upon by the publick breath of a popular assembly.

Cavendish's Report
(Eg. MS. 222, p. B 96)

Whatever my conduct has been, it has been universal. You Sir have a good memory & may remember my words. My opinion is that America cannot be governed here, that the detail — — — — — of their expences cannot be administered in a House of Parliament — — — — — with regard to interior measures, — — — — — The wisest deliberations of cabinet wisdom would shrivel into folly if once blown upon by the rude breath of a popular assembly.

The gaps, as reproduced from the manuscript, indicate that Cavendish's report is incomplete. It is evident, nonetheless, that in performance Burke again adhered closely to the substance of his draft. Yet in detail the passages diverge, and in a significant way. The final sentence of the first extract, for instance, is a particularly poised and polished composition. In some respects its counterpart in Cavendish is less effective. The proximity of 'wisest' and 'wisdom', for example, creates something of a jar. But in other ways the sentence Burke actually delivered is a more animated, imaginative and persuasive statement. The 'would become folly' of the draft, a rather inert phrase, is transformed into a more emotive appeal — 'would shrivel into folly'. The latter expression appears to complete a metaphor which was only implicit in the draft ('blown upon by the publick breath'). In a similar way the change from 'publick' to 'rude' may indicate a dislike of neutral and abstract terms in spoken discourse. It may well be that in the heat of debate Burke resorts more readily to metaphor, but it would be dangerous to draw general conclusions, however appealing they may be, from such scanty evidence. It is quite possible that the expression reported by Cavendish was reclaimed from another draft, now lost, or from a passage now deleted and indecipherable.

Verbal revisions of the kind I have just discussed are more striking, but not more significant, than changes which may occur in the rhetorical organisation of the speech. Burke will often retain prepared expressions but deploy them in a new way. Phrases which appear at one point in the draft may be transposed to a quite different location in the speech. In one case a rhetorical unit comprised of a pair of sentences in the draft is broken up and displaced in the course of delivery. Fulminating against ministerial inconsistency, Burke originally composed the following lines:

> Whilst here they Lightned and Thunderd; & our whole atmosphere was in flame in America nothing but breezes descended but mild dew & manna. Whilst here you were making a monstrous jumble of antique ferociousness & modern effeminacy in yr famous act of H. the 8th there you were yielding all.   (A. xxvii. 66)

In Cavendish's report — and hence, presumably, in Burke's performance — this rhetorical figure (structured by the repetition of 'whilst' and the successive patterns of hyperbole and ridicule) is dismantled. The concluding part of the harangue appears first, as 'a strong mixture of ancient ferociousness, & modern effeminacy' (Eg. MS. 222, p. B 112; it is possible that Burke actually said 'a *strange* mixture'). Ten pages later, and in a slightly modified form, the first section is finally delivered: 'whilst our atmosphere was full —————— & blazed with lightening in every part, in America every thing was mild' (ibid., p. B 122).

In spite of these structural changes, it is clear that Burke's speech relied extensively upon prior composition. His performance was 'extemporaneous' in the sense that it involved a degree of verbal revision and rhetorical reorganisation, but the form and substance of the speech were largely settled in advance. The function of the draft is by no means confined to its detailed literary activities. In a more general sense it provides a kind of rhetorical framework within the confines of which declamation can take place. For in this speech of 1770 Burke conducts an historical review of ministerial policy on America (and in this sense it is an anticipation of — indeed, a rehearsal for — his later and better-known *Speech on American Taxation*). The speech, in other words, is structured as a political narrative, and it is one of the functions of the draft to mark out its episodic character. Thus Burke organises his notes according to the successive 'periods' of colonial policy, from the repeal of the Stamp Act by the Rockingham Whigs in 1766 to the most recent ministerial measures.

At the same time — and this is evidence of its preliminary and preparatory status — Burke's draft issues instructions of a more precise kind, 'stage-directions' which suggest how an argument might be deployed or an issue presented, memoranda which note how ministerial attacks might best be countered or anticipated. Thus in a passage on the pernicious effects of the so-called 'Townshend's Duties', Burke describes their unfavourable reception in America, and draws attention to their essentially political character in a marginal note: 'State the reasons — by being uncommercial fixed upon us.' (A. xxvii. 67) Towards the end of the draft Burke begins to prepare more intricate manoeuvres and to consider the tactical presentation of his evidence:

> But the conduct of administration was the very reverse.
> A Circular Letter was sent — here the Circular Letter.
> Here the Letter —
> 1st. Compare it with the Kings Speech — What Laws did
> it propose to support but this — 2. What end did it answer
> to postpone the repeal.   (A. xxvii. 66)

From hints and suggestions such as these, together with the more elaborate literary preparation, Burke develops the impassioned analysis of colonial policy transcribed by Cavendish and inserted in his diary as the entry for 9 May 1770.

In the parallel readings that I have conducted both the limitations and possibilities of preparation become apparent. While Burke's effort was in no sense a 'set speech', written out in full and memorised in advance, the draft is yet far more than a mere citation of arguments. The relationship between draft and performance is complex, combinative, an action of the written and premeditated on the spoken and momentary. Burke saw the need for this combination of skills as early as 1747. In an entry in the minutes of the Trinity College Club (of which he was a founder member) he observed that

> as the business of this Society is principally our improvement of Eloquence, that it was well contriv'd that not only an action & extempore grace of speaking but also our invention should be regarded wch the premeditated Orations provide for. . . .   (Samuels, 1923, p. 251)

Almost half a century later he complimented the young William Smith for putting these skills into practice in a speech on the question of Catholic relief:

> The allusion with which you open to what had been said by a member who preceded you in the debate is a very happy one; and gives a spirited air of *impromptu* to the entire speech. It seems to show that though your general topics might have been revolved, your ideas were allowed to arrange and clothe themselves on the spot. (*Corr.*, VIII, 244)

What Burke again seems to have in mind here is a creative interaction of the impromptu and the premeditated, the spoken and the written. As Donald Bryant puts it, Burke's own literary practice enabled him to acquire 'precision, fluency, and grace in impromptu and extemporaneous speaking'. His 'habit of incessant writing', essentially linked to his oratorical art, was 'a way of forming his ideas, of generating his imagery, of planning his strategy, and, above all, of rehearsing his performance' (1966, p. 334). In Cavendish's diary we have the most accurate contemporary record of that performance. Its transformation into a text will be considered in the following chapter.

8

Performance and Text

Most eighteenth-century orators regarded their speeches as ephemera, the function of which was strictly parliamentary and occasional. As Prior, one of Burke's early biographers, put it, they 'contended as if their eloquence was only born to die with the debate of the day' (1826, II, 466). Fox, whose reputation as a parliamentarian was, if anything, greater than Burke's, seems to have been most reluctant to prepare his speeches for the press. Burke, on the other hand, aware at an early date that the speech might have an important extra-parliamentary function, was one of the first to realise its full literary and political potential as a printed text. While Wilkes and the city radicals maintained control of the newspaper press, Burke drew attention to the statesmanlike and neo-classical character of his politics by publishing full-dress parliamentary orations. For the speech, akin to the pamphlet in its range but observing a nicer decorum, was the most genteel of political productions. William Cobbett, himself a pamphleteer of note, was well aware of its prestige. In a letter of 1802 to Burke's protégé, William Windham, he discussed the various modes of political writing available to the statesman and concluded that

> A pamphlet would not do so well as the speech. It would be, in this case, not so congenial with the rank and character you hold. It would have more the appearance of an *extra-judicial* proceeding, if I may so express myself, and would have less weight. (Melville, 1913, I, 155-6)

Burke's practice of publishing his best parliamentary speeches may also have been influenced by rather more mundane considerations. It would have been difficult for a man accustomed to live by his pen to ignore such a rich quarry of material (one which had already cost him enormous labour). In this respect it may be significant that the *Letter to the Sheriffs of Bristol* (1777), the one important non-oratorical work published on Burke's authority between the *Thoughts on the Cause of the Present Discontents* (1770) and the *Reflections on the Revolution in France* (1790), was written at a time when the Rockingham Whigs were pursuing a policy of partial 'secession' from parliament. Moreover, Burke's return to the printed letter as his major mode of political writing in the 1790s coincides with the decline in his parliamentary and oratorical role which followed the break with Fox. It seems probable, then, that it was for a combination of reasons of strategy and convenience that in the central period of his political career Burke saw the printed speech as the primary means by which he could reach an extra-parliamentary public.

The first great product of this policy was the *Speech on American Taxation*, published in January 1775, and based, according to its preface, upon 'the notes of some gentlemen, members of the last parliament'. The most important source of these 'notes' was undoubtedly the parliamentary diary of Sir Henry Cavendish. Boswell records as much in his journal for 1776, while John Wright used the information to advertise his published extracts from the diary. And in the only surviving item of the Burke/Cavendish correspondence, a letter of 1 February 1775, the diarist thanked Burke for 'the two copies of your Speech'.[1] Burke had clearly dispatched these to Cavendish in return for the use of his notes. We should seem, on the face of it, to be presented with a perfect opportunity to conduct an extensive comparison of performance (Cavendish's report) and text (Burke's published speech). But in this case the analysis is obstructed by empirical difficulties of a typically mundane nature. For it is no longer possible to trace Cavendish's notes of Burke's speech. At the point in the diary at which they ought to appear, there is simply the declaration 'Mr. Edmund Burke's speech copied, and printed.' (Eg. MS. 255, p. 190) It was Cavendish's intention, ultimately unfulfilled, to publish his diary in full, in which production he no doubt planned wherever possible to use versions of speeches revised by their authors, rather than rely on his own inevitably incomplete accounts. In a section of the diary which he had begun to revise for publication there is the following note on George Grenville's *Speech on the Motion for Expelling Mr. Wilkes*: 'Print the printed Speech, which was taken from my minutes given to Mr. G. Note, Mr. Grenville's speech was printed by his order from the minutes of Mr. C. and is here reprinted.' (Eg. MS. 217, p. 150) As far as the *Speech on American Taxation* was concerned, then, neither Cavendish nor Burke would have thought it necessary to retain the original report.

Although this report is missing, a general survey of the Cavendish diary suggests that considerable revision and correction would have been required in order to prepare its fragmentary accounts for the public eye. Fortunately enough material survives to permit us to progress beyond mere conjecture. Among the Burke papers there is a manuscript endorsed: 'Mr. Burke's Speech on the Dissenter's Bill Ill taken in short hand but corrected by himself.'[2] This is Cavendish's account of the speech delivered on 17 March 1773, which Burke had begun to annotate, apparently with a view to publication. In many ways this is a valuable document. Burke's annotations offer us a rare opportunity to explore the relationship between a record of performance and a speech approaching its final and revised form. At the same time, however, the paper presents us with formidable problems of interpretation and even decipherment. Burke's more substantial marginal insertions are readily identifiable, but it is sometimes difficult to ascertain the status of the numerous additions and deletions inscribed on the face of the report itself. Fortunately another version of the report, uncorrected by Burke, appears in Cavendish's manuscript diary (Eg. MS. 263, ff. 59-70). In theory, Burke's revisions should come to light immediately on a simple comparison of the two documents, but it is evident that the second (uncorrected) report differs in some details from the copy used by Burke. It is significant that the uncorrected report has been detached from the rest of the debate as recorded in Cavendish's diary (Eg. MS. 243, pp. 282-357). It omits some of the more impenetrable passages in the copy annotated by Burke, and may well represent a later transcription of the original shorthand.

In view of the serious (though perhaps not insuperable) difficulties presented by this document, my conclusions will necessarily be somewhat tentative and provisional in character. My analysis will take the form of a parallel reading of passages taken from the corrected and uncorrected reports, followed by an attempt to identify and interpret Burke's additions and emendations. The probable state of Burke's copy before revision will, in each instance, be noted at the foot of the passages. In order to simplify matters, I have selected passages in which the copy used by Burke and the report preserved in Cavendish's diary seem to have been in close agreement.

Burke devotes a good deal of his speech to a refutation of the arguments put forward by Sir William Bagot who, earlier in the debate, had opposed wider relief for Dissenters. Bagot had praised the religious policies of the Roman state for allowing a measure of toleration within clearly defined limits. The Senate's attitude towards religious dissent, he argued, was a precedent which a British parliament would do well to follow. The Epicureans, for instance, 'were tolerated, they knew they were safe in their toleration. But great as they were, they never dreamt, they never took it into their heads, they never dreamt to go to the senate to be established Epicureans by law.' (Eg. MS. 243, p. 291) Burke disputes this account of Roman history in the following passage:

Cavendish (uncorrected) (Eg. MS. 263, f. 65)	*Burke's Revision* (A. xxxvi. 21)
The Honourable Gentleman must recollect the Roman law. It was clearly against any introduction of any foreign rights in a matter of religion — — — — — how they persecuted in the first introduction the rights of Bacchus before Christ, to say nothing afterwards. Heathenism therefore was, as in other respects erroneous, persecuting.	The Honourable Gentleman must recollect the Roman law — that was clearly against any introduction of any foreign rites in a matter of religion. You have it at large in Livy how they persecuted in the first introduction, the rights of Bacchus. There were moral reasons for this. But even before Christ to say nothing afterward they persecuted the Druids & others. Heathenism therefore was as in other respects erroneous was erroneous in point of persecution.

The copy on which Burke relied appears to have been almost identical with the uncorrected version reproduced above:

> The Honourable Gentleman must recollect the Roman law — that was clearly against any introduction of any foreign rites in a matter of religion ————— how they persecuted in the first introduction, the rights of Bacchus ————— before Christ to say nothing afterward ————— Heathenism therefore was as in other respects erroneous ————— persecuting.

'Foreign rites' is a substitution, apparently by Cavendish, for 'foreign rights', where the word 'rights' has been crossed through. All other emendations and additions in the revised copy seem to be Burke's, though 'was erroneous' might perhaps be attributed to Cavendish.

In this instance, when the gist of Cavendish's report is reasonably clear, Burke retains the argument while yet extending and embellishing it. He adds phrases and completes sentences, but does not alter the sense of the report in any material way. Burke's annotations may have been derived from several sources. It is possible that he took them from a sketch drawn up before the speech was delivered, a procedure he adopts later in the paper when Cavendish's report is seriously deficient.[3] It is most unlikely, however, that Burke had been able to prepare his comments on the Roman law in advance of the debate, for they appear to have been prompted by the arguments of Bagot. More probably he simply recalled the passage himself or relied on the memories of other members. In either case the text he produced is likely to have differed in some details from the speech he delivered.

At some points, particularly towards the end of the report, Cavendish was unable to provide more than a few detached words or phrases. Faced with such impoverished material, the desperate Burke twice scrawls 'cannot make it out' in the midst of a host of gaps and erasures. More characteristically, he makes good the deficiencies by drawing up marginal insertions and interlineations, containing arguments, illustrations and figures of speech which he may or may not have actually used in the debate. It is along these lines that Burke revises the following passage in which he continues his rebuttal of Bagot:

Cavendish (uncorrected) (Eg. MS. 263, f. 67)	*Burke's Revision* (A. xxxvi. 17)
I don't know what I would sacrifice — — — natural, or revealed religion. I would keep them both, & sacrifice neither. how? extend the doctrine of the Epicureans? nothing in the world propagates them so much as the suppression/ oppression of the poor, of the honest, of the candid disciples of them. — — — — — — — — — — — — — — — — — revealed religion makes them take a short cut out of slavery & bondage, into open, & direct infidelity.	I may be mistaken, but I take toleration to be a part of natural Religion — I don't know which I would sacrifice natural or revealed religion. I would keep them both. It is not necessary I would sacrifice either. I do not like this Idea of tolerating the doctrines of Epicurus: But nothing in the world propagates them so much as the suppression of the poor, of the honest, & candid disciples of the religion we profess in common I mean revealed religion, nothing sooner makes them take a short cut out of the bondage of sectarian Vexation into open, & direct infidelity than tormenting men for every difference.

Burke's copy of the report seems to have differed only very slightly from the one transcribed above from Cavendish's diary:

> I don't know which I would sacrifice. oh! natural or revealed religion. I would keep them both I would sacrifice neither. — — — — — how extend the doctrines of Epicurus nothing in the world propagates them so much as the suppression of the poor, of the honest, & candid disciples of them — — — — — — — — — — — — — — revealed religion makes them take a short cut out of the slavery of bondage into open, & direct infidelity.

The words 'oh!', 'how extend', and 'slavery of' have been deleted, presumably by Burke. For the most part he is again obliged to supply omissions and to link phrases — more the labour of an editor than an orator. But he also takes the opportunity to make stylistic improvements, even when the report makes adequate, if inelegant, sense. Thus 'I would sacrifice neither' becomes 'It is not necessary I would sacrifice either.' The somewhat tautological construction 'makes them take a short cut out of the slavery of bondage' is expanded into something altogether more particular and decisive: 'makes

them take a short cut out of the bondage of sectarian Vex-
ation'. There is little doubt, in either case, that the second
version is a distinct improvement, but we cannot assume that
it is equally representative of what Burke actually said.

Burke's large-scale additions to the report are obvious and
striking. Yet in a sense the document is at its most interesting
when Cavendish's notes are reasonably full, when they may
have furnished something approaching a verbatim record of
the speech. For at such moments Burke must have been con-
fronted with the reality of his own performance. One can
imagine that this re-acquaintance with the words one had
once spoken and lost might occasion a shock similar to that
produced by a recording of one's own voice with its curiously alien tones. Burke may often have undergone this kind
of experience when reading Cavendish's report. The following
passage, in which he describes the practices of the Epicureans,
may serve as an example:

Cavendish (uncorrected) (Eg. MS. 263, f. 65)	Burke's Revision (A. xxxvi. 21)
They defied all subscriptions. — — — — — no subscription to which they were not ready to set their hands. They made it a principle of their religion — — — — — They allowed all that you could, so will all free-thinkers for ever —	They defied all subscription. They defied all exterior Tests of conformity. There was no subscription to which they were not ready to set their hands nor no ceremonies they refused to practice. They made it a principle of their irreligion outwardly to conform to any Religion. These Atheists eluded all that you could do, so will all free-thinkers for ever.

In this case the copy annotated and amended by Burke seems
to have differed in some respects from the one now to be
found in Cavendish's diary. It may originally have read as
follows:

> They defied all subscription. There was no subscription to
> which they were not ready to set their hands. They made
> it a principle of their (ir)religion — — — — — They eluded all
> that you could do, so will all free-thinkers for ever.

The first syllable of 'irreligion' is an addition, inserted above
the line. The discrepancy between 'eluded' in Burke's copy

and 'allowed' in the diary report suggests that the latter may have been a re-transcription of the shorthand.

In general it is again clear that Burke's revised version preserves the argument and much of the language of the original. The additional sentences and phrases do not distort the sense of Cavendish's report. More interesting and problematical are the minor syllabic differences. The change from 'religion' to 'irreligion', for instance, might be interpreted in a number of ways, the probability of each interpretation being in inverse proportion to its appeal. Although the word appears as 'religion' in the manuscript diary, we cannot be certain that Cavendish did not himself, as an afterthought, change this to 'irreligion' in the copy he gave to Burke. Another explanation is that 'irreligion' was the word Burke originally used and afterwards remembered: in the heat and noise of the Commons it would have been easy for Cavendish to miss the opening syllable. It is possible, however, that Burke introduced the change during the process of revision. We might, then, read it as a delicate irony, an attempt to underline the poverty of a creed so indiscriminate as to be positively atheistic in its observances. In a similar way the shift from 'They eluded' to 'These Atheists eluded' sharpens the polemic and clinches a point which may only have been implicit in the report. Revisions of this kind will perhaps seem trivial and unworthy of our attention, so long as the substance of Burke's argument is clear. Yet in their contribution to the rhetorical style of the speech they may have an important cumulative effect. They suggest that Burke's revision was not only an effort of the memory but also a literary activity, a transformation as well as a completion of its source. Neither a verbatim record of performance nor a completely new composition, the revised version (and hence the printed speech) will be poised at a point somewhere between the spoken and the written word.

Burke's revision of this speech remains unfinished. Further work would no doubt have produced a text at a greater distance from its spoken form. In view of the practical difficulties involved in preparing parliamentary speeches for the press, it is not surprising that orators were sometimes faced with charges of distortion. It was perhaps easier for their opponents to cast doubt on the authenticity of the published speech than to counter the arguments it contained. George Grenville's *Speech on the Motion for Expelling of Mr. Wilkes* (1769), which, like Burke's speech, was based largely on Cavendish's diary, fell victim to just this kind of attack. In *A Letter to the Right Honourable George Grenville* an anonymous pamphleteer (perhaps Wilkes himself) ridiculed Grenville's attempts to embellish his speech. Claiming to have been a witness to the original performance, Grenville's reviewer questioned the authority of the printed text and implied, in a neat allusion, that Burke himself had been responsible for the final version:

> I was in the gallery, Sir, during the whole debate on the third of last February, and I recollect your arguments, which were sensible and cogent, altho' I do not remember all the *melliti verborum globuli* of the *Speech* published last Monday. The warmth of the colouring, the glowing touches, and soft graces have grown since under your *forming hands*, or those more elegant of a new friend, on whom nature has lavished all the powers of *the sublime and beautiful*. . . . (p. 2)

This no doubt exaggerates the extent of the changes, but my own analysis of Burke's use of the Cavendish diary suggests that, as a literary artefact, the published speech was a creative interpretation rather than a simple transcription of the performance it purported to record.

On the basis of this analysis we can speculate about the probable genesis of the text of Burke's *Speech on American Taxation*. More substantial than the *Speech on a Bill for the Relief of Protestant Dissenters*, but based on the same source, its revision would no doubt have presented a considerable task. The speech was finally published nine months after its delivery, a delay which, according to Burke, was determined solely by questions of policy. In another sense, however, we may conjecture that its late appearance was also the result of a lengthy process of revision, and was thus the outcome of literary as well as political considerations. There is some support for this interpretation in one of Richard Burke's unpublished letters. On 22 December 1774 he wrote to a supporter in Bristol about his brother's forthcoming pub-

lication: 'America — America — Well! The — — — — — is actually finished & revised. It is not yet determined whether it
shall come out 'till the meeting, or not. If not, you shall have
one immediately (if possible) but then, *seriously*, it will be
for your fireside solely.'[4] This letter may cast some doubt
upon Burke's claim that the speech had been 'for some
months ready for the press'.

The demand for secrecy, which Richard Burke is at pains
to emphasise in his letter, is a feature of the contemporary
attitude towards the printed speech. From the trouble taken
to conceal the identity of the 'publisher', together with the
nature of his source, it would seem that the publication of
parliamentary proceedings, even by a member of the House
of Commons, remained a matter of some delicacy. On 4
January 1775 Richard Burke made another curiously veiled
reference to the *Speech on American Taxation*: 'My Brother
is pretty busily employed in *what you know*.'[5] He 'does not
count it gracefull', we are told in a later letter, 'to be the publisher' of his speech (*Corr.*, III, 94). Burke was anxious to
turn the speeches he had delivered to a House of Commons
which remained largely unconvinced by his arguments into
an effective form of extra-parliamentary persuasion. But his
awareness that such a course of action might be considered
improper suggests the extent to which parliament still thought
of itself as a closed institution which should maintain the
privacy of its proceedings and jealously defend its privileges.

In this chapter I have been concerned with the process of
transmission by which a spoken performance became a published text. In order to summarise and develop my remarks, I
will briefly consider an event the dramatic character of which
was noted in the *Annual Register* for 1788:

> Her majesty, with the four elder princesses, sat in the centre
> of the duke of Newcastle's box. The queen was waited on
> by the duchess of Ancaster, lady Holderness, lord Aylesbury
> &c. She was drest plain without diamonds, and coming
> without state, the usual etiquette was dispensed with, and
> she suffered the ladies above mentioned, with the young
> daughters of lady Lincoln, to sit on the same seat with her.
> (XXX, 198)

The correspondent does not, as one might well think, describe a courtly visit to the theatre or an outing to the opera, but rather an elegant excursion to a trial. The scene of this aristocratic entertainment was Westminster Hall, its occasion the impeachment of Warren Hastings. Of all the great oratorical spectacles of the eighteenth century, this was the most exceptional and the most dramatic. It presented orators with an unprecedented opportunity for the extensive display of their eloquence. Burke's four-day opening address was as eagerly anticipated as any of Garrick's tragic performances. In his *Autobiography* Arthur Young recalls that 'tickets were sold at twenty guineas each'; his own afforded him 'many opportunities of much entertainment' (1898, p. 164).

While Burke's objective was the conviction of Hastings, and his immediate audience the assembled lords, his speeches had a spectacular effect on the public which had gathered to hear them. His description of the horrors of tax extortion in Bengal drew gasps from the galleries and, if one is to believe the reports, rendered Mrs Sheridan senseless. In so far as the trial of Hastings was a juridical affair, its proceedings are not strictly comparable to those of the House of Commons. Nevertheless, many of Burke's parliamentary speeches, and in particular those which take India as their theme, are themselves of a forensic character. Enacted within the walls of the Palace of Westminster, the impeachment can, with certain formal reservations, be regarded as an extension of the parliamentary drama. Indeed, the conduct and outcome of the impeachment suggest that the speeches of Burke and the other managers were *too* 'parliamentary'. Hastings's counsel, professional legal men, had a keener sense of the correct judicial procedures.

Indicative of the exceptional nature of this event were the measures taken to record its proceedings. An official shorthand writer, Joseph Gurney, was employed for the duration of the trial, and it is upon his accounts that the published versions of Burke's speeches are based. Gurney's reports, transcripts of which still survive, were published in 1859 almost in their original form (Bond, 1859-61). The products of a professional shorthand writer, they are far more reliable as sources than Cavendish's notes. In most cases Gurney was able to record the proceedings of the trial practically verbatim.

A comparison of the records of performance with Burke's revised version, therefore, would again appear to be possible. This time, however, it is not the report but Burke's own text which poses problems. For Burke's must be one of the most suspect, obscure and unreliable of all 'literary' texts, the more so whenever the publication was posthumous. The speeches against Warren Hastings fall into this latter category of texts, many of which may have been revised by Burke's editors.

William B. Todd, who has conducted the most extensive research into the bibliography of Burke, describes the opening day's speech against Hastings, subsequently printed in the *Works*, as 'later revision by Burke', but adds, in a cautionary note, that 'Even in the exceptional texts, as available in the revised *Works*, there is the constant danger of further revision by the executors.' (1964, pp. 232-3) In this way the extent, if any, of editorial intrusion remains unclear. Other evidence suggests that Burke had himself undertaken a good deal of revision. In a letter to George Paterson he wrote that 'As soon as I can look over and correct the short hand writer's notes, I shall send you the Extracts you wish of my speech in Westminster Hall concerning your Brother.' (*Corr.*, V, 381) Moreover, one of the transcripts in the British Library has been annotated by Burke himself (Add. MS. 24223, pp. 68-102). Headed 'Copy from Mr. Gurney's Shorthand Notes', its opening passages are extensively revised. Although its corrections are not always incorporated into the version of the speech published in the *Works*, this is not to say that the latter is an editorial fiction. More probably the surviving transcript was abandoned at an early stage of its revision, to be followed by more thorough correction. In any case, it should be emphasised that while these are formidable problems for the bibliography of Burke, they may yet have little bearing on the status of the printed speech. The object of the present inquiry is to evaluate the relationship between different kinds of text. The question of authorship is an important but separate issue.

Even when a source as impeccable as Gurney's is available, the printed text exhibits a great number of variants. The speech, indeed, is transformed into a text of an altogether distinct character. At a superficial level this may appear to be no more than a matter of tact, a keener observance of decorum. The second of the following passages, for instance, is careful to exaggerate Burke's posture of humility:

Bond, I, 1	*Works*, XIII, 2
The several Articles, as they appear before you, will be opened by the other gentlemen with more distinctness, and without doubt with infinitely more particularity. . . .	The several Articles, as they appear before you, will be opened by other Gentlemen with more particularity, with more distinctness, and, without doubt, with infinitely more ability. . . .

The revised text takes up a form of address in which the directness of speech is replaced by elaborate circumspection. It is a pattern that the rest of the speech will follow: thus 'we are bold to say' will become 'we are warranted to assert', while 'a banya has other names too' will appear as 'the Banyan is known by other appellations'. Changes of this kind do not simply add 'polish' to the surface of the speech. In that way of viewing it, the speech, as delivered, is understood as something 'unfinished', whereas considered in its own terms, rather than in retrospect, it presents a fully coherent rhetorical totality. What the printed text seems to establish, however, is always something more than a revision — almost, one might say, a different discursive structure.

The relative accuracy of Gurney's reports allows us to specify this difference in detail. The performance, to begin with, develops and communicates through a pattern of repetition. Reworking its arguments in the process of delivery, it makes a kind of internal commentary on itself, mounts successive and disjointed rhetorical efforts which may be relinquished or renewed:

Bond, I, 17	*Works*, XIII, 31
Your Lordships see here a regular system, a regular order, a regular course of gradation. . . .	Your Lordships see here a regular series of gradation. . . .

Bond, I, 32	*Works*, XIII, 61
if I have strength, if your Lordships are desirous of it, if I have not wasted your time in explanation of matters that I have already acquainted you with, I shall next beg leave to state to you . . .	if I have not wasted your time in explanation of matters, that you are already well acquainted with, I shall next beg leave to state to you . . .

In the performance Burke strives hard to find the correct mode of expression. Each previous attempt ('a regular system . . . a regular order'; 'if I have strength, if your Lordships are desirous of it') is, in a sense, discarded on the way, and yet remains an essential part of the rhetorical structure. In the printed version, on the other hand, a simple act of excision leaves a fixed and direct remark, a product which bears no trace of its process of production.

But the revised version does more than pare down the speech to its essentials. While, in performance, the speech had propelled itself forward in an effort of self-transcendence, the published text tends to deviate, so to speak, in a lateral direction. By thus enlarging its range of reference, it acquires a new kind of discursiveness. No longer a forensic instrument with the sole aim of securing a conviction, the speech can now afford to take on a wider rhetorical sweep. In the following passages, which describe the military exploits of the disciples of Mohammed, this is managed by the provision of a new topographical perspective:

Bond, I, 39	*Works*, XIII, 75-6
There can be no doubt that the enthusiasm which animated his first followers, the despotism that was connected with his religion, and the advantages that his followers had over the broken, disunited, countries of the world, extended its influence vastly.	The enthusiasm, which animated his first followers, the despotick power, which religion obtained through that enthusiasm, and the advantages, derived from both, over the enervated great empires, and broken, disunited lesser governments of the world, extended the influence of that proud and domineering sect from the banks of the Ganges to the banks of the Loire.

It is perhaps no accident that the final phrase of the revised version — 'from the banks of the Ganges to the banks of the Loire' — should, in its grandeur and its poise, remind us of the prose of Gibbon. For heroic geography of this kind is the spatial counterpart of historical narrative. Burke's text, indeed, takes on many of the characteristics of the *Decline and Fall*, not least in its ability to combine historical generalisation and detail. The printed text is distinguished most evidently by its concrete and descriptive qualities. The 'Gentu people' who,

in Gurney's report, 'have existed against bigotry, against persecution, against all the fury of foreign conquest', have, in
the revised version, 'existed in spite of Mohammedan and
Portuguese bigotry; in spite of Tartarian and Arabian tryanny;
in spite of all the fury of successive foreign conquest'. Narrative, having lost its wholly accusatory function, becomes
the field of historical elaboration.

At the same time the breaks and divisions which in the performance were no more than aids to the speaker, resting-
places at which he could restore the vigour of his discourse,
are emphasised to such an extent that they become the means
of signifying the formal qualities and achievements of the
printed speech. The function of such divisions is therefore far
from negligible. They remind us that the speech has now become a book:

Bond, I, 41	*Works*, XIII, 82
This brings me to the next era, that of Akbar Khan.	This view of the policy, which prevailed during the dynasty of Tamerlane, naturally conducts me to the next, which is the fourth era in this history – I mean the era of the Emperour Akber.

In the passages above there is an emphatic shift from performance to text, a transition with which I have been concerned throughout this chapter. This is not to say, however,
that the printed speech cannot, or need not, be differentiated
from other kinds of written discourse. Indeed, in the first part
of this inquiry Burke's speeches were presented as the distinctive products of a parliamentary drama. Not only the formal, but to some degree the actual character of the performance was retained in the printed text, the parentheses and
hesitations of the speech being preserved as plausible marks
of its authenticity. My more detailed comparison of performance and text, however, suggested that, in another sense,
the character of the speech was different in its revised version, that it had undergone substantial stylistic change. But
the speech is not now in some way more 'written' than
'spoken'. More accurately, it transforms and combines both
elements in its efforts to communicate and persuade.

As such it might stand as a model for Burke's idea of elegant and effective discourse. His recognition of the rhetorical advantages of a familiar and 'conversational' style is evident in the calculated informality of works such as the *Letter to William Elliot* and the *Letter to a Noble Lord*. His preference for this mode is stated clearly in a letter he wrote in 1793 to his friend Arthur Murphy, the translator of Tacitus:

> There is a style, which daily gains ground amongst us, which I should be sorry to see farther advanced by the authority of a writer of your just reputation. The tendency of the mode to which I allude is, to establish two very different idioms amongst us, and to introduce a marked distinction between the English that is written and the English that is spoken.   (*Corr.*, VII, 502)

Burke may well have thought of his published orations as embodying the mode of discourse he was so anxious to preserve: in which the discipline of writing is infused with the immediacy and sociality of speech.

In this respect the work he undertook in the specialised form of the parliamentary speech, some of the details of which I have surveyed, is related to a much broader cultural history. It would be too much to claim that the culture to which Burke belonged favoured spoken above written modes of communication. What *is* apparent, however, is its continued attachment to the convention of direct address, exemplified most obviously in the speech but also, in a more freely available medium, in the printed letter, a form which was put to a quite remarkable variety of uses in the eighteenth century. In works cast in this form, whether the subject be politics, travel, natural history, or whatever, the mode of direct address is a central and defining element. In letters on political themes the range and character of that address can vary considerably, according to the writer's objects. Sometimes the addressee is a named individual, as in Junius's accusations against the Duke of Grafton, where the printed letter presents a direct public challenge to an allegedly corrupt first minister. More commonly the form of address suggests the nature and qualities of the audience which the writer wishes to reach. Again this may be done by a letter to an individual, who will then be addressed as a kind of ideal reader, the representative of a wider social and cultural group. In order to understand the range of rhetorical possibilities afforded by the epistolary mode, one has only to turn to Swift's sequence of *Drapier's Letters*, where, in Letter V, the address is made to a prominent and sympathetic public figure (Viscount Molesworth); in Letter III, to a particular set of social classes ('the Nobility and Gentry of the Kingdom of Ireland'); and, in Letter IV, in its most open and challenging form, to 'the Whole People of Ireland'.

The convention on which the printed letter is based, and which links it formally to the speech, is that an act of communication between the writer and an identifiable reader (or set of readers) is taking place. In political discourse this convention of address is particularly significant. It allows the writer to discuss potentially abstract issues and arguments within the created social framework of a practical epistolary relationship. Indirectly it helps to define an audience, so that in many eighteenth-century letters on public affairs the address to a noble lord, public figure, or gentleman well-versed in politics, indicates that the writer's appeal is primarily directed towards a culturally privileged group of readers. The problem with this convention, however, was that its status *as* a convention (rather than a genuine act of address) was likely to become increasingly exposed. Changing conditions of publication and the pressures of an expanding readership made it difficult to sustain the myth of direct communication between writer and addressee.

It is not surprising, then, that eighteenth-century writers should sometimes admit that a valued contact with an identifiable audience has been lost. 'Reader, it is impossible we should know what Sort of Person thou wilt be,' Fielding concedes in *Tom Jones* (1974, II, 523). There is an interesting tension here because it was the novel, more than any other literary form, which was responsible for putting that relationship in doubt. It is perhaps for that reason that it was often regarded with hostility by the great Augustan writers. The fear of cultural degeneration, expressed so powerfully by Pope and Swift, is in part a fear of the consequences of an expanding literary market which, unresponsive to the rules of good taste, encourages hacks to flood the world with a torrent of useless periodicals, pamphlets and novels. A culture which had once seemed stable and coherent was now, it appeared, on the point of collapse. This complex set of historical developments is experienced formally as a problem of address. Professional writers like Fielding were conscious that their books were commodities, and that their literary progeny would have to be exposed to the mercies of a market composed of largely unknown readers. The creation of a fictional reader, so central to the rhetoric of *Tom Jones*, can be seen as a response to these changing cultural conditions. It allows the author to unfold a narrative which is anchored in a mode of direct address. Fielding sustains the illusion of this speaking presence throughout the novel, but it was not to become one of the primary conventions of the new form. In *Tristram Shandy* Sterne presents the problem clearly (and playfully) by means of an occasional division of addresss, whereby a kind of internal listener, a fireside 'Sir' or 'Madam', is intermittently buttonholed by the narrator, while for the most part his adventures are related to an assumed and impersonal reader outside.

Although the convention of address is discarded in a number of Burke's writings (most notably, perhaps, the *Thoughts on the Cause of the Present Discontents* and the *Appeal from the New to the Old Whigs*), it remained his most characteristic mode. For predominantly aristocratic Whig groups like the Rockinghamites continued to attach great importance to the ideal of a political discourse based on direct communication between gentlemen. The debates of the House of Commons provided an excellent model. Elsewhere in Burke's writing we can see a formal continuity between the mode in which day-to-day party transactions — letters requesting information, preferment, attendance, support, and so forth — were carried out and the mode thought appropriate for the more public task of political persuasion. In this way the convention of direct address had the effect of continually and publicly reaffirming the connections which allowed a high Whig political culture to cohere. Yet that culture could not entirely insulate itself from the pressures of political developments outside, and it is in this respect that Burke's role as spokesman and ideologist for the Rockingham Whigs is particularly significant. The early years of his parliamentary career coincided with the upsurge of political radicalism associated with John Wilkes, and with an increasingly innovative political press (some of the consequences of which I shall consider in the following chapters). The attitude of the Rockinghamites towards these developments was ambivalent: as an opposition group they sometimes sided with Wilkites on particular issues, without concealing their dislike and suspicion of Wilkite culture. Burke's own work was not entirely unresponsive to these challenges from 'below'. He was the most active communicator in the Rockingham group, and the one who was most aware of the need to secure extra-parliamentary opinion and support. Yet he undertook this task within literary forms and idioms which, like the parliamentary speech, were the products of a relatively closed political culture. Keeping faith with the established modes of direct address, while infusing them with an extraordinary passion and intelligence, he ensured that his audience would remain, for the most part, an audience of gentlemen.

PART THREE

The Anatomy of a Crisis: Burke, Wilkes,
and the Debate on the Middlesex Election

9

The Political Identity of Wilkes

In the foregoing chapter I began to consider the nature of
Burke's audience and the manner in which it was defined by
the convention of direct address. My aim in the final part of
this study is to broaden the basis of that discussion by examining the conflict and interaction of different modes of
writing within the context of a single political debate. The
political and constitutional crisis provoked by the activities
of John Wilkes and his supporters in the period 1768-70 was
fought out in a number of arenas and forms: in courts of
law, in parliamentary speeches and county petitions, in a war
of pamphlets and broadsheets, and in a series of popular
demonstrations, celebrations and riots. These manifestations
of crisis (or 'discontent', as Burke more cautiously chose to
call it) have been studied by a number of historians and
critics.[1] Their historical significance, it has been argued, lies
primarily in the emergence of an alternative political culture
which represented the interests of those excluded from the
networks of power which centred on parliament. The crisis
of the Middlesex Election provided a focus for this increasingly vigorous counter-culture and led it to develop institutions (such as the Society of the Supporters of the Bill of
Rights) and modes of representation and argument which
were to play a leading role in the formation of British radicalism. In this way the mobilisation of opinion during the Wilkes
controversy set a precedent for the later and more sustained
radical campaigns which culminated in the crisis of the French
Revolution.

My object in the following chapters is to trace the genesis
of the pamphlet debate on Wilkes and to consider the significance of the different styles and idioms in which it was

disputed. It is in the context of this debate that the particular qualities and characteristics of Burke's *Thoughts on
the Cause of the Present Discontents* (1770) can best be
understood. The *Thoughts* is commonly regarded as the most
coherent and able justification of party to have been published in the eighteenth century, and as such has been acclaimed
as a major contribution to English political thought. While
this judgment may seem unexceptionable in itself, it has led
to a relative neglect of the rhetorical character and functions
of Burke's pamphlet. For from another point of view the
Thoughts can be seen as an essentially polemical work, one
of the outstanding productions to emerge from the debate
on the Middlesex Election. One of my objectives here will
be to determine the manner in which Burke's pamphlet is
related to this debate. Is it an entirely independent utterance, or part of a more general controversy? In order to
answer this question, it will be necessary to undertake a
relatively broad survey of the political writing of the period
1768-70. In so doing I hope to identify some of the terms,
modes and concepts — as well as issues — which mark the
development of the debate.

In the following survey the final chapter alone will be
devoted to Burke. It may be felt that I have given undue
attention to the work of relatively obscure pamphleteers.
But I would argue that the lesser-known tracts of the period
are worthy of analysis not only because they enhance our
historical understanding of Burke's *Thoughts* but also because
it is only through them that we can become familiar with the
language and rhetoric which characterise different political
cultures. Any study of political discourse which wishes to
go beyond a simple summary of the arguments must be prepared to extend its formal inquiry to even the most ephemeral
of tracts. In my view, the Wilkes controversy is open to just
such an approach, one which should enable us to explore the
literary dynamics of a political crisis.

It is important, however, that the problems of method that
may be involved here should be recognised. For instance, the
assumption that a single debate can be isolated for formal
and analytical purposes may prove to be unfounded. I shall
go on to argue that the case and career of Wilkes impose a

certain coherence on the political writing of the period in question, so that the debate on the Middlesex Election has a relatively closed structure. But it is also necessary to note the moments at which issues apparently exterior to the immediate concerns of the controversy are raised. It is one of the characteristics of a crisis that it should develop rapidly from its first causes and begin to produce new situations and issues. This was a problem faced by the Rockingham Whigs when they took part in the petitioning movement of 1769. It was their policy that these petitions, drawn up in towns and counties throughout the land, should be solely concerned with the constitutional questions raised by the Middlesex Election, but other groups saw them as convenient vehicles for a more general campaign of protest. In a similar way supporters of Wilkes sometimes combined their defence of the cause of liberty with more mundane economic demands, such as for a rise in the rate of wages. The changing contingencies of social and political life have a tendency not only to inspire but also to disrupt the rhetoric which seeks to express them. This complex interplay between form and circumstance, a concern throughout this study, will be examined further, and its problems in some respects recast, in this final part of my inquiry.

In November 1764, when he had already been in exile in Paris for almost a year, John Wilkes was pronounced an outlaw, following his condemnation by parliament and the courts for the publication of the allegedly seditious *North Briton*, no. 45 and the allegedly blasphemous *Essay on Woman*. He finally broke his exile in February 1768, returning to London, where a new phase of his extraordinary career was to begin. A considerable proportion of the political pamphlets published during the period 1768-70 is concerned to a greater or lesser degree with the issues raised by Wilkes's return and the subsequent disputed election for Middlesex[2] (see table of dates, p. 142). Within this body of writing there are striking variations of strategy and form. Quite different conceptions of literary decorum and of what constitutes politics or proper political activity seem to be at work. One of the primary distinctions which emerges between different groups

WILKES AND THE MIDDLESEX ELECTION:
A TABLE OF DATES

1768

Feb. 6 Returns to London, a declared outlaw, ending four
years of exile abroad.

Mar. 23 Stands unsuccessfully in the parliamentary election
for the City of London.

28 Elected to the Commons as member for the County
of Middlesex.

Apr. 27 Remanded in King's Bench prison in connection with
his outlawry.

May 10 Serious disturbances following his committal, cul-
minating in the 'Massacre of St George's Fields'.

June 8 Outlawry declared void on a technicality.

18 Sentenced to twenty-two months' imprisonment for
publication in 1763 of *North Briton*, no. 45 and
An Essay on Woman.

1769

Feb. 4 Expelled from the House of Commons. New writ
issued for Middlesex.

16 Re-elected unopposed.

17 Commons resolves that Wilkes is 'incapable of being
elected a member to serve in the present Parliament'.

Mar. 16 Re-elected unopposed; election declared void.

Apr. 13 Re-elected for Middlesex; Colonel Luttrell second in
poll. Election declared null and void.

May 8 Luttrell formally admitted as member for Middlesex
in Wilkes's place.

Nationwide petitioning movement on the issue of
the Middlesex Election begins.

1770

Apr. 17 Wilkes released from prison after having served his
full term.

23 Burke's *Thoughts on the Cause of the Present Discontents* published.

of tracts is the degree to which an individual agent or character
is presumed to be an essential element in the writing of politics.
One set of pamphlets conceives of politics as a kind of drama

in which a named individual — often Wilkes himself — takes the central role. Whether the writer is sympathetic or antagonistic towards that individual is immaterial, at least from a formal standpoint. Many pro-Wilkite and anti-Wilkite tracts are virtually indistinguishable in terms of the modes of writing they adopt. But another network of pamphlets, consisting largely of those of parliamentary origin, almost completely suppresses the character and politics of Wilkes, highlighting instead the legal and constitutional questions raised by the Middlesex Election. This and the following chapter will consider these two polemical strategies in turn. A third and concluding chapter will examine Burke's contribution to the debate.

Some useful reflections on the merits of different methods of argument and persuasion can be found in the work of one of the principal polemicists involved. 'Junius' was the pseudonym of a writer whose identity remains uncertain, and whose scathing and brilliant letters on political affairs caused a sensation when they appeared in the *Public Advertiser* during the critical months of 1769 and 1770. The accusation and condemnation of named public figures which marks so many of the *Letters of Junius* has sometimes been imputed to a defect of personality in their author. Conjecture of this kind would see Junius as the victim of a deep-seated sense of personal grievance which can find outlet only in the most savage irony. But in a footnote to Letter XXVI (7 October 1769) Junius offers another explanation, based upon opposition to a particular political doctrine, and allegiance to the ruling principles of satire described by Pope in a letter to Arbuthnot.[3] *'Measures not men'*, Junius declares,

> is the common cant of affected moderation; — a base, counterfeit language, fabricated by knaves, and made current among fools. Such gentle censure is not fitted to the present, degenerate state of society. What does it avail to expose the absurd contrivance, or pernicious tendency of measures, if the man, who advises and executes, shall be suffered not only to escape with impunity, but even to preserve his power, and insult us with the favour of his Sovereign!   (Junius, 1978, p. 130)

In rejecting the slogan of 'measures not men' (one associated in particular with the Elder Pitt) Junius forges a direct link between a political principle and a mode of writing. The state of the nation demands a polemical strategy — a kind of literary impeachment — by means of which individual statesmen will be brought to account. In this way the savage indignation which impels and controls so many of the *Letters*, and which so often takes the form of personal accusation, is justified by the author on moral, social and political grounds. The animosity of Junius may be seen from this perspective as a necessary procedure as well as a heartfelt conviction. In Junius vilification is refined into a high political art. More often than not, the *Letters* conceive of politics as the expression and self-realisation of an identifiable individual. It is the purpose of this chapter to consider some of the writings of 1768-70 which share this point of view, and to examine some of the ways in which the identity of the political agent is defined and presented there.

The tone assumed in Burke's *Thoughts on the Cause of the Present Discontents* is one of lofty detachment, indicative of the author's reluctance to engage in merely personal disputes. Yet Burke was no advocate of the doctrine of 'measures not men'. In the *Thoughts* he explicitly rejects 'the cant of *Not men, but measures*', describing it, in a remark which was no doubt intended as a hit at Chatham, as 'a sort of charm, by which many people get loose from every honourable engagement' (II, 337). His own creed, expressed most cogently in the celebrated advocacy of party, is that personal connections are the basic elements of political life. Later in his career Burke would often select a particular figure as the focus of an attack or, if the occasion demanded it, as the subject for a panegyric. But the general strategy of the *Thoughts* is to cast a philosophical eye over the state of the nation, to investigate a system rather than expose an individual. In a characteristic passage Burke explains his disinclination to carry the attack to the Earl of Bute, who, under the title of 'the Favourite', had long been selected by opposition writers as one of their principal targets. 'Where there is a regular scheme of operations carried on,' Burke remarks, it is the system, and not any individual person who acts in it, that is truly dangerous. This system has not arisen solely from the ambition of Lord Bute, but from the circumstances which favoured it. . . . We should have been tried with it, if the Earl of Bute had never existed. . . . (II, 258)

This measured analysis of circumstance is quite contrary to the strategy favoured by Wilkes and his supporters (and, for that matter, by many of his adversaries). For it is precisely on 'the individual who acts' that the writings of the Wilkites are based. Political issues are presented through a protagonist or leading figure, a freeborn individual whose character and actions rather than any abstract argument constitute the starting-point of the tract. In order to understand the role of Wilkes in the debate on the Middlesex Election, we' need to look back to the *North Briton* of 1762-63, where the tendency I have described is already well established. For the *North Briton*, produced by Wilkes in collaboration with the poet Charles Churchill, is distinguished above all by its mastery of political perspective and impersonation. It is as if the selection of an individual standpoint was understood to be the first principle of political writing. The early issues of the journal are a case in point. For there political satire is most commonly conducted through the assumption of a series of ironic guises. Often the writer is identified, in accordance with the journal's title, as a Scot, and hence a countryman of the despised Earl of Bute, but this viewpoint is always subject to modification. In *North Briton*, no. 6, for example, we are addressed by an unashamedly chauvinistic spokesman for the Scottish nation, who looks forward eagerly to 'the completion of all our views, the intire possession of the revenues of this whole country'. By no. 10, however, there has been a slight but significant change in tone. Once again the writer is a Scot, but the quieter, more cautious and pragmatic nature of the advice given heralds the development of a new political character. Replying to a letter attributed to a 'Presbyter' who advocates the immediate abolition of episcopacy in England, Wilkes's 'moderate' Scot admits the desirability of the design but counsels caution: 'discretion steps in, and teaches us to consider this event as placed at a great distance, surrounded with difficulties, and to be brought to pass by slow degrees'. Wilkes was astute enough to realise that understatement is as useful a rhetoric as harangue, making the Scottish threat more credible rather than less.

The shifting and fictional viewpoint which characterises the *North Briton* prevents the writing from hardening into stereotype and alerts the reader to the possibility of new sequences of irony. Perhaps the most striking instance of the technique is to be found in *North Briton*, no. 38, which Wilkes casts in the form of a letter from the Pretender, in exile at Rome, to his supposed ally, the Earl of Bute. A number of the *North Briton* papers are framed as straightforward and unironic indictments of the Bute administration. But from the standpoint of the Pretender – as adopted in no. 38 – the charges which have been hurled at Bute throughout the journal are matters for commendation rather than censure. What any self-respecting Whig would have condemned apoplectically as conspiracies against the constitution are from this perspective manifestly expedient, if unremarkable, courses of action. The polemical skill of the piece lies in its lack of self-consciousness, its failure ever to notice just how outrageous its insinuations are. The stigma of Jacobitism comes naturally, almost inevitably, and without emphasis. Thus Wilkes's 'Pretender' declares that 'We have had the truest pleasure in hearing of the noble provision you have made for so many of our staunch friends, and of the considerable posts, both of honour and profit, which you have bestowed on them.' It is not so much that Wilkes expects the accusation of Jacobitism to be taken seriously; rather that the very standpoint and conception of the letter ridicule Bute's policies by showing them in an unexpected and ludicrous light.

A number of the *North Briton* papers are written in this style. Ideology and politics are presented, so to speak, at one remove, in a distorted but still recognisable form, through a gallery of character types. From a polemical point of view, this can be seen both as a strength and a weakness. Like Swift's brilliant *Examiner* papers, on which it is no doubt modelled (in no. 11 Swift is acknowledged as 'the *father* of all political *humour*'), the *North Briton* is extremely rich in its creation of ironic masks and in its development of grotesque modes of argument. Satirical dialogues, ironic prophecies, absurd catalogues and perverse tables of merit are deployed in rapid succession, so that at times the *North Briton* reads like a glittering political entertainment or cabaret in the mould of Fielding's satirical ballad operas. But on the other hand, Wilkes's liking for caricature, his need to personalise political issues, and his acutely theatrical consciousness might all be blamed for the lack of direction from which the journal suffers. Rarely does the *North Briton* achieve any decisive polemical continuity. In one sense this may be a problem inherent in the weekly journal form: the *Examiner* itself, for all its fine wit, is a diffuse and sometimes uneven collection. But Wilkes in particular is always liable to be sidetracked by the prospect of some witty but disruptive digression. In the course of nos 39 and 43, for instance, he cannot restrain himself from mocking the clumsy oratory of William Beckford, who as a prominent radical and power in the city was really a political ally. In no. 43, which is largely an attack on the financial mismanagement of the nation, the ridicule of Beckford, if not politically unwise, at least seems gratuitous. 'That acute reasoner and sound scholar has more than once assured us, that he will always argue *à priori, from facts, a priori, I say*,' reports Wilkes of Beckford, whom he likes to depict as a client of Dulness. It is evident in such remarks that in the *North Briton* the exercise of wit can take priority over the logic of politics. It might be argued that this lack of self-discipline is of major historical importance, that in the critical years of the 1760s it was responsible for both the popular appeal and political limitations of Wilkes.

Like later Wilkite writings, the *North Briton* is distinguished by its wealth of forms and the multiplicity of voices at its command. The modes in which Wilkes appears to be most successful are the ironic, the indirect and the fictive. At first sight this might seem to run counter to the general view of Wilkes's achievement. John Brewer (1976) has attributed the political success of Wilkes to his capacity for self-projection, the process by which abstract political concepts such as 'Liberty' become indistinguishable from the personality of Wilkes himself. But this determined act of self-mythification, performed in the symbolic world of Wilkite propaganda and the rituals of the crowd, was, it seems to me, a controlled and politic operation, orchestrated, as it were, from the outside by Wilkes himself. Or to put it another way, the *persona* of 'Wilkes' was foremost among the voices at his command. In a conception of politics which afforded the individual a central role, Wilkes's greatest effort was naturally devoted to the construction of a political self.

The literary forms used to project this self were therefore of decisive political importance. The historic and public status of Wilkes is commonly dated from the controversy concerning general warrants — from the intense legal conflicts, that is to say, which followed his prosecution for seditious libel. This view would see Wilkes's achievement of a popular political identity as subsequent to the furore over his final *North Briton* paper in April 1763, but it may well be that the process of definition is already implicit in the writing of that journal. There are occasions, for instance, when the character of Wilkes himself is used to provide a focal point. *North Briton*, no. 21 is written in reply to the *Auditor*, an organ of the Bute administration. Arthur Murphy, author of this journal, had published a potentially damaging account of an alleged altercation in Winchester, involving Wilkes, at the time a colonel in the militia, and a schoolboy son of the Earl of Bute. On the face of it, no. 21 is simply a necessary and largely defensive rebuttal of this version of the colonel's conduct. At the same time, however, much of the apology is framed in terms of contemporary political debate. In a passage attacking Dr Burton, then Master of Winchester School, for his failure to intervene in the dispute, Wilkes is cast in an heroic and popular mould, while the unfortunate Burton is lampooned as little more than a tool of the administration, as one who 'will ever distinguish between persons in, and out of power; between a Colonel engaged in the barren cause of Liberty, almost alone, and a favourite with a troop of slavish courtiers at his heels, and bishopricks at his command'. Written by Charles Churchill (possibly with the connivance of his colleague),[4] this unashamed fusion of personal and public concerns seems to herald the coming apotheosis of Wilkes and Liberty.

In Churchill's somewhat fanciful description Wilkes becomes a martial figure, engaged 'almost alone' in an unequal
political contest. In a handbill circulated by Wilkes ten days
before the publication of the celebrated *North Briton*, no. 45
this image is developed further. Wilkes dismisses the recent
resignation of Bute as a mere ploy. The Scot's influence, it is
claimed, far from diminishing, will remain as malevolent and
destructive as ever, for henceforth it will be exerted through
Grenville, Halifax and Egremont, the nominal heads of the
new administration. In this new and alarming conjuncture
Wilkes is once again cast as a figure in a political romance:

> The NORTH BRITON has been steady in his opposition
> to a *single*, insolent, incapable, despotic minister; and is
> equally ready, in the service of his country, to combat
> the *triple-headed, Cerberean* administration, if the SCOT
> is to assume that motley form.
>
> (Wilkes and Churchill, 1763, II, 228)

In this passage Wilkes is engaged in the creation of a political
mythology, one which will be extended and to some degree
redefined during the crises of 1768-70. But we should note the
skill with which Wilkes, while projecting himself in heroic
fashion, at the same time manages to belittle his enemies.
For there may be at least a hint of irony here, a suggestion,
perhaps, that the new administration will prove altogether
unworthy of the sublime and classical imagery at the service
of its opponents. It is as if Grenville and his colleagues, the
very tamest of hell-hounds, were incapable of appearing in
anything more dignified than a political mock-heroic. This
combination of ridicule and high seriousness is characteristic
of the rhetoric of both Wilkes and Junius. For Wilkes, Bute
is at once a knave and a fool, a despot clad in motley. Junius,
as we shall see, strikes a similar attitude towards a later first
minister, the Duke of Grafton, whom he presents as a rake
whose malice is equalled only by his dullness.

From the standpoint of his supporters, Wilkes's heroic
political stature, developed in the papers of the *North Briton*
and made secure by the controversy concerning general
warrants, was further confirmed by the events of 1768-70.
Incarceration in King's Bench prison and expulsion from the

House of Commons followed in rapid succession. To his sympathisers it must have seemed as if his career had become a catalogue of suffering, persecution and grievance. According to the Wilkite author of the *Letter to the Right Hon. Thomas Harley* (1768), 'He has not only been a hero; he has almost been a martyr in the glorious cause of liberty.' (p. 31) This epically inflated and almost sacred terminology features regularly in pamphlets dedicated to the formation of the political identity of Wilkes. As John Brewer has demonstrated, it is often accompanied by another kind of panegyric which figures him as a master of satire and a monarch of wit. In the letter to Harley the author laments Wilkes's failure in the election for the City of London of March 1768. For Wilkes would have brought more than political benefits to the city; he is also the man to vindicate it from the aspersions cast by Alexander Pope, his predecessor in satire: 'A little of Mr. Wilkes's mercury mixed with the City lead, might have freed the metropolis from the opprobrium, under which it has long laboured, of being the seat of dulness.' (p. 12) In this tract, and in others of its kind, heroism and wit are two of the major components of Wilkes's political personality. Combined with a third, a studied and insolent class consciousness, they appear again, and in perhaps their most splendid form, in one of Wilkes's own productions, the *Letter to His Grace the Duke of Grafton* (1767). This pamphlet contains an account of Wilkes's arrest by general warrant and his subsequent appearance before Secretaries of State Halifax and Egremont:

> I . . . turn'd to Lord Egremont, and said, 'Your Lordship's verbal orders were to drag me out of my bed at midnight. The first man, who had enter'd my bedchamber by force, I should have laid dead on the spot. Probably I shou'd have fallen in the skirmish with the others. I thank God, not your Lordship, that such a scene of blood has been avoided. Your Lordship is very ready to issue orders, which you have neither the courage to sign, nor I believe to justify.' No reply was made to this. The conversation drop'd. Lord Halifax retir'd into another apartment. Lord Egremont continued sullen and silent, about a quarter of an hour.

I then made a few remarks on some capital pictures, which were in the room, and his Lordship left me alone. (pp. 22-3)

This is magnificently impudent autobiography. Wilkes highlights not only his fearless confrontation with authority but also his refusal to observe social distinctions and the forms of conduct generally assigned to them. He uses the language of deference ('your Lordship') only to underline his own moral superiority. The witless aristocrat is vanquished by the intrepid, eloquent and self-possessed man of taste — Wilkes, the connoisseur, who while under arrest finds time to appraise the decorations in the drawing-room. The passage is, of course, massively conceited, but it is a politic form of conceit rather than an unthinking vanity. For the confident superiority of Wilkes's prose is based on the recognition that it is precisely a triumphant display of arrogance that his audience expects and desires. In this sense there is little point in questioning the accuracy of Wilkes's account or his good faith as a narrator. More important is his ability to dramatise his own character and to organise a myth out of his own career.

In pamphlets of this kind, where a central figure personalises complex political forces and issues, the same forms, techniques and procedures will often recur. Wilkes's letter to Grafton is one of a number of tracts which are cast in narrative — or, more precisely, biographical — form. In the 1760s biography offered definite advantages to the pamphleteer. It might be said, for instance, that the career of Wilkes was used to give a sense of coherence to the period of political instability which followed the accession of George III. For Wilkes seemed to personify some of the outstanding issues of the reign: the legality of general warrants, the electoral rights of freeholders, the right to report the proceedings of parliament, and the more general issue of the freedom of the press. Quite disparate issues might then find a kind of unity in the person of Wilkes. Pamphlets which take this direction tend to forgo the logic of abstract argument in favour of a system of politics based on the portrayal of character and the narrative of a career.

I have already suggested that writings of this class may be

very similar in form, even when their politics are diametrically opposed. Pro-Wilkite tracts like the letter to Grafton or the equally biographical *Letter on the Public Conduct of Mr. Wilkes* (1768) are countered by tracts in which Wilkes is satirised as the anti-hero of a kind of scurrilous biography. Wilkes the martyr gives way to Wilkes the rake. Andrew Henderson's *Letter to the Right Honourable the Earl of T[empl]e* (1768) reads more like the history of a libertine than a study of the contest between Wilkes and the state. Blurring the polite distinction between public and private conduct, and lacking any conceptual realm, Henderson's pamphlet sites its politics in a record of petty domestic transactions. Wilkes, we are told, 'run in debt with his seedsman, his cheesemonger, and at the time of quitting the kingdom, was in arrears to his landlord for three years rent' (p. 8). In this way Henderson exploits the stereotypes of eighteenth-century biography and fiction for political purposes. It is the kind of literary caricature practised — admittedly with a little more panache — by Wilkes himself. Henderson's description of the death of Charles Churchill, who comes in for similar treatment, might be seen as the final episode in a rake's progress:

> C————ll the genius soon dropped; he went over to see his patron, and drinking too freely of new wine at Boùloìgne, he died of a surfeit, unrelenting and unprepared, bewailed by few, except such as were sorry for his impieties, and the ungenerous treatment he gave to his own spouse, to whom he became unfaithful; and decoy'd a girl of eighteen years from her parents, people of credit and reputation.   (p. 30)

This potentially endless list of crimes, out of some compendium of contemporary vice, is brought to a close with a description of Wilkes 'roaming through the provinces of France and Holland', chief scoundrel in a political picaresque.

Narrative seems to be one of the modes most appropriate to politics of this essentially personalised kind. It is not surprising, then, that the career of Wilkes should have been selected as the theme of a full-scale satirical novel, *The History of Jack Wilks, a Lover of Liberty* (1769). In the orthodox political pamphlet, which thrives on argument, riposte and direct address, the function of narrative is generally secondary and supportive. In the novel, however, narrative is the central element, the discourse of personal conduct and social relations. It is the realm in which politics can be explored and portrayed in terms of the moral and social life of the individual. In *The History of Jack Wilks* the narrative once again takes the form of a rake's progress, though in this case the satirical stance is sometimes tempered with sentiment. Wilkes's commitment to the principles of liberty is ridiculed in a series of disreputable episodes, the general effect of which is to reduce his politics to a mere apology for self-gratification. 'A mistaken love of Liberty', complains his unfortunate mistress, 'must degenerate into licentiousness.' (I, 125) Authors of works such as this no doubt felt they had struck a telling blow against the Wilkite cause. But it is at least arguable that their efforts were based upon an ideological misapprehension. For it is more than possible that Wilkes really gloried in the name of rake. Tracts like *The History of Jack Wilks* may, then, have actively promoted the mythology Wilkes was concerned to create, a mythology in which his reputation for sexual prowess played no small part. Many of his opponents, carried away by their righteous moral indignation, take this myth at face value. They commit the error of fighting their politics on a terrain that Wilkes has chosen for himself, where the only real issue seems to be his own personality.

In the tracts I have just considered Wilkes is cast as an opportunist and a rake, the Lovelace of political life. His presence in narratives of this kind might be seen as the inevitable consequence of a uniquely scandalous personal life. But Wilkes was not the only political figure to be carica-tured in this way. In the period 1768-70 the anti-biography, as I would call it, is one of the forms most favoured by those who participate in the politics of the individual. The finest examples of this kind of writing are to be found in the *Letters of Junius*, where the victims – unlike Wilkes – are often occupants of the highest offices of state. Junius's con-tributions to the genre are worth examining in some detail, if only to show that personal invective and scandal may be as regular in design and structure as the most elegantly de-tached of *belles-lettres*. In Letter XII (Junius, 1978, pp. 67-74), a great ironic composition, the victim and addressee, as so often in Junius, is the Duke of Grafton. The rhetorical effect of this letter depends very largely upon its mercilessly direct form of address. Grafton is transfixed by the insistent and accusatory 'You' with which Junius spearheads the attack. He is introduced to us as a duke without decorum, a minister who lacks the conscience even to varnish his misdeeds. His parliamentary conduct is denounced as crudely manipulative, for Grafton bypasses the time-honoured modes of political argument. Instead he appeals directly to the baser instincts:

> You neither address yourself to the passions, nor to the understanding, but simply to the touch. You apply your-self immediately to the feelings of your friends, who, con-trary to the forms of parliament, never enter heartily into a debate, until they have divided.

This ironic assault on Grafton, a voluptuary, as it were, even in the House, serves as a brilliant prologue to the history of a rake.

The portrait itself falls into three main parts. Junius begins by inverting the forms of the complimentary biography. Panegyrics of this type are often prefaced by the recital of a long and illustrious lineage which is intended to establish the social and political credentials of the subject. Junius parodies this convention in a scornful reference to Grafton's some-what irregular descent from Charles II:

> you may look back with pleasure to an illustrious pedigree, in which heraldry has not left a single good quality upon record to insult or upbraid you. You have better proofs of your descent, my Lord, than the register of a marriage, or any troublesome inheritance of reputation. There are some hereditary strokes of character, by which a family may be as clearly distinguished as by the blackest features of the human face. Charles the First lived and died a hypocrite. Charles the Second was a hypocrite of another sort, and should have died upon the same scaffold. At the distance of a century, we see their different characters happily revived, and blended in your Grace.

In this passage, which combines historical allusion and ironical address, Grafton is pilloried in two ways: politically, since a Caroline heritage should be anathema to any true Whig, and morally, since Charles II was not only a Stuart but also a profligate, at least by repute. We are often reminded of this moral inheritance as the anti-biography of Grafton unfolds.

The second element of Junius's account, the satirical sketch of an aristocrat's education, had found perhaps its most perfect form in the lines on the 'young Aeneas' in Pope's *Dunciad* (IV, ll. 275-336), and especially in the address to Dulness:

> Thro' School and College, thy kind cloud o'ercast,
> Safe and unseen the young Aeneas past:
> Thence bursting glorious, all at once let down,
> Stunn'd with his giddy Larum half the town.
>
> (IV, ll. 289-92)

The unfortunate Grafton is destined to fill this role, to become the 'young Aeneas' of the *Letters*, the raffish graduate of race-course, coffee-house and back-benches:

> You had already taken your degrees with credit in those schools, in which the English nobility are formed to virtue, when you were introduced to Lord Chatham's protection. From Newmarket, White's and the opposition, he gave you to the world with an air of popularity, which young men usually set out with, and seldom preserve. . . .

But as far as Junius is concerned, Grafton's indiscretions have by no means been confined to his youth. The duke's familiarity with the morals of a rake had only been confirmed by his divorce from Anne Liddell and subsequent remarriage to Elizabeth Wrottesley, 'a near relation of one who had debauched his wife', as Junius puts it, with customary delicacy, in Letter XIII. The improprieties of this connection are a true epitome of Grafton's character and career. It is at this stage, therefore, that Junius draws the veil over the duke's personal history: for 'marriage is the point on which every rake is stationary at last'.

The biographies and mock-biographies I have discussed, whether they be panegyrical or ironic in intention, tend to mould rather than analyse the political identities of their subjects. Other pamphlets, however, favouring a less obviously partisan approach, attempt to put their political evaluation on a more systematic basis. Concerned in particular with the question of patriotism, they seek to arrive at a set of criteria according to which electors may accurately assess the probity and politics of their candidates. In a useful discussion John Brewer (1976, pp. 96-111) has shown how the Elder Pitt, with varying degrees of success, projected himself in the role of the Patriot. In the period under review, and indeed earlier in the century, the term had a more specific meaning than it has today. It denoted a definite ideological and political stance. The patriot was the figure who personalised and set into motion the doctrine of 'measures not men'. Pitt, for instance, claimed to be above the sordid connections of party and free from the taint of political corruption. Independence of this sort — including a refusal to engage in merely 'factious' opposition — was seen as an essential prerequisite of patriotism, the disinterested service of one's country. These qualities are the most visible marks of the patriot, who in these pamphlets is, as much as the rake, a stock type, with fixed moral and ideological characteristics. By the late 1760s the figure of the patriot already had a considerable history. William Arnall's pamphlet *Opposition No Proof of Patriotism*, reissued in 1770 to coincide with the controversy concerning Wilkes, had first been published as far back as 1735. This would seem to indicate a definite continuity in political thinking, argument and presentation. In the period 1768-70, when some saw the Middlesex Election as a crisis of faction, there are a number of pamphlets which offer their readers the means by which a politician's claims to the virtues of patriotism may be assessed. Those with a theoretical bias inquire into the anatomy of the ideal patriot. Others, with a more pressing sense of circumstance, present a preliminary account of patriotism in order to pronounce judgment on active political figures such as Wilkes and Chatham. Taken together, these tracts are exemplary products of the class of political writing we have been considering, in that the political subject, whose definition and analysis they perform, is the very *raison d'être* of the work.

For this reason it is worth looking in some detail at the

criteria observed by such 'tests' of patriotism. Almost invariably the dynamics of political activity are located not in periodic party conflict, or in the economic state of the nation, but deep within the politician's breast. The search to determine the features of the patriot becomes, more often than not, a study of personality in which the procedures of moral and psychological inquiry are eagerly annexed. Political discourse of this kind is distinguished by its opportunism rather than its rigour, by its readiness to employ a language or technique which may, on the face of it, lie well outside its field. In some cases this may lead to problems of definition, when the classification of a pamphlet as 'political' should be recognised as tentative and provisional. *An Essay on Patriotism* (1769), for example, speaks of the urgent need for a patriotic leadership, and laments, in a general way, the growing civil unrest, but for the most part reads more like a philosophical treatise than a contribution to political debate.

In Burke's view, the remedy for political instability and disorder was to be found in party, defined by him as the honourable combination of men of like views. In the *Essay on Patriotism*, on the other hand, faith is placed in the probity of the individual patriot. Attention turns away from the immediate significance of political actions and is directed instead towards those forces of character which are seen to promote them. For this writer, then, patriotism is not to be regarded as a political programme, a set of policies to be taken up or discarded. It is an attitude of mind, an affection, a passion, a moral and psychological attribute, involuntarily held. Properly constituted, the subject cannot help but be a patriot, for patriotism exists below conscious conviction, in the very elements of human nature. It follows that political choices and decisions, foremost among which is the ritual of election, must rest upon a process of psychological scrutiny. The author of the *Essay* is in no doubt of the procedures to be followed:

> Before any Man's Claim . . . to Patriotism is allowed, the Bias of his Mind is to be examined, his internal Character to be weighed, and a Trial must be made, whether his Nature is capable of an Affection so exalted, as that of Love to his Country.   (p. 22)

It is not enough to say that in this tract, and in others of its kind, political judgments are made with reference to the character of an individual. For what is really at stake here is the particular theory of character — as a psychological configuration of passions and affections — which gives those judgments their particular quasi-scientific form.

In its adoption of this somewhat theoretical approach, discerning patriotism in the tissues of personality rather than in the contingencies of action, the *Essay* does have a concrete end in view: the distinction of the True Patriot from the False. The entire apparatus of the seventy-page pamphlet, divided, treatise-like, into parts and sections, is devoted to this end. Indeed, the high-sounding preoccupation with method is somewhat at odds with the limited political objectives of the tract. In a pompous introductory statement the author warns that

> it will be necessary to enquire into the Nature and Origin of this truly virtuous and extensive Affection of the Mind; so that from hence we may be able to form some general Rules by which to distinguish such a noble and sublime Passion, from all Counterfeits and injurious Pretensions.(p.5)

Other pamphlets on patriotism are less concerned with the exposition than with the application of this mechanism of judgment. I have already mentioned those election addresses which describe the qualities of the True Patriot in order to direct the choices of their readers at the polls. *An Address to the Electors of Great-Britain*, published to coincide with the election of March 1768 (in which Wilkes was one of the successful candidates for Middlesex) concludes with a 'Test of Patriotism', a set of practical suggestions towards an estimate of the moral and political rectitude of the candidates. In contrast to the relatively complex procedures of the *Essay*, the criteria offered here tend to be direct and manifest actions, of a personal and unprompted kind, such as an attempt to reduce the national debt. In tracts such as this political questions are often answered by moral solutions. Political corruption, viewed in the *Address* as the dominant feature of the electoral system, is not to be eradicated through concerted action or public policy but rather by a patriotic 'love of virtue and detestation of vice'. It is in terms of such moral generalities that patriotic candidates are identified and defined as 'men . . . of unblemished characters, whose words are sacred, and whose hearts are upright, fearing God, and devoted to their country's welfare' (pp. 14-15). The preference throughout, it would seem, is to avoid any standards of judgment which might savour of the language of faction. By way of contrast, the *Cautionary Address to the Electors of England*, published at about the same time, issues a series of unashamedly political criteria to guide the election choice. Candidates deserving of rejection are the adherents of Bute, 'in general, every Man whatever, who has acted under the Banner of the the Favourite' (p. 29). At the head of those deemed worthy of selection are 'those approved Patriots, who opposed the late pernicious Peace' (p. 31).

Wilkes himself would certainly fit into this category. Other than Chatham, he is the figure most frequently associated with the ideology of patriotism in this period. Having been worshipped as a hero and a martyr, or, conversely, denounced as a rogue and a rake, it was perhaps inevitable that Wilkes should be further classified in terms of an opposition between the True and False Patriot. His supporters are careful to argue that even his most conspicuous moments of triumph should be regarded as a contribution to the national interest. Wilkes, they declare, is no rabble-rousing Sacheverell:

> He did not make a vain foolish progress through several counties, like the mad Tory Parson in Queen Anne's time. He went only once into Buckinghamshire, and he chose the king's birth-day for the time of his coming among his constituents at Aylesbury, that the rejoicings on his return to them might distinguish that auspicious day.[5]

The strategy followed here is to assume a posture of self-effacement, and yet to elevate Wilkes to a public stature, to involve him in a fusion of private and patriotic celebration. The choice of the birthday of George III is by no means a random one. With a fine sense of irony, it allows Wilkes to appear at once both a dutiful subject of the monarch and a potential rival to his authority. Simultaneously, as it were, Wilkes is able to engage in both panegyric and parody.

It is this second aspect of his conduct, the subversive character of his politics, that Wilkes's opponents wish to highlight and expose. One line of attack is to confer upon him the identity of the False Patriot, to present him as an ingenious but despicable master of the art of political deceit. This, as its subtitle suggests, is the polemical policy pursued by *A Mirror for the Multitude; or, Wilkes No Patriot* (1769). In this pamphlet the exposure of the mock-patriot is akin to the technique of unmasking, the formal and theatrical identification of a political villain. As if it were still caught up in the political thinking of seventeenth-century drama, the *Mirror* conceives of the state as a theatre of deception and intrigue, patrolled by unsuspecting patriots, who are duped by 'the base Artifice, false Colourings, and foul Misrepresentations of crafty, sinister Male-contents' (p. 43). The Malcontent is defined, again in neo-Jacobean terms, as one excluded from the centre of power, whether this be the court of James I or the administration of Grafton: 'those who are not, and ought not, to be admitted into the Administration, become Malecontents because they are not admitted' (p. 48). There is an interesting overlap here between two stereotypes of political writing, the Malcontent and the False Patriot. Both, and this is their point of unity, are psychological configurations, political deviants troubled by an imbalance of the humours. The author of *The History of Jack Wilks* had described liberty as Wilkes's 'ruling passion', a trait of character rather than a political ideal. In the *Mirror* he is, more darkly, a man disturbed by 'luciferian passions', the chief agent of misrule in a nation which itself suffers from a welter of 'restless, flagitious Affections' (pp. 4-5). In this way the pamphlet performs on its protagonist an anatomy of 'political melancholy', an affliction later diagnosed in Samuel Johnson's *The Patriot* (1774). Wilkes appears like a figure out of a morality play, 'a Person gigantic in Vice' (p. 24), a False Patriot and ally of the inhabitants of 'those sable Regions, where hideous mis-rule, tumultuous Rage, and alarming Clamour prevail' (pp. 27-8).

A Mirror for the Multitude is no masterpiece of political writing. There is something extravagant in its hell-fire oratory, while its portraits of Wilkes, apparently based upon preconceived notions of character, are unconvincing. But not all of the works I have considered in this chapter are content simply to reproduce stereotypes. Some writers show a critical awareness of their own techniques and objectives. In short, there is a sufficiently wide range of achievement to suggest that invective and panegyric, the styles of address appropriate to the politics of personality, need not be regarded as inferior literary forms. Junius is certainly convinced of the high seriousness of his *Letters*. In his view, the satirical portrayal of individual politicians is an acceptable and even distinguished mode of political discourse. In an interesting passage he defends this approach in terms of a contrast between character and caricature, between the aesthetic worth of the portrait and the cartoon:

> Every common dauber writes rascal and villain under his pictures, because the pictures themselves have neither character nor resemblance. But the works of a master require no index. His features and colouring are taken from nature. The impression they make is immediate and uniform; nor is it possible to mistake his characters, whether they represent the treachery of a minister, or the abused simplicity of a king.   (Junius, 1978, p. 62)

It is probable that in this defence of his portraits of Grafton and George III Junius owes a good deal to the aesthetics of Fielding and Hogarth. For the distinction Junius makes between the 'master' and the 'dauber' is similar to that drawn in the famous preface to *Joseph Andrews* between the ridiculous and the monstrous, the comic and the burlesque – a set of oppositions further illustrated in Hogarth's etching 'Characters and Caricaturas' (1743). Like his predecessors, Junius regards his work as both aesthetically and morally superior to the burlesque efforts of the 'common dauber'. He would no doubt have agreed with Fielding that 'it is much easier . . . to paint a Man with a Nose, or any other Feature of a preposterous Size, or to expose him in some absurd or monstrous Attitude, than to express the Affections of Men on Canvas' (Fielding, 1967, pp. 6-7). Wilkes turned this theory of character portrayal to polemical ends. In *North Briton*, no. 17 he mounted a fierce attack on Hogarth following that satirist's allusions to Pitt and Lord Temple in the powerful political print entitled *The Times* (1762). In a deliberate reversal of the painter's aesthetic ideals he complains that Hogarth has declined into the politics of caricature, that he has joined 'the miserable tribe of party etchers . . . entering into the poor politics of the faction of the day, and descending to low personal abuse, instead of instructing the world, as he could once, by manly moral satire'. *The Times* certainly signalled a growing political emphasis in Hogarth's work, but Wilkes's lofty criticism is disingenuous. For there is evidence enough in the *North Briton* of his own liking for – indeed, mastery of – the very mode of presentation he censures. In the course of the journal one is liable to stumble upon passages which might almost be intended to serve as illustrations of the technique of literary caricature. In no. 36, a satirical catalogue of the '*hereditary* virtues and vices' of the royal families of Europe, Wilkes remarks that 'Pride and bigotry have marked the imperial house of *Austria*, equally with the coarse, big lip' – where the emphasis on a single detail of physique, and its association with the moral condition of the subject, seems a textbook example of the caricaturist's art.

What Wilkes devised in such passages was a politics of spectacle rather than concept, a literary equivalent of the political cartoon. Other pamphleteers of the period sought similar effects. The analogy with the visual arts is implicit in the title of the entertaining *Original Camera Obscura; or, The Court, City, and Country Magic-Lanthorn* (1768). Two other pamphlets concerned with Wilkes, the *Dialogue between the Two Giants at Guildhall* (1768) and *Harlequin Premier* (1769), adopt theatrical conventions, including those of pantomime and farce, in their efforts to create popular political spectacle. Wilkes's use of such techniques was not confined to the portrayal and vilification of his political opponents. He also applied them to himself. Indeed, one might be forgiven for viewing his entire career as a triumphant exercise in self-caricature. It seems appropriate, then, that Brewer should describe the historical significance of Wilkes in terms of his innovations in political method. An undoubted virtuoso in the literature of politics, Wilkes used his polemical talents to force himself into the public consciousness, to register his importance as a public figure. It might even be

argued that he was responsible for a new understanding of
the term 'public', for forging a new concept of that realm of
life. For now we would say, almost without hesitation, that
a 'public' figure is the creation of that apparatus we know
collectively as 'the media'. Wilkes, I would guess, was involved
in this process at a formative stage in its history. For the
most part the techniques and procedures which secured his
public status were those of the press in its various political
forms: the pamphlet, the broadsheet, the journal, and the
newspaper. But as an elected (if ultimately disqualified)
member of parliament Wilkes was also subject to an older
and more ceremonial set of practices, in which the citizen
was made public by due process of law. In the debates of
1768-70 Wilkes is caught between these two modes of estab-
lishing his political identity. It is a division which runs through
much of the political literature of the period, giving it a quite
distinct historical character.

The opposition between 'personalities' and 'issues' is a
perennial one in political argument. The debate on the
Middlesex Election shows that it is not as simple as it might
appear. 'Personality', at first sight the most obvious of things,
may in practice be understood in a number of ways. In the
fine *Letter to Samuel Johnson* (1770) the 'identity' – or
'personality' – of Wilkes is a central political question. Much
of the early part of the pamphlet is a sustained and mocking
riposte to *The False Alarm*, Johnson's contribution to the
debate. But in due course this satire of what Wilkes regards
as an 'effusion of servility and bombast' gives way to a more
considered analysis of the development of Johnson's argument. Wilkes's expulsion from the House of Commons in
February 1769 is one of the major issues. Johnson, in common
with other pro-ministerial writers, argued that this expulsion
had rendered Wilkes incapable of re-election, at least to the
present parliament. Wilkes's reply to this point is framed in
such a way as to make a qualitative distinction between the
private individual and the political subject, between, in this
case, citizen John Wilkes and the elected member for Middlesex.
In this way of viewing it, each election creates a new member,
even if the personal identity of the successful candidate remains unchanged: 'A fresh writ is issued, and a NEW MEMBER

is returned to Parliament. The same individual, perhaps, as a man; — — — but I repeat it, a NEW MEMBER.' (Wilkes, 1770, p. 18) This distinction is fundamental to what amounts to a general theory of election. In applying it to his own case, Wilkes conducts the argument carefully and with no little skill:

> The immediate effect of the expulsion is a political *anni-hilation*. A subsequent return is *not* of the nature of a political resurrection. It has no reference to a former delegation; it sends the member, as a new existence, un-conscious, unaccountable for former parliamentary delin-quencies; his political identity is destroyed; he is become, in the eye of common sense, in the established idea of Parliament, in the express language of the law, to all intents and purposes. ANOTHER MEMBER.   (ibid., p. 22)

In this chapter I have argued that Wilkes is the prime exponent of a mode of writing in which personality is itself a central political issue. But here he propounds a theory which seems to run in a quite different direction. The identity of the office-holder is not derived from within as an attribute of the will or as an expression of the ego, but is imposed from without as a creation of the electoral process. If Wilkes was in some respects an opportunist, always ready to make out a case for himself from whatever materials lay to hand, his argument cannot in this instance be dismissed as no more than a piece of convenient sophistry. As a theory of representation, it seems to conform to the conventional parliamentary wisdom of the time. One of Wilkes's most persistent opponents in the debate on the Middlesex Election argued from exactly the same principle in order to put a contrary case — that the nature of Wilkes's offences made him incapable of re-election. In his *Letter to Junius* (1769) Nathaniel Forster cites a case in which an MP had been expelled from the House, yet readmitted on relinquishing the office which had created his incapacity. According to Foster's interpretation of this precedent,

> The same Mr. Wollaston, who was expelled, was not again elected. The same *individual*, if you please, walked into the house, and took his seat there; but the same *person in law* was not again admitted a member of that parliament from which he had been discarded.   (p. 12)

In this exposition election is presented as a sort of legal mystery which, as if by magic, transforms the private individual into a public entity. Arguments of this kind may now seem arcane, and of interest only to specialists in electoral law, yet they have a direct bearing on Wilkes's historical role. For in defining his political identity in such terms he engages in an abstract, legalistic and parliamentary discourse which is quite at odds with the language of, say, his *Letter to the Duke of Grafton.* It is a measure of Wilkes's versatility that he was able to operate successfully within different political cultures. A one-time associate of Temple, Grenville and Pitt, he was at ease in the established political world, familiar with its attitudes and manners, and able to confront it, when necessary, in its own language. Indeed, some of his most telling ironies arise from his intimacy with the very objects of his ridicule. But he was also able, in ways which I have attempted to describe, to forge a more popular political identity and to project a cause which could mediate the demands and desires of those unrepresented by the ruling political interests.

10

Legal Argument and the Middlesex Election

At the beginning of *The False Alarm* (1770) Samuel Johnson dismisses Wilkes summarily and contemptuously from the argument he is about to present. He will not demean himself by crossing swords with one who has been condemned both as an outlaw and a libertine:

> The character of the man thus fatally excepted, I have no purpose to delineate. Lampoon itself would disdain to speak ill of him of whom no man speaks well. It is sufficient that he is expelled the House of Commons, and confined in jail as being legally convicted of sedition and impiety.
>
> (Johnson, 1977, p. 319)

Johnson's determination to exclude the personality and politics of Wilkes from the debate is shared by many of the writers who discuss the issues raised by the Middlesex Election. Few of the pamphlets to be considered here go beyond the odd jibe at — or embarrassed apology for — the personal history of Wilkes. In part this neglect is no doubt a studied and tactical one. Writers who favour the ministerial position (among whom we may include Johnson) are anxious to play down any manifestation of discontent. To this end the crisis of the Middlesex Election is dismissed as little more than the effect of faction, with no root cause in the system of government, while the activities of the Wilkites and the character of Wilkes himself are simply deemed unworthy of the consideration of serious men.

Wilkes features scarcely more prominently in the writings of the parliamentary opposition and its allies. This can again be interpreted as a tactical move, a decision to fight on constitutional issues rather than on the less promising ground of

Wilkes's reputation. This defensive attitude, characteristic, in particular, of the Rockingham Whigs, is condemned as hypocritical in a pamphlet entitled *A Seasonable Address to the People of London and Middlesex* (1770). In the view of this author, Wilkes 'has been, in every debate relating to his election, formally disowned, contemned, and vilified, by those who espoused the cause; while they adopted his argument they were ashamed of his person' (p. 7). A reading of the anti-ministerial propaganda of 1768-70 lends some weight to this charge. The constitutional issues raised by the actions of Wilkes are exploited to the full, while Wilkes himself, as character, politician and popular political symbol, is disavowed. For generally speaking, the aristocratic groups which made up the opposition remained dedicated to the exclusion of the extra-parliamentary forces marshalled by Wilkes.

Nevertheless, there may be more to this proscription of Wilkes than simple political opportunism. Considerations of decorum and literary form may also play a part. Johnson's reference to 'lampoon' is a case in point. His claim that Wilkes has sunk even beneath the dignity of lampoon is a deliberate exaggeration, but the more important point is that he sees his own work as qualitatively distinct from a mode of writing in which personality is a principal object of concern. In *The False Alarm*, it is implied, the very nature of the discourse rules out such an approach. According to Johnson, moreover, the conventions of public life themselves require that Wilkes should be ostracised. Expelled from the House of Commons and deprived of his liberty, he is in effect a legal and political nonentity. There is evidence to suggest that this kind of thinking, by which personal identity could be defined in legal terms, came habitually to Johnson. Thus his curious gloss on the line from *King Lear*, 'Edgar I nothing am', reads: 'As Edgar I am out-lawed, dead in law; I have no longer any political existence.' (Johnson, 1968, p. 677)

Although Burke, author of the greatest anti-ministerial pamphlet of the period, would have contested Johnson's argument, the procedures he adopts have similar consequences for the presentation of Wilkes. For as we have seen, the overriding aim of Burke's *Thoughts* was to expose a political *system*. It is as if the individual cannot be reckoned among the elements of the inquiry, as if the person of 'Wilkes' cannot be admitted as a concept until his identity has been stripped away. This point is best illustrated by a passage in which Burke offers his interpretation of ministerial attitudes towards Wilkes and his supporters:

> all excesses on the side of liberty, or in pursuit of popular favour, or in the defence of popular rights and privileges, were not only to be punished by the rigour of the known law, but by a *discretionary* proceeding which brought on the *loss of the popular object itself.*   (II, 295)

Burke alludes here to the expulsion of Wilkes from the House of Commons, the decision that he was therefore incapable of re-election, and the final resolution that Colonel Luttrell should be chosen in his place. But more striking is the process by which Wilkes, the hero of popular politics, or, according to one's demonology, 'a Person gigantic in Vice', is transformed into a quite abstract formulation, 'the popular object itself'. The personality of Wilkes dissolves, so to speak, into a logical proposition or form of words.

It will be the aim of the next chapter to assess Burke's pamphlet and to remark upon its distinctive qualities. While his treatment of Wilkes is not dissimilar to that found in many contemporary writings, the range of the *Thoughts* is exceptionally broad. By way of contrast, an entire network of pamphlets written in 1769 and 1770 might be described as narrowly legalistic in approach. In works of this kind Wilkes and the Middlesex Election are considered as instances in a complex, quasi-legal debate, the general and constitutional significance of which is held far to override that of the particular case from which it arose. While pro-ministerial and opposition pamphleteers will present quite different interpretations of legal precedent, the privileges of the House of Commons, and the state of the law regarding elections, it is true to say that in a larger sense they occupy the same ground. The occasional ferocity of some of the exchanges does not conceal the fact that writers on either side of the question share certain assumptions about the terminology and modes of analysis proper to the debate. It will be my purpose in the present chapter to examine some of these assumptions.[1]

It is perhaps significant that a prominent figure in the debate on the Middlesex Election, at least in its early stages, should have been William Blackstone, member of parliament for Westbury, but better known as the author of the celebrated *Commentaries on the Laws of England*. The close relationship between legal and political argument which characterises the debate is somehow personified by this great jurist. His learned remarks on election law, gathered in the *Commentaries* (1765-69, I, 169-70), were applied to the case of Wilkes, and regarded as entirely authoritative, by a great many of the polemicists involved. But Blackstone's judgment on the case itself, given in the course of parliamentary debate, proved more controversial. Opposition speakers argued that his approval of the disqualification of Wilkes was contrary to the legal opinion set out in the *Commentaries*. Thus in the debate on the petition against the return of Luttrell (8 May 1769) George Grenville declared his preference for 'the opinion given by the learned gentleman, in his work on the Laws of England, to what fell from him this evening' (Cavendish, 1841-43, I, 430). Blackstone's list of the legal grounds upon which a candidate might be proscribed did not include that which had been invoked against Wilkes. Whatever one might think of the merits of this vexed dispute, one of its most striking features is the determination shown on all sides to confine the debate to legal grounds.

Yet in a case which concerns the rights of electors as well as the privileges of parliament, political sentiments are always likely to intrude. Blackstone claimed only to be expounding a code of law, but in *The Question Stated* (1769) William Meredith claimed that political considerations had swayed his judgment. 'I shall continue to prefer the *Thoughts* of the Professor,' he remarked sarcastically, 'to the *Words* of the Politician.' (p. 20) Blackstone's rejoinder was indignant: in *A Letter to the Author of 'The Question Stated'* (1769) he assured his readers that he had 'industriously avoided saying any thing on the political Merits of the principal Question in Dispute' (p. 8). A broad view of the pamphlet literature devoted to the Middlesex Election would suggest that Blackstone's distinction is a difficult and tenuous one. The boundaries between legal and political argument become increasingly hard to discern. Or, to put it another way, it appears that political issues have somehow been transposed, so that the forms and procedures of law themselves become the principal bones of contention.

In this sense, and from an historical perspective, the debate on the Middlesex Election seems to occupy remarkably narrow ground. We might recall that Wilkes's candidature for Middlesex in 1769 had been declared invalid on the grounds that his earlier expulsion from the House of Commons had rendered him incapable of re-election, at least to the present parliament. This decision was announced through a resolution of the Commons acting alone, and the right of the House to create an incapacity of this kind became a fundamental issue in the ensuing debates. Wilkes, the array of forces he represented, and the political principles for which he stood, are all ruled virtually out of court. For the real concern is whether or not the action by the Commons was legitimate.

This way of viewing the controversy has a formal analogue, described concisely in the short title of William Meredith's famous anti-ministerial tract, *The Question Stated*. For in a procedural sense the primary aim of the pamphlet is to resolve the whole crisis — the immense political and constitutional ramifications of the Middlesex Election — into a single *question*. 'Stating the question' is an activity which typifies the pamphlets, both pro- and anti-ministerial, engaged in the argument. In many cases this may no doubt be considered as a mark of their parliamentary origin. For the drafting of a question was one of the practices any serious participant in parliamentary debate was bound to undertake. It is worth recalling that such questioners were obliged to exclude any derogatory reference to private character and to refrain from any personal form of address. In a similar way the naming and delineation of an individual, so important in tracts considered in the preceding chapter, finds little place here. While not all of the pamphlets which present a legal argument were written by MPs, they do broadly conform to a parliamentary mode of discourse. The dramatisation of character is no longer seen as the writer's task. More crucial is the ability to define a question with clarity and precision.

In Meredith's pamphlet that question, the rhetorical turning-point of the discourse, is phrased in legal terms. 'By what Law', he asks, 'was Mr. Wilkes rendered incapable, so that the Freeholder of Middlesex, by acting in Defiance of that Law, should be disfranchised, for having given him his Vote?' (p. 20) From this point on the pamphlet takes the form of an answer to the question it has itself asked. More particularly, the question prompts and authorises a review of legal precedent, the powers of the Commons, and the rights of freeholders, cited by Meredith in order to demonstrate that the declar-ation of Wilkes's incapacity was illegal. In this respect the question has a vital but relatively straightforward function. It is rhetorical in a precise sense of the word, since it defines the subject-matter and directs the movement of persuasive discourse.

In some other pamphlets, however, the stating of the ques-tion is a more complex affair. It occupies the bulk of what is perhaps the lengthiest work to come out of the controversy, *A Fair Trial of the Important Question* (1769). The preamble to this tract is indicative of its preoccupation with the for-malities of debate:

> I shall . . . shew what is *not* the question. . . . I shall state what the real question is; and, for preventing all ambiguity, shall explain the terms necessary to the understanding of it. . . . I shall lay down what I apprehend to be the prin-ciples and grounds, upon which the question ought to be tried. (pp. 3-4)

In keeping with the judicial metaphor implicit in its title, the *Fair Trial* develops an apparatus by means of which the ques-tion can be stated and its merits ascertained. The title of the tract, then, seems to promise a calm and non-partisan approach to the Middlesex Election, an abstract legal inquiry. It is soon obvious, however, that the pamphlet is sited in the midst of a paper war. Combining formal exposition with polemical intent, it seeks energetic combat with two ministerial tracts.[2] Never-theless, it is to the procedures rather than the politics of these pamphlets that the author objects. Thus the *Fair Trial* com-plains that 'where terms are promiscuously used, without sett-ling or affixing their precise signification, it is impossible the argument can proceed with real force, or conclude to fair demonstration' (p. 19). If only the terms could be fixed, the author seems to suggest, the dispute might finally be resolved. It is arguable, however, that the quarrel about terms is no more than a projection of entrenched political viewpoints.

In Letter XVI Junius, perhaps following Meredith's example, remarks on the formal inadequacies of contributions to the debate and offers his own version of the question at issue. In so doing he is determined to exclude all extra-judicial criteria:

> The consideration of what may be reasonable or unreasonable makes no part of this question. We are enquiring what the law is, not what it ought to be. . . . I do not mean to admit that the late resolution of the house of commons is defensible on general principles of reason, any more than in law. This is not the hinge on which the debate turns.
> (Junius, 1978, p. 88)

There is a kind of confidence about this passage which, if impressive as rhetoric, is somewhat misplaced in view of the larger development of the controversy. For an inquiry into 'what the law is' turns out to be a most involved affair. Indeed, it was precisely in the attempt to distinguish the legal from the extra-legal, and to decide upon the admissibility of political criteria, that the main grounds for dispute in the Middlesex Election lay. In *A Word in behalf of the House of Commons* (1769) Jeremiah Dyson, a one-time Clerk to the House, adopts an unashamedly legalistic stance. In a discussion of Wilkes's expulsion he remarks that 'As to what regards merely the *propriety and wisdom* of the measure, it is not proposed to enter into that part of the argument', for this is 'a consideration of far inferior moment to the question of its legality and justice' (p. 7). Burke, on the other hand, was much readier to consider questions of policy. As Cavendish (1841-43, I, 427) records, he asked the Commons whether anyone would 'pretend to say, that this House, in judging of the rights of the freeholders, ought not to have policy in its eye? Are we such judges dropped from heaven, that we shall not put parliament in mind how the people will like this?' Questions of reason and policy, which Junius is reluctant to admit into the argument, are for writers such as Burke fundamental to the debate. What emerges from the controversy is not, as Junius would have it, the certainty and solidity of legal argument but rather its inexactitude, its capacity for contention, and its readiness to accept and mediate political opinion.

This is perhaps most evident in the appeals made by writers of opposing political viewpoints to different codes or bodies of law. In his attack on the administration in the *Letter to Dr. Blackstone* (1770) William Meredith compiles a list of the relevant sectors: 'the Decision of the Middlesex Election could not be defended on any Principle of common Law, is directly in the Teeth of the Statutes, and a Contradiction to that Law and Custom of Parliament which is to be found in the Journals' (p. 29). Nowhere is it argued that Wilkes, expelled on a charge of seditious libel, had been punished according to *statute*: Blackstone's *Commentaries* demonstrated that this was not the case. But the action taken by the Commons against Wilkes — especially the decision that he could not be re-elected — was vigorously defended on the authority of the law and custom of parliament. Nathaniel Forster, for instance, in his *Defence of the Proceedings of the House of Commons* (1770) claimed that the resolution was not of a legislative, discretionary, and therefore unconstitutional character, since the House was only enforcing the legal provisions necessary to its existence as a political body. Every senate, he declared, must have

> a *law* of *parliament*. . . . Because no assembly or body of men can subsist, without rules and orders for its regulation and government. This law has been always, and in all its stages, clearly distinguished from the common law of the land. (pp. 14-15)

Wilkes's punishment by the law of parliament, pronounced by the Commons sitting as a judicial body, was therefore as constitutional as any decision made according to statute law.

Forster's position was that the House of Commons itself constituted the final court of appeal in questions concerning the exercise of its privileges. But pamphleteers who joined in the attack on the administration wished to refer disputed cases to the judgment of the common law, described by William Dowdeswell, one of Burke's political allies, as the legal embodiment of 'sound reason and well-established practice' (1769, p. 1). Unlike Junius, then, Dowdeswell thinks it legitimate to question the 'reasonableness' of the decision. In the wake of a concept such as 'reason', however, opinion of all kinds, not necessarily legal in character, is likely to enter the argument. 'Sound reason', not perhaps the most definite or rigorous of categories, is employed as such by a number of the writers involved. It is a feature of the Wilkes case, then, that what is projected as a judgment strictly by law will before long take up ground on the farthest shores of jurisprudence.

The *Fair Trial*, for instance, is unrelenting in its demand for precision. Pro-ministerial pamphleteers are castigated at every turn for their looseness in definition and demonstration, and for their egregious or unscrupulous philological blunders. And yet the *Fair Trial* itself resorts to authorities which are either ill-defined for the purposes of inquiry or 'legal' only in a loose sense of the word. The author puts much faith in the sovereignty of the British constitution, so often the object of eighteenth-century myth and fancy, as if its bearing on the case was self-evident:

> We summon up the first and fundamental principles of the constitution, which proclaim with a loud voice, that the House of Commons cannot have the power attributed to them. (p. 128)

On the face of it, this appeal is not out of place. The verdict of history was not required to demonstrate that the case of Wilkes and the Middlesex Election was a great constitutional issue. And as E. P. Thompson (1980, pp. 237-8) has recently pointed out, a constitution like that of Britain is not nugatory just because it is unwritten. Nevertheless, in pamphlets such as the *Fair Trial* its prestige tends to be invoked uncritically, as a substitute for argument. There is consequently some basis to the claim made by John Shebbeare in his *Eighth Letter to the People of England* (1770) that the failure to interpret, explain or anatomise the constitution had been a flaw running through the entire debate:

The term constitution, unapplied to the constituent parts of it; and to the exercise of the legislative, executive, and other powers of which it is composed, conveys nothing more than a mere abstract idea, inoperative and unproductive. (p. 9)

In a direct criticism of the *Fair Trial* itself he gets close to determining the mythical, oracular and fetishistic quality of the constitution in so much of the political discourse of the time. 'The error . . .', Shebbeare concludes, 'arises solely from the considering those things to be emanations from the constitution, which form that constitution itself.' (p. 23) Shebbeare's objections are trenchant. In pamphlets like the *Fair Trial*, where legal demonstration is the very essence of the undertaking, the constitution stands beyond comment or proof, a body of traditions and practices the origins of which are lost in the mists of time.

In the *Fair Trial* the testimony of the constitution is backed up by a number of authorities of more or less judicial character. Some are presented as actual bodies of law, whether they have been codified or not. Thus the argument against the disqualification of Wilkes is based in part on the principles of 'the Law of Nations'. Rather less concrete systems of law may also be pressed into service. Anxious to refute the idea that disqualifications, such as those barring the election of minors, could be enacted solely by a resolution of the Commons, the author claims that 'Scripture itself, speaking according to the Law of Reason, tells us, the heir, while a child, is under tutors and governors until the time appointed.' In this second reference — 'the Law of Reason' — we seem to have moved away from constituted legal authority towards a notion of the eternal verities underpinning the system of justice. This trend continues as the author endeavours to explain the thinking behind the electoral incapacities suffered by various groups: that of the clergy is 'founded in the nature and reason of things, which is the first and highest of all legal incapacities'. The objections which debar returning officers from election are 'founded upon the principles of reason and natural justice, which are acknowledged grounds of the Law of England'.[3]

I do not wish to imply that propositions of this kind were futile — far from it. Those who complained that the treatment meted out to Wilkes and the freeholders of Middlesex was unreasonable were, in my view, on very strong ground. The point I would emphasise, however, is that this widening of the area open to argument is at odds with the kind of discourse in which the author of the *Fair Trial*, and many other writers opposed to the administration, had chosen to enter. They move uneasily from grandiose appeals to the spirit of the constitution to a more narrowly legalistic mode of argument. This successive expansion and contraction of the grounds for dispute may not indicate a lack of conviction so much as a rhetorical uncertainty, upon which Nathaniel Forster, an acute and consistent supporter of the ministerial line, is only too pleased to pounce. Forster's *Defence of the Proceedings of the House of Commons* ridicules William Dowdeswell's *Sentiments of an English Freeholder* for an alleged attempt to smuggle extra-judicial concepts into a strictly legal argument:

> If one species of law will not answer this purpose, perhaps two, or three, or half a dozen, may do it completely. At one time it is the law of sound reason, and common sense; at another, the common law of the land; by and by we find it, the law of natural justice; and at length, the law of inanimate nature, with infinite propriety as well as emphasis stiled, the *common law of all nations*, is made to bring up the rear. . . . There can be no such thing as a half-legislative authority. (p. 7)

Tempering his sarcasm, Forster goes on to argue that the legitimacy of the common law depends upon 'some external stamp of authority' rather than on a jurisprudential idea like the rule of reason or natural justice. Whether or not Forster is an adequate jurist, his argument does carry a certain weight. It is a shrewd rhetorical if not a watertight legal analysis. For it points to the uncertainty of an opposition which, while deeply committed to the language, law and customs of an unreformed parliament, exploits a controversy the origins and primary significance of which lie in extra-parliamentary activity.

On occasion pamphleteers are led, almost unawares, into unmistakable declarations of ideology and allegiance. It is in the historical analysis of precedents for the expulsion of an MP that these political sentiments are at their most explicit. Many discussions of the Middlesex Election are in effect inquiries into case law. The journals of the House of Commons are scoured for evidence which might lend support either to the privileges of parliament or to the rights of freeholders. Precedents of outstanding importance are discussed endlessly, and quite contrary conclusions concerning their relevance to the Wilkes affair are reached. This juridical procedure is sometimes disturbed by outbursts of polemic. The supposedly impartial review of precedents becomes explicitly partisan. In *The Question Stated* (1769) Meredith considers the expulsion of Walpole in 1712, an important precedent for the expulsion of Wilkes, and one which, perhaps against the writer's better judgment, arouses his political ire:

> 'Twas the Cause . . . of the House of Hanover, and the Vigor with which he supported it, that made Sir Robert Walpole's Expulsion necessary. . . . But I am only now to state the Case, and see whether it authorized our Decision in the Middlesex Election. . . .   (pp. 36-7)

There is a definite sense of reluctance here, as Meredith quells the voice of protest and resumes the more limited task he has set himself. It is an indication of the difficulties experienced by political writers who felt obliged to fight on legal terrain. The author of the *Fair Trial* shares Meredith's distaste for the precedent established by the expulsion of Walpole, and in this case an impatience with the niceties of judicial review finds unambiguous expression in the language of politics:

> 'Tis the precedent of times I am not much in fancy with; of a House of Commons led by a Tory Ministry, the enemies of the House of Hanover, to whose malice and wicked designs against the liberties of this country, Sir Robert Walpole was, on account of his opposite attachments, sacrificed. . . .   (p. 77)

Not only is the objection made upon political grounds, but the language itself changes from the pedantic mode of an attorney (which typifies the tract) to the bluff and open manner of an old-style Hanoverian Whig.

In this chapter I have tried to uncover some of the discrepancies which occur when a political issue is fought out in legal terms. Perhaps even more significant, however, than these tensions which are internal to the debate is the general lack of concern shown for the politics of Middlesex, in which, after all, the dispute had its origins. When Nathaniel Forster, for instance, deigns to mention the freeholders who had elected Wilkes, he finds it difficult to conceal his contempt. Some pamphleteers had argued that once Wilkes had been expelled from the House of Commons it was the duty of his constituents to decide, through the electoral process, whether he was fit to be readmitted. Thus, in the view of the anonymous author of *A Vindication of the Right of Election* (1769), expulsion restores 'to the people the Right of Election, enabling them to *reconsider* their choice, and proceed to a new election' (p. 19). In Forster's opinion, such a course of action would be improper. A decision reached by the Commons sitting in its rightful judicial capacity might be overturned by the political whim of the electorate. In making this point in his *Defence of the Proceedings*, Forster quite abruptly introduces a social element into his argument, basing it upon certain assumptions about class:

> that a cause, solemnly tried and adjudged at a tribunal as respectable at least as any tribunal upon earth, should be sent down for a rehearing and a rejudgment to a set of free burgesses, most of which are, in no respect, in the higher ranks of civil society, and many of them unfortunately in the very lowest, involves a degree of ridicule in it, which exceeds expression; and would imply a total subversion of order in the state.   (pp. 43-4)

In his insistence on a legal definition of the crisis Forster comes close to calling into question the right of election itself.

Those who opposed the disqualification (as opposed to the expulsion) of Wilkes are generally more respectful of the rights of the freeholder. This is sometimes apparent in the forms of address adopted in their pamphlets. Thus William Dowdeswell, who represented Worcestershire in the House of Commons, entitled his work *The Sentiments of an English Freeholder.* It should be stressed that this defence of the free-holder's interests is a defence of the political *status quo*, not a programme for electoral reform. Moreover, it is this pre-dominantly defensive attitude which leads pamphleteers like Dowdeswell to argue in legal and constitutional rather than overtly political terms. They conceive of the vote as a legal privilege rather than a natural right, as a privilege secured by — indeed, inherent in — the possession of property. According to Constantine Phipps's *Letter from a Member of Parliament* (1769), the freeholder's suffrage 'was a part of his Freehold, and inherent in his Person by Reason thereof; and to which he had as good a Title as to receive the Profits of his Soil' (p. 40). The decision to disqualify Wilkes and to appoint Luttrell in his place is, from this point of view, tantamount to an act of dispossession. In some ways this argument resembles Locke's discussion of the concept of property in the second of the *Treatises of Government*, where it is under-stood to include definite rights as well as material goods. Thus Locke speaks of a man's 'Property, that is, his Life, Liberty and Estate' (1967, p. 341). In Phipps's view, the right to vote is inseparable from the possession of the freehold: both are, as it were, essential attributes of the freeholder's person. William Meredith makes a similar point in *The Ques-tion Stated*, while emphasising that the connection between the suffrage and the right of possession is expressed concretely in law: 'The same Law that *bounds* the Freehold, *fences in* the *Franchise* likewise.' (p. 53) Meredith's metaphor, deliber-ately playing on ideas of possession and enclosure, actually has the effect of limiting our conception of the franchise, and hence of actively maintaining the exclusion of those outside the electoral process.

In this respect his argument is characteristic of the ideology of parliamentary Whiggism which identified political rights with the possession of property. For anti-ministerial writers like Meredith the point at issue in the debate on the Middlesex Election was the alleged abrogation of an existing legal right. It was to this question alone that they wished to confine the argument. The measures of government could then be de-nounced as unconstitutional and characterised, in accordance with Whig tradition, as the actions of men bent on assuming arbitrary power. In this way the relatively narrow question of legality came to dominate the entire pamphlet debate, to the extent that those involved sometimes seemed oblivious to political developments out of doors. In the case of opposition pamphleteers this apparent myopia may well have been self-induced. Their dilemma was that they wished both to exploit and to limit the crisis. They sought to manage the debate so as to inflict the maximum possible political damage upon their ministerial adversaries, and yet to prevent it from developing into an argument about the justice of the political system of which they formed a part.

The policy which opposition groups such as the Rockingham Whigs adopted on the Wilkes affair was in this sense entirely representative of their general historical position. Indeed, it might almost be described as a classical 'Whig' stance. But in the increasingly volatile political conditions of the late eighteenth century it was a position in which they would sometimes find themselves embarrassed or outflanked. There is a small instance of this in a pamphlet written by one of the shrewder anti-Wilkites, John Shebbeare's *Eighth Letter to the People of England* (1770). Shebbeare tries to draw out and expose the logic of opposition writers who had backed the rights of the freeholders of Middlesex against the powers and privileges asserted by the majority in the House of Commons. If it was illegal for the Commons to disqualify Wilkes, he argues, then 'the laws which have precluded some subjects from the privilege of being elected, and others from the right of election, are equally repugnant to the constitution' (p. 18). Opposition Whigs in parliament might reject this inference, but they would have been aware that the meddlesome Shebbeare was not alone in making it. Pro-Wilkite dissenters, radicals and activists were increasingly likely to reach and act upon the same conclusions. It is true that they would often continue to characterise themselves as 'Whigs', but the retention of that label could not conceal the nature of their challenge. The crisis of the Middlesex Election marked an important stage in the growth of a body of radical opinion which the relatively broad and flexible ideology of Whiggism would find itself unable to accommodate.

In the works of the controversialists I have discussed in this chapter there are clear and significant differences in emphasis. But more generally one is struck, when reading these tracts, by the homogeneity of the discussion. The same arguments, illustrations and precedents are encountered again and again. While I have tried to show how the assumptions which lie behind an argument sometimes break down in practice, it would be equally true to say that the degree of unanimity with which these assumptions are held is surprising and significant. In the pamphlets I have been considering here the crisis of the Middlesex Election may be reflected not so much in a diversity of opinion as in a failure to break out of conventional patterns of thinking. In a crisis an exceptionally large number of writers focus on a single issue. Many feel the need to rejuvenate the argument, but, as Bryant (1973) found in his study of the parliamentary debates of the period, new questions, ideas and solutions are generated only with the utmost difficulty.

I would suggest that in political writing tensions and obstructions of this kind are one of the formal manifestations of a crisis. 'Crisis' is a term which is used rather loosely in political affairs. It is conceivable, nonetheless, that the signs by which a crisis is popularly identified, and the forms through which it is encountered and felt, could be determined with some precision. There are a number of methods one might adopt in order to achieve this. Today the most favoured technique is the survey of public opinion through selective poll. Alternatively, one could perform statistical analyses of the newspaper coverage of certain events. One might go on to examine the political tensions within leading parties and institutions, or attempt to quantify the degree of social and economic unrest in the country. These methods, all of which are no doubt open to various revisions and objections, are beyond the scope of this study. But a more formal approach, undertaken through a reading of political tracts, may be within compass. We might familiarise ourselves, for instance, with the rhetorical conventions which govern the works of a particular period. We could then look at the ways in which these conventions have been disrupted – or perhaps even consolidated – by the perception and experience of political change.

In the course of the debate on the Middlesex Election the letters of Junius, which range in form from personal abuse to abstract argument, register these effects more acutely than any other text. From January 1769 to the publication of Burke's *Thoughts* in April 1770 Junius wrote and published almost forty letters. While by no means all of these are directly concerned with the Middlesex Election, there is no doubt that this is the dominant issue. It is not simply that it provides the subject-matter for a good many of the letters. More interestingly, it is felt as a crisis for the text itself, one that is experienced so keenly that it precludes or disrupts the usual procedures of political debate and review. Junius himself draws attention to this problem in Letter XXXIX, written shortly after the prorogation of parliament in May 1770 (Junius, 1978, pp. 193-203). John Cannon, Junius's most recent editor, describes this letter as 'a grand review of the state of the nation', and this certainly seems to be the writer's intention. The end of the parliamentary session is seen as a proper time for taking stock, for engaging in a general survey of the commonwealth. Junius suggests that this is the approved procedure for commentators on public affairs: 'The prorogation of parliament naturally calls upon us to review their proceedings, and to consider the condition in which they have left the kingdom.' In an earlier chapter I examined some of the criteria according to which the state of the nation was assessed in the writings of Burke. Among other concerns, Junius looks at the condition of the colonies, Lord North's 'application of the revenue', and the politics of the Court. And yet one feels, at least in the first two instances, that the account is somewhat cursory, even half-hearted, and lacking in Junius's usual and effective combination of formal logic and brilliantly ironic wit. It is not that Junius is unconcerned with these sectors. More accurately, one might say that an acute sense of crisis has made a general review of the state of the nation, undertaken in the conventional style, seem an irrelevance or even a luxury:

> At any other period . . . the scandalous disorders, which have been introduced into the government of all the dependencies in the Empire, would have rouzed the

attention of the public. . . . But the daring attack upon the constitution, in the Middlesex election, makes us callous and indifferent to inferior grievances. No man regards an eruption upon the surface, when the noble parts are invaded, and he feels a mortification approaching to his heart.

In this passage the crisis is thrown back as an indictment against the administration. But it is also experienced and reproduced as a disturbance in the rhetoric of the letter itself.

Writers on both sides of the question share this sense of crisis, though it must be admitted that legal argument is not always the most urgent or enlivening of styles. Many pamphleteers, perhaps tiring of the minutiae of the debate, conclude their works with graphic descriptions of riot-torn streets and Wilkite demonstrations. The events of 1768-70 may not have been on the scale of a *grande peur*, but Johnson was certainly wrong in dismissing the whole affair as a false alarm. Indeed, from a parliamentary standpoint, 'alarm' was a not unjustifiable response. In the seventeenth century, broadly speaking, the House of Commons had posed itself as the defender of the rights of the people against the arbitrary dominion of the Crown. By the late 1760s, as a direct consequence of the Middlesex Election, it was increasingly seen as an opponent of the rights of the common freeholder, as a usurper of the franchise which had created it. For a moment it seemed as if the interests of the electorate (not to mention those of the unenfranchised people at large) might run counter to those of an unreformed House of Commons. This conflict was expressed in the resolution that Colonel Luttrell, with a minority of votes, should sit as member for Middlesex in place of Wilkes, the freeholders' choice. It is notable that many of the writers I have considered in this section regard the admission of Luttrell rather than the expulsion of Wilkes as the really critical and unprecedented act. In his *Letter from a Member of Parliament* Constantine Phipps argued that the resolution had changed the character of the entire controversy, for 'It was no longer a speculative or temporary Injury to one Sett of Electors, but an actual Violation of the Rights of every Elector in the Kingdom, that became the

Subject of the Debate.' (p. 15) In the opinion of Junius (1978, p. 66), the admission of Luttrell was a crucial moment in the whole argument about right. In effect, it marked the creation of a new *question*.

Only after this critical point does the paper war really gather head. From then on the political stimulus which propelled the argument in the first place gives way, so to speak, to a dynamic internal to the debate itself. In a pattern of development which is characteristic of controversies of this kind, statement provokes counter-statement, and accusation fuels riposte. As pamphlet answers pamphlet, and as controversialists return again and again to the fray, it seems as if the debate has begun to generate its own energy, until objective political conditions — in our case the failure of the petitioning movement of 1769 — signal the end of this phase of the crisis and reimpose external constraints. Few of the writers involved have the capacity or desire to reflect upon the genesis of the debate, upon its lines of development, its advances, retreats and discontinuities. Burke does so briefly in his *Thoughts*, but perhaps the best contemporary summary is provided by George Rous in his provocative *Essay on the Middlesex Election* (1770):

> we may . . . observe the opinions of men not immediately unfolding, but enlarging by degrees in the late important affair of the Middlesex election. At first the right of expulsion *ad infinitum* was admitted on all hands; that incapacity followed was denied by few; nay, the vote of a void election passed without opposition in the House, upon no better reason than that resolutions once made are binding during that session. The first stand was made on the admission of Mr. Lutterell [*sic*]. Self-evident as the consequence is, this was the only part for which the nation had not seen a precedent, and the novelty rather than the principle first excited alarm. Men who wrote in their closets found it necessary to controvert the point of incapacity; till, after frequent discussion, latter publications, more liberal, have attempted to limit, upon constitutional principles, the power of Expulsion itself.   (postscript, pp. 6-7)

Rous's account of the debate is selective and one-sided, a

survey of opposition rather than ministerial opinion. Nevertheless, the passage is of particular interest for its description of the progress of a political argument. It can be seen that, in Rous's view, while the debate developed in time and gathered forward momentum, its logic moved, as it were, in reverse. Anti-ministerial writers, more sensitive to political acts than political concepts, first baulked at the admission of Luttrell, then contested the disqualification of Wilkes, before reaching what Rous sees as the first principle at the heart of the crisis, 'the power of Expulsion itself'. In the following chapter I will look at a pamphlet which is placed chronologically at the very end of this process — Burke's *Thoughts on the Cause of the Present Discontents.*

11

Philosophy in Action

In the last two chapters I tried to identify and analyse the most important modes of political argument encountered in the debates of 1768-70. While few of my remarks were directly related to Burke, it was part of my purpose to recover the rhetorical context in which the *Thoughts on the Cause of the Present Discontents* should be read. This is not to say that the lesser-known pamphlets I discussed are to be dismissed merely as aids to reading Burke. Communications which have, according to literary judgments, proved ephemeral, may turn out to be indispensable for the study of political writing. They may embody or act upon preconceptions with which we are unfamiliar. They will have a structure, even a rigour, and a metaphorical life of their own. Above all, they make up the body of a debate which engendered outstanding contributions such as Burke's. From this point of view — from the standpoint of a theory of political discourse — the development and general characteristics of the debate are more significant than any of its individual participants, Burke included. Nevertheless, I would argue that quite apart from its literary qualities and its contribution to political thought, Burke's pamphlet is of particular interest on account of the peculiarity of its relation to the debate on the Middlesex Election. It is the purpose of this chapter to reach an understanding of this relationship and to mount a more general inquiry into the rhetorical organisation of the tract.

My reading of the controversies of 1768-70, and of the political history of Britain in its first decade under George III, has convinced me that the specific qualities of the *Thoughts*, the particularity of its context, allusion and effect, have often been underestimated. Historically the pamphlet has been regarded as a veritable compendium of general political principle. It has been welcomed for its eloquent propositions concerning government and applauded for its celebrated definition of party. Thus C. B. Cone, a professional historian and a biographer of Burke, highlights the 'philosophical' content of the *Thoughts* and tends to play down the importance of the context in which it was composed: 'Certain portions of the pamphlet, dedicated to an analysis of political conditions in 1770, have meaning only for historical specialists. But other sections of it will remain relevant as long as political freedom exists.' (1957-64, I, 195) In view of the style in which the *Thoughts* is written, this emphasis should perhaps come as no surprise. Burke is evidently concerned to argue in a general, even a theoretical mode. Some external confirmation of this is to be found in letters written prior and immediately subsequent to the publication of the tract. Writing to Rockingham in November 1769, Burke draws attention to the formality of the *Thoughts*. He finds it necessary to offer an apology for the theory his pamphlet contains. 'I find some difficulties as I proceed', he admits, 'for what appear to me self evident propositions, the conduct and pretences of people oblige one formally to prove.' (*Corr.*, II, 107) Other Whigs in the Rockingham group seem to have had doubts about Burke's method. Sir George Savile, who made detailed comments on one of Burke's drafts, regarded the pamphlet as a somewhat speculative venture. His bluff pragmatism is sometimes reductive – as in his remark that 'whoever answers it would say its all about who shall be in and who shall be out' – but it does serve to highlight the character of Burke's mode of exposition: 'doesn't it grow more theoretical than is necessary. Perhaps not. Yet People in general Skip over mere truths.' (*Corr.*, II, 120) Interestingly enough, Burke himself appears to accept that the pamphlet lacks the urgency of polemic. 'I know', he tells Rockingham, 'how ill a long detail of Politicks not animated by a direct controversy, wants every kind of help, to make it tolerable.' (*Corr.*, II, 109) In a single phrase – 'not animated by a direct controversy' – Burke seems to dissociate his work from the debate on the Middlesex Election, even though the composition of the *Thoughts* and the paper war concerning Wilkes largely coincided.

There is no doubt that Burke's pamphlet is often general and even theoretical in character. All the same, it may depend upon specific conditions which make its 'theory' possible, and indeed necessary. In this respect, and in spite of Burke's disavowal, the Middlesex Election may be of considerable importance. For throughout Burke's career it seems, somewhat paradoxically, that the production of theory is consequent upon the experience of crisis. The greatest expression of this is undoubtedly the *Reflections on the Revolution in France*. In that text Burke describes the requisite response to what is the most agonising crisis he can imagine, the collapse of monarchy and empire:

> we behold such disasters in the moral, as we should behold a miracle in the physical order of things. We are alarmed into reflection; our minds (as it has long since been observed) are purified by terrour and pity. . . .   (V, 157)

As I remarked in Chapter 3, this passage is of great interest for its application of an aesthetic principle, Aristotelian in origin, to the experience and perception of political events. But it is also a most suggestive account of the psychological genesis of general propositions about politics. In Burke's words, 'we are alarmed into reflection'. 'Alarm', the immediate response to a crisis, is a term which reverberates through the debate on the Middlesex Election and is sounded at strategic moments in the course of the *Thoughts on the Cause of the Present Discontents*. 'There is something particularly alarming in the present conjuncture,' Burke writes at the beginning of the tract (II, 220). Later, in a direct reference to the Wilkes affair ('an hardy attempt . . . *to alter the right of election itself*'), he tells us that 'the nation is alarmed at it' (II, 293). Samuel Johnson's pamphlet of 1770 registers the term in its title — *The False Alarm* — while claiming that too frequent expressions of alarm have exaggerated the importance of the Wilkes affair. In the passage just quoted from the *Reflections* Burke forges a connection between 'alarm', in the realm of feeling, and 'reflection', an intellectual activity which works on and modifies the original response. In this way the crisis of the French Revolution triggers off a complex mechanism of sensation and cognition. The ideological challenge posed by the Jacobins gives rise to thought as well as passion. An enthusiastic declaration of faith is quite insufficient. Unquiet times demand a theory too. The 'reflections' incorporated into the title of the text itself are the outcome of the whole process of thought and feeling. 'Reflection' may seem a rather curious and even inadequate term to describe the activity of a work which is, among other things, a clarion-call for action. And yet the juxtaposition of enthusiastic address and theoretical exposition is wholly characteristic of its style and manner.

It is also, in a quieter and less spectacular fashion, a feature of the *Thoughts* of 1770. In this pamphlet, I would suggest, Burke's excursions into political theory do more than fulfil the doctrinal requirements of the Rockingham Whigs. They also respond to the civil disorders and political crises of the late 1760s, pre-eminent among which was the affair of the Middlesex Election. In the opening pages of the *Thoughts* Burke introduces his thesis in the manner of a philosopher rather than a politician. The title itself leads us to expect this, a discourse consisting of 'thoughts', the products of meditation and reflection, composed at a certain distance from the urgent press of public affairs. This distance is taken as a precondition for the whole project. It puts the inquirer into a privileged position from which he can seek out the *cause* of discontent. This is not in everyone's power. In Burke's view, most right-thinking subjects respond immediately and intuitively to effects but fail to identify causes. Writing of the 'system of favouritism' which he denounces as the root of political evil, Burke observes that 'The people, without entering deeply into its principles, could plainly perceive its effects, in much violence, in a great spirit of innovation, and a general disorder in all the functions of government.' (II, 259) It is left to the enlightened inquirer to uncover the 'principles' which lie behind discontent, much as it was the task of the aesthetician, in Burke's *Philosophical Enquiry*, to discover the *'Origin* of our Ideas of the Sublime and Beautiful'.

The opening pages of the *Thoughts* are indeed reminiscent of both the epistemology and nomenclature of the *Philosophical Enquiry*. Political analysis takes the form of an empirical investigation into the relations of cause and effect. Consequently Burke's introductory remarks are couched in heuristic terms like 'examine', 'cause', 'enquiry', 'discovery' and 'error'. These excite definite expectations about the nature of the discourse which is to follow; it will be non-partisan, and entered into on the assumption that at the heart of the problem to be examined there lies a single truth or 'cause' which may be identified with philosophical precision. In this way Burke looks forward to the discovery of 'the true source of the mischief' (II, 218), a tactful phrase which implies that he is not prejudging the issue.

It is interesting that Burke should share this desire for philosophical certainty with one of his political adversaries. In *The False Alarm* Johnson, like Burke, is concerned to establish an epistemological framework for his analysis. The conclusions he reaches may be entirely at odds with those of Burke, but both writers find it necessary to outline the general principles and criteria according to which they will proceed. The preamble to Johnson's pamphlet undertakes this task in a characteristic manner, combining worldly scepticism with a philosophical regard for truth. He accepts that the 'science of government' has fallen behind the progress of natural philosophy. Unfortunately it is detained by the very political passions it seeks to understand. And yet Johnson implies that in time political theory will gain comparable increases in knowledge and insight. It is in this spirit that he considers the controversy over the admission of Colonel Luttrell. Writing in a language which is at this point, if not throughout the tract, that of disinterested philosophical inquiry, Johnson sees the case as one in which error and good faith are by no means incompatible: for, after all,

> Every diffuse and complicated question may be examined by different methods, upon different principles; and that truth, which is easily found by one investigator, may be missed by another, equally honest and equally diligent.
> (Johnson, 1977, p. 324)

Johnson's remark has the ring of an extract from some science of logic. For here, as in the opening pages of Burke's *Thoughts*, the writer is presented not so much as a committed and partial pamphleteer but rather as an honest 'investigator' engaged in a single-minded pursuit of political truth.

It would be easy enough to dismiss this stance as a simple rhetorical ploy, an unscrupulous attempt to annex the prestige of philosophy for polemical ends. In my view, this would be to underestimate the complexity of Burke's *Thoughts*. For in his finest writings rhetoric and inquiry are mutually sustaining, involved together in the production of political thought. The nature of the philosophical method may then itself bear close analysis. In the *Thoughts* there is a particular emphasis on observation and perception as the means by which the cause of discontent is to be isolated and identified. What may at first sight seem little more than a trope or mannerism on Burke's part, a simple accident of metaphor, is in effect an allusion to the mode of inquiry. 'I keep my eye solely on this system,' he declares (II, 259) in the course of his allegations concerning the notorious 'plan of favouritism'. Later, developing his argument that parliament has been 'usurped' by the Court, he insists that 'In speaking of this body, I have my eye chiefly on the house of commons.' (II, 286) The motive forces of the political world, its complex relations of cause and effect, are to be discerned by recourse to an empirical method. A keen and experienced eye is the key to political understanding.

These acts of perception may have their basis in the sensuous materialism of the *Philosophical Enquiry*. Burke argues there that our ideas concerning the sublime and beautiful can be traced back to their material causes in the natural world. Similarly, and in the realm of ideology, Burke's empirical method often leads him to conceive of political issues as concrete objects of inquiry. This is an approach adopted throughout Burke's career. In the early *Observations on . . . 'The Present State of the Nation'* (1769) he advances a critique of 'the policy of this country with regard to America', viewing it as an 'object . . . wholly new in the world. . . . All the reasonings about it, that are likely to be at all solid, must be drawn from its actual circumstances.' (II, 165-6) The experimental method is applied to a similar object in the *Speech on Conciliation with the Colonies* (1775). In his consideration of the penal acts inflicted on the colony of Massachusetts, Burke protests that

> in wishing to put an end to pernicious experiments, I do not mean to preclude the fullest inquiry. Far from it. Far from deciding on a sudden or partial view, I would patiently go round and round the subject, and survey it minutely in every possible aspect.   (III, 61-2)

It is not entirely clear from this remark whether the 'subject' is to be understood as the colonial policy or the locality and polity of 'America' itself. In either case the important point is Burke's determination to eschew abstraction. He describes this empirical mode of political inquiry most clearly in the *Letter to a Member of the National Assembly* (1791) when replying to the charge that he has failed to suggest a remedy for the crisis in France:

> I must see with my own eyes, I must, in a manner, touch with my own hands, not only the fixed, but the momentary circumstances, before I could venture to suggest any political project whatsoever.   (VI, 53)

As Chapman (1967, p. 146) puts it, there is at the heart of Burke's political experience 'a realm of impression or tact' in which his political ideas originate.

It is largely on account of this empirical approach that Burke's contributions to political thought have been so valued. For this is the epistemology which underpins his noted pragmatism, his concern with experience, and his refusal to countenance the merely 'abstract' in politics. As a method in aesthetics, however, it has often been found wanting. A common objection to the *Philosophical Enquiry* is that it belittles the role of the mental and imaginative faculties in aesthetic experience. Thus Canavan, a great admirer of Burke, concedes that in the *Philosophical Enquiry* 'he did not know what to make of abstract ideas which were not reducible to sensible elements' (1960, p. 38). I would suggest that this empirical outlook is responsible for similar limitations in Burke's political thought. In the first place, the observer tends to be caught up within the relations of power – is part of the very object – which is to be investigated, a problem Burke certainly encounters in the course of the *Thoughts*. More importantly, perhaps, it might be argued that certain questions in politics — questions of right, duty, sovereignty, obedience, possession, and the like — are necessarily conceptual and abstract in character, and hence irreducible to the simply institutional or objective.

In order to illustrate this point, we might look at Burke's proposition in the speech on *Conciliation* that

> Abstract liberty, like other mere abstractions, is not to be found. Liberty inheres in some sensible object; and every nation has formed to itself some favourite point, which by way of eminence becomes the criterion of their happiness.   (III, 49-50)

Like many such declarations in Burke, this sounds decidedly plausible. The rejection of the 'abstract' in favour of the 'sensible' reminds us again of the terminology and method of the *Philosophical Enquiry*, with its ultimate reliance on the 'sensible qualities' of things. And yet Burke's maxim may underestimate the power of ideas. It might be said, for instance, that 'abstract' need not mean 'unreal'; that the relations, ideas and rights gathered under the name of 'liberty' have a definite conceptual existence; that they may have force and effect even if they cannot be 'touched'. In other words, there may be significant political questions which are not wholly intelligible from the outlook of a philosophy of sensation. This is a difficulty Burke himself seems to encounter in this part of the speech. It may be straightforward enough to repudiate an abstract mode of liberty, but it is more difficult to find a 'sensible object' in which freedom can be said to inhere. Later in the passage Burke does attempt this. Reviewing the history of the colonies, he concludes that

> Their love of liberty, as with you, fixed and attached on this specifick point of taxing. Liberty might be safe, or might be endangered in twenty other particulars, without their being much pleased or alarmed. Here they felt its pulse. . . .   (III, 51)

The right to tax themselves, then, would appear to be the 'favourite point' or 'sensible object' in which the liberty of the colonies is embodied. It is defined here by Burke as 'a fundamental principle, that, in all monarchies, the people must in effect themselves mediately or immediately possess the power of granting their own money' (III, 50-1). In this way of viewing it, taxation is both a privilege and a duty. It is a rightful power which has apparent and significant effects. But it is difficult to conceive of it as a 'sensible object', as Burke appears to do. In this kind of argument, we might conclude, taxation is hardly less 'abstract' an idea than the concept of liberty itself.

In the preceding chapter I suggested that abstract formulations of this kind are to be found in the *Thoughts on the Cause of the Present Discontents*. Burke chose a somewhat theoretical and apparently unspecific mode of expression — 'the popular object itself' — by which to allude to Wilkes. In my view, this mode of indirect allusion is a leading feature of the rhetoric of the *Thoughts*. I would suggest that the general and 'philosophical' demeanour of much of Burke's writing in the tract is sustained by a fine particularity of reference, that beneath the detached surface of the *Thoughts* lies a dense network of allusion in which the issues raised by the Middlesex Election are of the first importance. In this respect one of the principal achievements of the tract is to frame a most discreet and serviceable discourse which can carry a general meaning with a particular application. In a style of this kind — which Macpherson has well described as a mode of 'empirical generalisation' (1980, p. 24) — Burke's deepest feelings about the function of politics are realised. For the politician, in Burke's famous phrase, is 'the philosopher in action'. The political pamphlet should then be the field of a theoretically informed practice. Ideally it should fuse the twin elements of thought and action into a dynamic, inquisitive and enlivening language.

The possibility that the rhetoric of the *Thoughts* may operate at more than one level is raised by a letter Burke wrote to Richard Shackleton shortly after the publication of the pamphlet in April 1770. 'It is the political Creed of our Party,' he declared in confident mood, but added that 'many parts will be unintelligible to you I confess for want of knowledge of particular persons and facts; but on the whole I think you must enter into the design' (*Corr.*, II, 136). The first part of this statement is more often quoted than the second. On first reading the *Thoughts* it is easy to overlook Burke's frequent allusions to 'particular persons and facts'. It will now be necessary to identify some of the more significant of these allusions and, more importantly, to indicate their rhetorical function.

Many of them are related in some way to Burke's presentation of the Wilkes affair. The disqualification of Wilkes and the installation of Colonel Luttrell are decisive instances in Burke's thesis that the influence of the Court has become excessive. And yet Burke's first references to the Middlesex Election are surprisingly coy, couched in the covert and indirect idiom of official discourse. Prompted by his rejection of the view that the power of the aristocracy had increased, they take the form of an ironic concession, introduced in pedantically negative terms:

> I will not affirm, that there may not have lately appeared in the house of lords a disposition to some attempts derogatory to the legal rights of the subject. . . . Those attempts in the house of lords can no more be called aristocratick proceedings, than the proceedings with regard to the county of Middlesex in the house of commons can with any sense be called democratical.   (II, 245)

Burke's allusion to 'the proceedings with regard to the county of Middlesex' is made with all the detachment and formality of some learned history of parliament. A little later, and in the same style, he speaks of 'the transactions relative to Saint George's Fields' (II, 253), a remarkably restrained reference to the bloody massacre of 10 May 1768 which had become an opposition *cause célèbre*. Allusions of this kind may seem slight and unemphatic, but their rhetorical function is of some importance. They prepare the ground for the more particular consideration of the Middlesex Election which is to follow. Their detachment and indirection lend Burke's pamphlet a certain dignity and ensure that it remains aloof from the more boisterous polemical activities of the Wilkites, 'a species of men', according to another of Burke's allusions, 'to whom a state of order would become a sentence of obscurity' (II, 277).

On other occasions, and as part of a tissue of references to the Middlesex Election, Burke will turn a particular instance into an apparently general case. Contemporary readers of the *Thoughts*, with the Wilkes controversy fresh in mind, would have been able to grasp Burke's strategy. Many would have delighted in his rhetorical skill. But it is now easy to read the pamphlet as if it comprised a series of exclusively general statements. The following extract, in which Burke launches a vigorous attack on the 'king's friends' and their alleged failure to preserve public order, may serve as an illustration:

> Unable to rule the multitude, they endeavour to raise divisions amongst them. One mob is hired to destroy another; a procedure which at once encourages the boldness of the populace, and justly increases their discontent. Men become pensioners of state on account of their abilities in the array of riot, and the discipline of confusion. Government is put under the disgraceful necessity of protecting from the severity of the laws that very licentiousness, which the laws had been before violated to repress. Every thing partakes of the original disorder.   (II, 278)

Burke writes here in a style which is somehow both urgent and controlled. The malevolence and deceit of government are exposed by a most acute and poised irony ('the array of riot, and the discipline of confusion'), which is capped by a finely-turned paradox ('that very licentiousness, which the laws had been before violated to repress'). The patrician tone of Burke's writing, and his evident concern for the public weal, stand as a rebuke to a cabal whose pursuit of self-interest has led only to chaos.

This passage is clever and energetic enough, but on the face of it Burke's accusation remains somewhat unspecific. Much of it reads like an exercise in the language of general description. Burke's use of the present tense — as in the allegation that 'one mob is hired to destroy another' — adds to this effect, as if he were describing the habitual conduct or fixed policy of government. And of course this is exactly the impression he wishes to make. At the same time, however, it should be recognised that such generalities rest upon a detailed sequence of allusions. It is probable that Burke refers here to the events of the Middlesex by-election of December 1768 and their controversial aftermath. In the course of the election, clashes between Wilkite crowds and supporters of the Court party led to the death of one George Clarke. As a result, Lawrence Balf and Edward MacQuirk, underlings of the Court denounced by Burke as 'pensioners of state', were tried for murder and convicted as charged. In March 1769 these menial anti-Wilkites were granted a royal pardon, which Burke styles as the 'disgraceful necessity' of a criminal government. In a slightly different interpretation, Paul Langford (*Writings and Speeches*, II, 287n) reads the passage as an allusion to the St George's Fields Massacre of 1768 — another disturbance which involved supporters of Wilkes. It may well be that Burke has both of these riots in mind, thus adding weight of evidence to his eloquent general charges. In this way the passage can be read both as a detailed case history and as a general survey of the state of the nation.

The final line of the passage I have just quoted — 'Every thing partakes of the original disorder' — deserves further consideration. It too is a generalisation, drawn, no doubt, from the disturbances at Brentford and St George's Fields, but alluding, more obviously, to the widespread discontent into which the *Thoughts* as a whole inquires. And yet, as a generalisation, it is on a different plane from the others I have discussed. It is a line more typical of the counter-revolutionary writings than of the *Thoughts*. It has the kind of moral universality so beloved by those critics who see Burke as the vindicator of a Christian Natural Law. The statement is indeed characteristic of Burke's political writing at its best. In the midst of a series of allegations against the government, the language reaches a pitch of metaphysical excitement. For the 'original disorder' is an epic phrase, culled from the politics of the sublime. It alludes not only to the savage riot at Brentford in 1768 but also, in a glorious hyperbole, to a Satanic state of chaos (see Boulton, 1963, pp. 55-6). In its context, then, it is more historical, more concrete, and more specific than the 'Natural Law' theorists would allow. Yet it remains more splendid and more forceful a phrase than we have any right to expect from a stolid party man. The rhetorical strength of the line depends upon its fusion of disparate elements, upon the audacity with which Burke connects the empyreal to the mundane.

If the sublimity of this phrase is somewhat unusual in the *Thoughts*, the passage as a whole is not. Indeed, the allusive method is fundamental to Burke's purpose in the pamphlet. It is a mode in which the particularity and urgency of polemic may not be inconsistent with the calm detachment of inquiry. In the course of the pamphlet Burke will make an observation which at first sight, and in keeping with his general approach, appears to be hypothetical or unsubstantive in character. It is as if the case he describes is to be understood as a possible outcome rather than the actual state of affairs. Viewed from another perspective, however, the *scenario* becomes a definite statement of fact, historical and specific rather than general and speculative. It is a technique Burke sometimes uses in the *Thoughts* to usher in accusations of a personal nature. Those figures who were regarded by the Rockingham Whigs as political renegades are often his prime targets. In an early passage Burke remarks upon the method by which the hated 'cabal' of Court politicians seeks to undermine the discipline of opposition parties. Speaking in very general terms, he starts to examine the whole process of political seduction and betrayal: 'They find out some person of whom the party entertains an high opinion. Such a person they endeavour to delude with various pretences.' (II, 251)

At this stage Burke's allusions are deliberately veiled ('some person', 'such a person'). It might well be assumed that he has no particular victim in mind, or that his is an argument based on hearsay rather than personal experience. Burke continues in the same mode, but is careful to drop significant hints or clues for the attentive reader to recognise and apply. 'When such a person', he goes on,

has broke in this manner with his connexions, he is soon compelled to commit some flagrant act of iniquitous personal hostility against some of them (such as an attempt to strip a particular friend of his family estate), by which the cabal hope to render the parties utterly irreconcileable.
(II, 252)

Burke's language remains relatively unspecific, but he alludes in parenthesis to a recent and controversial case. The 'particular friend' in question was the Duke of Portland, a prominent member of the Rockingham Whigs. His claim to the forest of Inglewood in Cumberland had been passed over by the Crown in 1767. Instead the estate had been granted to Sir James Lowther, son-in-law to the Earl of Bute, an action denounced by opposition groups as an improper and dangerous exercise of Crown prerogative. Instrumental to these proceedings was the Duke of Grafton, a one-time associate of Portland and the Rockingham Whigs, and, in Burke's eyes, a true political turncoat. Historical considerations apart, it is necessary to disentangle this long detail of politics in order to make sense of the rhetorical strategy of the *Thoughts*. For Grafton, identifiable from the allusion to the Lowther affair, is the figure with whom Burke is concerned throughout the passage (a fact which he noted himself, together with a host of other such allusions, in his own copy of the 1792 edition of the *Works*). In effect, then, we are presented with a review of Grafton's political career from the standpoint of a committed Rockinghamite. The rhetorical significance of Burke's method is clear. His references to some quite abstract 'person' lend his pamphlet all the grandeur of generality. They imply, in their very obliquity, that he is above the petty disputes of faction and devoid of animosity. No doubt it was on these grounds that Burke was able to claim, in a letter to Charles O'Hara, that his work had been received, even by its victims, as 'a piece of Gentlemanlike Hostility' (*Corr.*, II, 139). But at the same time Burke is careful to indicate — and this is the function of the parenthesis — that the passage can be read in a more particular way, as a detailed commentary on the political conduct of the Duke of Grafton. In this way the pamphlet retains a directly polemical function.

Burke's analysis of the Middlesex Election is governed by the rhetorical principles I have just described. In my view, the crisis concerning Wilkes helps shape Burke's *Thoughts*, but it is some time before his concern is made explicit. To begin with, preparing the ground with delicacy and skill, Burke creates in the reader an undercurrent of interest in the controversy. He works quietly, through allusion and through the careful repetition of phrases which are resonant of the political struggles of 1769. One might instance his use of the term 'discretionary'. Rehearsed *ad nauseam* by opposition pamphleteers who saw the disqualification of Wilkes as a 'discretionary' and unconstitutional proceeding, this epithet had become a veritable keyword of the debate. Burke uses the word in a variety of contexts, not always in direct allusion to Wilkes, but nevertheless forging a significant link with the terminology of tracts on the Middlesex Election.

In the pages in which Burke unfolds his historical view of parliament there is more extensive allusion to the crisis. He begins his account as if he were engaged in writing some treatise on the constitution, a general inquiry into the origins, powers and relations of the House of Commons. The style in which he chooses to introduce his remarks is decidedly formal, with an undertone of apology: 'I hope I shall be indulged in a few observations on the nature and character of that assembly; not with regard to its *legal form and power*, but to its *spirit*, and to the purposes it is meant to answer in the constitution.' (II, 286) This is not at first sight the language of polemic, yet Burke's studied rejection of strictly legal criteria may have a specific political end in view. For it is more than likely that he intends his comments to be taken as a critical allusion to the kind of abstruse legal argument which had been used, as we saw in the preceding chapter, to justify the disqualification of Wilkes. Continuing in the same, apparently indirect manner, Burke reminds us that the House of Commons 'was not instituted to be a controul *upon* the people, as of late it has been taught, by a doctrine of the most pernicious tendency. It was designed as a controul *for* the people.' (II, 288) In the midst of his excursion into constitutional theory Burke once again finds it appropriate to refer to the particular case ('a doctrine of the most pernicious tendency') by which it is both authorised and animated.

If at this stage Burke finds it sufficient simply to allude to the recent crisis of the Middlesex Election, he will before long enter more directly into the controversy, as we shall see in a moment. In this respect his pamphlet is related to the others I have examined, but in an unusual and characteristic form. Burke is not quite a participant in the debate, but there is no doubt that it shapes his thinking. While he affects a certain detachment from the case of the Middlesex Election, it nevertheless provides his pamphlet with a central rhetorical impulse. The *Thoughts*, then, lies on the very periphery of the debate which nurtured it. Paul Langford has recently remarked that

> The great political crisis associated with the affair of the Middlesex Election might naturally be supposed to have turned Burke's thoughts, at the close of the session of 1768-9, in the direction of a major public initiative to exploit the evident popular concern with the issues raised by Wilkes. But the pamphlet, when it emerged nearly a year later, in April 1770, actually had little to say about the Wilkes affair, though it plainly assumed a certain knowledge of the essential arguments on the part of the reader.
> (*Writings and Speeches*, II, 242)

I would argue that the pamphlet's underlying concern with the Middlesex Election is rather greater than Langford suggests, but he is correct, I think, to describe the relationship in somewhat negative terms. In most cases Burke's writings were provoked by a specific *occasion* (whether it was a parliamentary debate, a request for information, a pamphlet which required rebuttal, or a political crisis) which underpins the general maxims they expound. On the face of it, the *Thoughts* is an exception, but it might be said that the Middlesex Election, to which Burke often alludes, is, so to speak, the 'half-acknowledged' occasion behind the tract. James T. Boulton may have a similar idea in mind when, quoting phrases from Burke's correspondence, he remarks that the *Thoughts* is 'not a publication "animated by a direct controversy" but a statement of a "political Creed" given extra relevance and a particular focus by the furore over Wilkes' (1963, p. 15; see also Mansfield, 1965, p. 154).

There are perhaps four reasons we can offer for the peculiarity of this relationship. In the first place, Burke's pamphlet underwent a lengthy period of composition and revision (see Bryant, 1956) which distanced it historically both from the heat of the crisis itself and from the paper war to which that crisis gave rise. We first hear of the *Thoughts* when, in a letter of 29 June 1769, Rockingham tells his protégé that he is 'exceeding glad you have begun to look over the Papers of the system of the last 9 years' (*Corr.*, II, 39). Thus Burke was meditating on the *Thoughts* when the argument on the Middlesex Election was at its height, but his pamphlet was not published until 23 April 1770, when the debate had more or less ebbed away. The relative autonomy of the *Thoughts* may then have been inevitable, or perhaps purposeful — most probably both. Rockingham's remark suggests a second explanation for this sense of detachment. From the outset, it would seem, the objective Burke had in view was much wider and more general than a consideration of the political affairs of Middlesex. He aimed at nothing less than an exposure of the entire 'system' of politics which, in his view, had been inaugurated on the accession of George III. This 'historical' point of view was also adopted by Burke in the parliamentary debates of the period. In the preamble to his speech on the St George's Fields Massacre (8 March 1769) he remarked that:

> I was in no Sort of haste to bring the matter under your consideration. Near ten months have elapsed since this unhappy Transaction; four since the meeting of Parliament. I postponed it from day to day Because I wished that this enquiry should stand upon Ground — entirely general; and entirely publick totaly seperated from every temporary View, and even from the suspicion, of any partial or any personal End or purpose whatsoever. . . .
>
> (*Writings and Speeches*, II, 224)

The *persona* Burke creates for himself here is remarkably similar to the one we encounter in the *Thoughts*. Thirdly, and this is a related point, Burke may well have felt out of sympathy with the narrowly legalistic approach to the controversy which many pamphleteers had adopted. In general his own political writing avoids the pedantry under which the debate on the Middlesex Election laboured. Finally, Burke was probably as nervous about the Wilkes affair as he was indignant. He may have been reluctant to give too central a place to a crisis which had begun to raise issues of a radical nature.

When Burke does come to consider the controversy in some detail, he is careful to distinguish his style and method from those of the earlier pamphleteers. Referring to the disputed right of the House to declare a candidate incapable of election, he remarks that 'The arguments upon which this claim was founded and combated, are not my business here. Never has a subject been more amply and more learnedly handled, nor upon one side in my opinion more satisfactorily.' (II, 293) Burke takes a stand on one side of the question (and may have William Dowdeswell's *Sentiments of an English Freeholder* in mind when he offers his words of approval), but he regards the debate itself as finished and of a mode quite different to his own. 'I too have thought on this subject', he informs us, 'but my purpose here, is only to consider it as part of the favourite project of government; to observe on the motives which led to it; and to trace its political consequences.' (II, 293-4) Nevertheless, Burke does give some consideration to the legal and constitutional aspects of the Wilkes affair. Like many of the opposition pamphleteers whose work I have discussed, he draws a distinction between *making* law and *declaring* it; in the case of the Middlesex Election, he argues, the administration has confused these functions. But in general Burke is somewhat impatient with the legal niceties of the case. He will not involve himself in endless inquiries into precedent. It is the spirit rather than the letter of the law which interests him:

> When any construction of law goes against the spirit of the privilege it was meant to support, it is a vicious construction. It is material to us to be represented really and *bona fide*, and not in forms, in types, and shadows, and fictions of law. (II, 304)

Burke's discussion of the Middlesex Election is generally less abstruse than that of many of his contemporaries. But his main concern is to put the Middlesex Election into context, to demonstrate that it is an important element in the more wide-ranging conspiracy which he describes as a 'system of favouritism', a rule by double cabinet.

In practice, the procedures Burke employs to forge these links — to portray the persecution of Wilkes as part of some grand design of the Court — are as much rhetorical as demonstrative. Once again he exploits key terms from the debate on the Middlesex Election to suggest a collusion between apparently disparate areas of ministerial policy. In Burke's view, the principle of 'occasional and personal incapacitation' (as practised in the exclusion of Wilkes) had been an essential part of the strategy of the Court. For this kind of external and unconstitutional influence had undermined the popular character and independence of the House of Commons. The whole scheme was made more secure by certain innovations in the civil list and in the discharging of the civil list debt, practices which were intended, Burke felt, to ensure that parliamentary control over the revenues of the Crown should be fatally relaxed. The historical accuracy of Burke's account is not at issue here. Even if we were to regard it as entirely fictional, we would still need to understand its rhetoric and rationale. Of particular importance in this respect is Burke's attempt to link the principle of disqualification and the new demands on the civil list as twin elements in a coherent and mischievous design. Burke's method is allusive rather than analytical. In a notably sarcastic passage his suggestive manipulation of terms prepares the reader to hail the spectre of conspiracy:

> in order firmly to establish the precedent of *payment previous to account*, and to form it into a settled rule of the house, the god in the machine was brought down, nothing less than the wonder-working *law of parliament*.
> (II, 313-14)

Burke goes on to describe certain procedural ruses employed to legitimise the fraud. But for our purposes his emphasis on the phrase 'law of parliament' is the more important point. We saw in the preceding chapter that apologists for ministerial policy justified the disqualification of Wilkes on the grounds that there was a *law of parliament* which granted the House of Commons absolute jurisdiction in questions involving its own privileges. It is out of such carefully drawn parallels — between the Middlesex Election and the civil list debt — that Burke builds up the great myth of intrigue which lies at the heart of the pamphlet.

It is a 'myth' not primarily in the sense that it is untrue but rather in the sense that it is coherent and suggestive. Historians sometimes dismiss Burke's account as simple fiction, without paying much attention to the rhetoric which made it so plausible and ideologically attractive to his nineteenth-century admirers. The passage on the civil list is a good example of Burke's rhetorical skill. Having placed his dark hints to good effect, he finally gathers them together, making both the parallel and the accusation explicit:

> The power of discretionary disqualification by one law of parliament, and the necessity of paying every debt of the civil list by another law of parliament, if suffered to pass unnoticed, must establish such a fund of rewards and terrours as will make parliament the best appendage and support of arbitrary power that ever was invented by the wit of man. (II, 317)

In this passage, and perhaps throughout the pamphlet, the Middlesex Election is one of the main points of evidence, one of the few really concrete instances of demonstration, upon which the conspiracy theory is based. Though often presented in a veiled and detached way, it nevertheless prompts and to some degree directs the principles for which the tract has become famous.

Much of this chapter has been concerned with the rhetorical function of the Wilkes case. At this stage I would like to extend my review of the *Thoughts* and conclude this inquiry with some more general observations on the structure and success of the pamphlet. I have drawn attention here to Burke's use of the language of inquiry and the technique of allusion. It is by these means, I have suggested, that a concern with the consequences of the Middlesex Election is mediated, together with a more general fear that the constitution itself is under threat. But Burke's approach may not be ideally suited to the incitement of alarm. It may be difficult, from the stance of a relatively detached observer, to create a sense of urgency, to make the perils of the crisis quite palpable. In this sense the 'philosophical' and general viewpoint which Burke adopts initially, while clearly advantageous in some respects, may actually inhibit the persuasive function of the pamphlet. I see this as part of a general problem of form and tone encountered by Burke in the composition of the *Thoughts*. It is a question which concerns the selection of the most appropriate and effective voice to project in political discourse at this juncture. Should one be identified as a philosophical and non-partisan inquirer — a private citizen delving into his stock of political maxims — or as a committed and polemical activist? These questions of audience, stance and address are central to our understanding of the *Thoughts*. Boulton (1963, p. 72) has drawn attention to a passage in which Burke clearly has a particular audience in mind. Resuming his onslaught on the hated cabal, he claims that 'It was to be avowed as a constitutional maxim, that the king might appoint one of his footmen, or one of your footmen, for minister' (II, 234) — a revealing remark which suggests that Burke's ideal reader is of definite and privileged social origin. But if Burke has a consistent image of his audience, his conception of *himself*, as author of the address, may be less stable and secure. Any assessment of the tract should therefore take into account its possible shifts in voice and tone; once these have been identified, we should go on to ask whether they are strategic and calculated, or involuntary and forced.

I remarked earlier on Burke's attempt to combine the language of general principle with a more forceful and polemical address. It is a manoeuvre which Burke conducts with immense skill, so much so that one is often as impressed by the rhetorical dexterity of the work as by the reflections on party for which it has been celebrated. At times it is possible to trace Burke's movements, to watch his fine modifications of tone and stance. At an early stage in the pamphlet Burke intimates that while his inquiry into discontent will be thoughtful, it will also be energetic and practical. He may proceed in rather general terms, but it is not his aim to write a leisurely and reflective essay on the ways of the world. In the following passage Burke seems to adopt the style of the moralist, but only in order to present the viewpoint of the politician:

To complain of the age we live in, to murmur at the present possessors of power, to lament the past, to conceive extravagant hopes of the future, are the common dispositions of the greatest part of mankind; indeed the necessary effects of the ignorance and levity of the vulgar. Such complaints and humours have existed in all times; yet as all times have *not* been alike, true political sagacity manifests itself, in distinguishing that complaint which only characterizes the general infirmity of human nature, from those which are symptoms of the particular distemperature of our own air and season. (II, 219)

In effect, Burke offers two quite distinct ways of responding to widespread expressions of discontent. The first is to undertake a lofty and unspecific survey of the manners of mankind. The second approach is to focus more narrowly on the particular and circumstantial. Implicit in Burke's remarks, I think, is the view that the moralist's tendency to universalise issues is inadequate in the face of acute political crisis. Indeed, from the perspective of the moralist it is difficult to identify the crisis in the first place.

In this sense the apparently moralistic opening of the passage may be seen as a quiet and elegant parody, an imitation of the kind of viewpoint Burke feels unable and unwilling to adopt. There is something Johnsonian for once in Burke's turn of phrase, and it is more than possible that the passage is intended as a discreet reply to *The False Alarm*, published four months earlier. For Johnson's pamphlet develops in an entirely contrary direction. He certainly enters into the case of the Middlesex Election with some relish, assailing the anti-ministerial forces with keen irony and considerable venom. Yet in the long run he casts doubt on the importance of the entire polemical enterprise. It is his philosophical outlook as much as his political conviction that leads him to take up a stance which is diametrically opposed to Burke's. He brushes aside the controversy of the Middlesex Election with a weary and weighty scepticism: 'it will not be easily found, why, among the innumerable wrongs of which a great part of mankind are hourly complaining, the whole care of the public should be transferred to Mr. Wilkes and the freeholders of Middlesex' (Johnson, 1977, p. 333). Unlike Burke, Johnson neglects the particular in favour of the universal complaint.

Towards the end of *The False Alarm* the voice of the moralist is increasingly in evidence. In Johnson's view, the process of election, which lay at the very heart of the debate on Wilkes, has a merely momentary significance when compared with the more profound movements of moral history and the natural cycles of growth and decay:

> We have found by experience, that though a squire has given ale and venison in vain, and a borough has been compelled to see its dearest interest in the hands of him whom it did not trust, yet the general state of the nation has continued the same. The sun has risen, and the corn has grown, and whatever talk has been of the danger of property, yet he that ploughed the field commonly reaped it, and he that built a house was master of the door. . . .   (ibid., p. 334)

It might almost have been with this passage in mind that Burke stressed that 'all times have *not* been alike'. Certainly its sentiments run counter to his own, and not just in a narrow, 'party' sense.

For while Johnson's determination to play down the importance of the Wilkes affair is part of his polemical strategy, I would argue that this is reinforced by a kind of distaste for the very activity of politics. As a political writer this sets Johnson quite apart from Burke. The calmly disengaged tone of much of the *Thoughts* is never allowed to obscure Burke's belief that political action (within, it is true, narrowly circumscribed limits) is the only remedy for popular discontent. This is not to say that thought and action always achieve a perfect union in the work. The particularising and polemical impulse is usually held in check, informing and inspiring the progress of the argument without threatening to disturb it. But there are moments when Burke injects a somewhat jarring and impatient note, as if he were inclined to rebel against the orderly and moderate stance he had chosen to adopt. I think this is the case when Burke describes the fall of Pitt and Newcastle early in the king's reign. Burke's political sentiments are undisguised at this point, but thus far he has been careful to avoid any language which might smack of faction. His exposition has been notably restrained and temperate in tone.

Abruptly his prose quickens and changes pitch as he recalls the events which had shaken the political world ten years before:

> Every one must remember that the cabal set out with the most astonishing prudery, both moral and political. Those who in a few months after soused over head and ears into the deepest and dirtiest pits of corruption, cried out violently against the indirect practices in the electing and managing of parliaments, which had formerly prevailed.
>
> (II, 240)

The detection of hypocrisy provokes a sudden flight into metaphor. Burke's expression of disgust ('soused over head and ears . . .') anticipates the abrasive language of his counter-revolutionary tracts and, perhaps most of all, his violent denunciations of Hastings.

But personal invective of the kind bestowed upon Hastings would be out of place in the *Thoughts*. As we have seen, it is Burke's aim to set out an historical and diagnostic view of discontent, a general inquiry free from personal rancour, for 'it is the system, and not any individual person who acts in it, that is truly dangerous' (II, 258). Many of Burke's texts are written in opposition to such a system, whether, as in this case, it be a domestic 'system of favouritism', or the system of East India Company rule in Bengal, or the revolutionary system of government in a republican France. But in his most incisive and spectacular writings this careful mode of analysis is focused and enlivened by more particular forms of challenge and address. An intimate sense of audience (found in many of the printed letters and speeches) will often be combined with a passionate denunciation of the agents of political wrong. In the *Thoughts*, on the other hand, no named individual is on trial. Only rarely is the hated cabal given any personal identity. There is no outstanding malefactor to impeach. In this respect it is interesting that the epigraph Burke chose for his pamphlet should have been taken from Cicero's *Verrine Orations*, a classical specimen of forensic eloquence which takes the form of an indictment against a single man. There are a number of reasons why Burke may have felt the quotation to have been appropriate. Cicero's concern with the treachery, subversion and ingratitude of Verres would no doubt have seemed to match his own suspicions of the Court. But he may also have been attracted by the form of Cicero's work, and by the dramatic, almost heroic attitude struck by the prosecutor himself.

Before he led the action against Verres, Cicero had been best known in criminal proceedings not as a prosecutor but as a counsel for the defence. In justifying this change in role Cicero portrays himself as a resolute spokesman for the public interest, an advocate who has taken on the mantle of a patriot. In an introductory speech intended to establish his right to present the case against Verres, Cicero declares that the task before him is

> in form . . . an act of prosecution: but it may fairly be regarded as equally an act of defence. I am, in fact, defending a number of individuals, and a number of communities; I am defending the entire province of Sicily; and therefore, in prosecuting only one single man, I feel that I am almost remaining true to my established custom — that I am not wholly abandoning my mission as rescuer and helper.
> (Cicero, 1928, I, 7)

There is little doubt that this stance appealed deeply to Burke. Cicero's prosecution of Verres was a model for those who wished to rid the state of corruption. In an impeachment which, as Canter (1913-14) has demonstrated, owed a good deal to Cicero's example, Burke was himself to display all the zeal of a *novus homo* in the service of the commonwealth. In the *Thoughts*, however, this side of Burke, his more public and declamatory idiom, is generally played down. Perhaps wishing to dissociate himself from the vituperation and self-delight which had characterised the Wilkite tracts, he presents himself as, at the most, a quietly dignified and reluctant polemicist. The outbursts of indignation which just occasionally disturb his pamphlet remain significant, for they may point to a slight hesitancy in its rhetoric, as if Burke, with Cicero, would as much be an inquisitor as an inquirer.

For much of the *Thoughts*, however, Burke is content to write in the guise of a private citizen, one of those who, in times of crisis, are 'justified in stepping a little out of their ordinary sphere' (II, 217-18). When writing the pamphlet, Burke was the member for Wendover, and already a prominent figure among the Rockingham Whigs, yet he finds it convenient to create an alternative identity for himself, to appear as an independent gentleman deeply concerned for the public weal. It is as an elector, then, rather than as a representative, that Burke chooses to address his audience, a fact that is not often recognised in studies of the *Thoughts*. Following his colleague, William Dowdeswell, an MP whose views on the Middlesex Election had been published as *The Sentiments of an English Freeholder*, Burke claims to offer the viewpoint of a *constituent*. Like the majority of freeholders in the county of Middlesex, he is opposed to the power of discretionary disqualification which the House of Commons had exercised against Wilkes:

> when this submission is urged to us, in a contest between the representatives and ourselves, and where nothing can be put into their scale which is not taken from ours, they fancy us to be children when they tell us they are our representatives, our own flesh and blood, and that all the stripes they give us are for our good.　　　(II, 306-7)

In a similar vein Dowdeswell asks whether we should 'stand back with reverential awe, and bow in humble silence to gods of our own creating!' (p. 3) Both Dowdeswell and Burke find that the indignation of the freeholder makes for forceful rhetoric, but voiced too passionately — acted out too convincingly — it might prove counter-productive, might come to sound almost Wilkite in tone. Burke therefore makes sparing use of such outright protestation. He is careful to steer clear of the more radical issues raised by the Middlesex Election, to divert attention away from the potentially explosive conflict of interests which had emerged between the House of Commons and a body of its constituents. In his view — the view of a parliamentary spokesman for a largely aristocratic political cause — the real roots of discontent are to be found in the Court rather than in an unreformed House of Commons.

The *Thoughts*, an exceptionally able and rhetorically astute performance, is notably free from the suffocating legalism and narrow parliamentarianism which characterise so many of the pamphlets I discussed in the preceding chapter. By writing in the person of a private gentleman (though one possessed of firm and mature political convictions), and by considering the Wilkes affair as an intrinsic part of a more general constitutional crisis, Burke greatly broadens the basis of his pamphlet's argument and appeal. While other pamphleteers of the period wrote as if they were addressing an audience made up exclusively of lawyers, the *Thoughts* invites the attention and canvasses the support of interested gentlemen at large. This sense of an audience, together with other factors — Burke's clear preference for a political system founded on connections within the great landed families, his defence of the constitutional liberties of the subject against the alleged depredations of a Court cabal, and the elegant empiricism of his argument — makes the *Thoughts* a classic piece of high Whig political discourse. Yet as I have intimated, Burke is consciously engaged in a kind of rhetorical balancing act. As the spokesman for the Rockingham Whigs, he was required to present a reasoned and powerful case against the ministry without allowing his adversaries a pretext to make the counter-charge that his aristocratic party was colluding with dangerous Wilkites and reformers. In the event the most severe criticism of the *Thoughts* came not from ministerial pens but, as Burke himself acknowledged, from pamphleteers representing radical and extra-parliamentary opinion. The *Thoughts*, he declared in a letter to his friend Shackleton,

> have had in general I flatter myself the approbation of the most thinking part of the people; and the Courtiers admit that the Hostility has not been illiberal. The party which is most displeased, is a rotten subdivision of a Faction amongst ourselves, who have done us infinite mischief by the violence, rashness, and often wickedness of their measures, I mean the Bill of rights people but who have thought proper at length to do us I hope a service, by declaring open War upon all our connection.   (*Corr.*, II, 150)

This candid account of the rift between parliamentary and extra-parliamentary tendencies within the opposition has an importance which goes beyond the immediate reception of the *Thoughts*. Twenty years before the French Revolution Burke already finds himself under fire from radicals and reformers — 'the Bill of rights people' — who, spurred on by the crisis of the Middlesex Election, had begun to define a programme which put them beyond the pale of respectable Whig opinion. This growing ideological divide was to become one of the central and determining elements of British politics as the century drew to a close. Thus the conflict which Burke describes in his letter to Shackleton re-emerged at moments of crisis throughout his political career. Some of his most accomplished antagonists in the debates of the 1790s were spiritual descendants of the radicals who had attacked him in 1770. Mary Wollstonecraft, the radical and feminist who replied to the *Reflections* in her *Vindication of the Rights of Men* (1790), was indebted to the example of her predecessor, Catherine Macaulay, who published a persuasive critique of the *Thoughts*. Macaulay — 'our republican Virago', as Burke called her (*Corr.*, II, 150) — denounced his pamphlet as an apology for oligarchy, the elegant product of a faction whose adherents 'under the specious pretensions of public zeal, are to all appearances only planning schemes of private emolument and private ambition' (1770, p. 31). Under the pressure of this developing antagonism it would become increasingly difficult for Burke to maintain the poised and dignified Whig manner which characterises so much of the *Thoughts*. For that manner was shaped by political circumstances and presuppositions which by 1770 had already begun to break down. No longer was the old body of Whig magnates securely in control of the affairs of the nation. The claims of parliamentary Whiggism — that the aristocratic Whigs represented a 'natural' governing class, the ideal product of a perfectly balanced constitution, and the true defender of the rights of the people — were being contested and even reviled. In the 1790s Burke would have to reassert and redefine these claims in a style which was altogether more fierce and emphatic than the concerned but controlled discourse of the *Thoughts*.

Towards the end of the pamphlet the man who had begun by presenting a case for the electors is increasingly likely to adopt a partisan and parliamentary viewpoint. This change in identity is not marked, decisive, or even obviously calculated, but is the result of a gradual shift in tone, so that at the close we seem to be in the hands of one who has experienced the vicissitudes of high political life for himself. Burke now speaks as one with a practical understanding of the value of party. The effect is more didactic than speculative:

> Of what sort of materials must that man be made, how must he be tempered and put together, who can sit whole years in parliament, with five hundred and fifty of his fellow citizens, amidst the storm of such tempestuous passions, in the sharp conflict of so many wits, and tempers, and characters, in the agitation of such mighty questions, in the discussion of such vast and ponderous interests, without seeing any one sort of men, whose character, conduct, or disposition, would lead him to associate himself with them, to aid and be aided, in any one system of publick utility?   (II, 340)

Burke's expression of incredulity seems quite unforced. It is the eloquence as much as the substance of the passage which marks it out as the work of a parliament man. In this controlled and authoritative key Burke brings the rhetoric of the *Thoughts* to a close. It may be felt that I have given undue priority to this rhetoric. For the pamphlet's quality of allusion, the quiet hints which link its general maxims to the particular political conditions of the 1760s, hardly make it Burke's most vehement or colourful text. It is more highly esteemed as a dissertation on party than as a piece of polemic. But rhetoric may be a quite unspectacular mode of writing, not an enemy of thought but its boon companion. It is the mode in which thought is energised and in which philosophy is translated into action. I therefore see no reason why we should relegate rhetoric to the lesser arts. The desire to persuade is not a dishonourable passion. It is as likely to create an idea as to sully one. It may take part in the shaping of a thought, or be born in the very instant of belief.

12

Conclusion

The *Thoughts on the Cause of the Present Discontents* is perhaps the most even and controlled political work Burke ever published. It is, as he put it himself, 'a piece of Gentleman-like Hostility' in which the polemic observes the decorum of reasoned debate. Together with the two celebrated parliamentary speeches on America, it established Burke's reputation as a liberal and rational Whig, a principled opponent of the excessive and unconstitutional use of state power. The writings of the 1790s, however, were seen almost from the moment of their publication as initiating a sharp break in Burke's thinking about politics. His long campaign against the allegedly improper political influence of the Court gave way to a more urgent and vehement polemical effort, designed to mobilise all the forces of the state against the Antichrist of innovation. The tone of his economic writing also changed. In the 1770s it was characterised by the optimistic and even heroic view of commerce presented in the works on America; in the 1790s by the grim and punitive 'realism' of the scarcity tract. And in the *Reflections*, with its conception of society as an organism to which the individual is attached by the indissoluble ties of nature, custom and birth, Burke broke decisively with the liberal Whig creed of social contract and natural right. The causes, extent and significance of these changes have been at the centre of the debate about the alleged 'inconsistency' of Burke's political thought.

Most studies which have considered this problem have done so either from the point of view of British political history or from the broader perspective of the history of political ideas. In an obvious sense my own approach to the ideological in Burke has been more 'literary' in its emphasis. Primarily I have been concerned with the significance of the developing form and style of Burke's political writing — with what I described earlier as the 'internal' history of his work. Properly understood, however, this project in itself implies the necessity of a synthesis between the two kinds of study — between the survey of Burke's literary practice and the historical estimate of his career. It is the necessity of understanding the practice of writing itself, in all its elements and relations, as a political act. Seen in this way, the question of Burke's consistency cannot be resolved simply by comparing the positions he stated at various points in his career, or even by exposing an underlying pattern (or patchwork) of ideas. It is an ideological question, a question of tone, manner and feeling as well as of concept, and hence a question which involves the full range of meanings and representations embodied in his work.

Considered outwardly, in terms of genre, Burke's political writing, across a period of almost thirty years, shows little evidence of radical change. Throughout this period he continued to work within the literary forms — notably the parliamentary speech and the 'private' letter — appropriate to a 'closed' political culture. At the same time, however, we can see in his work an attempt to adapt those forms, not so much because he wished to create a new public, along Wilkite lines, but because he felt the need to reach an existing one more effectively. The *Thoughts* is a case in point. Concealed within the pamphlet are elements of a relatively closed form of address. It was originally conceived in the form of a letter to a retired member of parliament (see *Corr.*, II, 52), and, as we have seen, Burke at one point makes plain his assumption that he is addressing an audience of propertied men. Yet for the most part, and notwithstanding its partisan objects and origins, the pamphlet rises above the mode of direct appeal to interested parties. Its language of principle encourages a broad range of response to Burke's political argument. The same can be said of the parliamentary speeches he published. Burke retains the authority and prestige of the original form, but submits his case to the judgment of a wider audience — the political nation 'out of doors', as parliamentarians of the period liked to put it.

Within these customary forms of argument there are important shifts of tone and emphasis which bear more directly on the question of Burke's consistency. The most important change occurs in the *Reflections* of 1790, where the intended audience is at least as wide as it had ever been in Burke, but where the form of address is more narrowly pedagogic and the style more diverse, emotive and unstable. The address to 'a very young gentleman at Paris' establishes a literary relationship based on an assertion of authority rather than on the rational exchange of views among equals. The important general propositions about politics which Burke makes in the course of the pamphlet retain something of this mood of instruction. As Williams (1983, p. 77) puts it, Burke's address to the young Depont 'permits the decisive tone of the reflections, from settled wisdom (English politics) to inexperience (French politics)'. It is evident that more than a question of mere 'style' is at stake here. The manner of address shapes and informs both the argument and the outlook of the *Reflections*. The connection is made explicit when, in a discussion of the National Assembly's alleged mismanagement of the armed forces of France, Burke pours scorn on 'the fantastick vagaries of these juvenile politicians' (V, 384). The youth of the correspondent who had asked for Burke's views on the revolution in France paves the way for a general charge of callow ineptitude. Burke was to make further use of the address to a younger man in other works of the 1790s. In the *Letter to a Noble Lord* he exploits the Duke of Bedford's political inexperience — 'Let me tell my youthful censor . . .' (VIII, 12) — for rhetorical advantage. In the *Letter to William Elliot* and the *Letters on a Regicide Peace* he speaks as a dying prophet to a younger generation, urging his disciples into action in defence of a ruling class which he saw as dangerously complacent. There is, then, a nice irony in the fact that in *A Vindication of Natural Society*, the parody of Bolingbroke's philosophy which Burke published at the very beginning of his literary career, he should have anticipated the rhetoric of the master/pupil relationship which he was to use so effectively in his final years ('You are, my Lord, but just entering into the world; I am going out of it,' (I, 79) he announces to the imaginary addressee of the *Vindication*). Broadly speaking, then, there is a development

of manner in which the appeal to a common experience, shared
by writer, reader and addressee, which characterised the earlier works, gives way to a more peremptory mode of argument
in the writings of the 1790s.

As I suggested in the first part of this study, this development in address is linked to some significant changes in political idiom. It is as if the conventions of polite argument,
whereby an exchange of views can take place even between
those who disagree, have been rendered obsolete by the threat
of the French Revolution. The old questions, and the old
manner of disputing them, no longer seem important. Burke's
tendency towards violence in debate, which had sometimes
shocked his milder-mannered parliamentary colleagues even
in pre-revolutionary days, becomes increasingly pronounced.
In seeking to communicate his sense of crisis he alternates
rapidly between the twin extremes of fierce denunciation and
sentimental acts of homage. When he writes in this strain, it
is in a language consonant with his earlier concept of the
sublime – a language which operates primarily on the passions,
and which presents the affairs of the political world in terms
of an imagery of apocalypse. In this way the style of Burke's
political writing in the 1790s is significantly less 'parliamentary', less imbued with the historical and secular idioms of
the House of Commons, than the earlier work. Instead the
French Revolution is experienced within a framework of
ideas and images which are often frankly religious in origin.
This is the language – of increasing importance in the 1790s
– which has been seen as evidence of Burke's allegiance to
the principles of Natural Law, according to which the social
and economic system he sought to uphold is understood as a
temporal expression of the divine order of things. The celebrated passage on contract in the *Reflections on the Revolution in France* is perhaps the best example of this mode:

Each contract of each particular state is but a clause in
the great primaeval contract of eternal society, linking the
lower with the higher natures, connecting the visible and
invisible world, according to a fixed compact sanctioned
by the inviolable oath which holds all physical and all
moral natures, each in their appointed place. This law is

not subject to the will of those, who by an obligation above them, and infinitely superiour, are bound to submit their will to that law. The municipal corporations of that universal kingdom are not morally at liberty at their pleasure, and on their speculations of a contingent improvement, wholly to separate and tear asunder the bands of their subordinate community, and to dissolve it into an unsocial, uncivil, unconnected chaos of elementary principles.

(V, 184-5)

Burke's espousal of the kind of conservatism represented here — one based on an appeal to metaphysical principles — has provoked recurrent debate. Various attempts have been made to explain how it relates to the more pragmatic argument from circumstance which typified the earlier work (see Brady, 1962), and to reconcile it with the 'modern' and unambiguously capitalist outlook of the economic writings. It was largely on the evidence of passages such as the one on contract that 'Natural Law' interpreters of Burke felt justified in according his work the status of a coherent political philosophy. Recent critiques have been more dismissive of Burke's excursions in this elevated style. They are now often regarded as mere flights of rhetoric designed to divert attention from the inadequacies of his logic. The strength of this attitude lies in its recognition that Burke's primary object as a political writer was not to enunciate a theory but to organise and persuade. Its weakness is that it is based on a narrow understanding of the nature and scope of 'rhetoric'. The disfavour in which rhetoric is commonly held — the tendency to associate it with insincerity, sheer opportunism, or uncontrolled emotion — is especially limiting when applied to a political writer such as Burke. It can lead to a neglect of those areas of his work which have proved to be ideologically the most powerful. To criticise Burke for abandoning the path of logical argument is in this sense beside the point. For central to his endeavour in the 1790s is a certain attitude towards, knowledge of, and engagement in the realm of feeling. Burke succeeds in his ideological task in so far as he is able to induce the reader to live out, and experience as 'true', the values and beliefs of the dominant culture of his time. For that reason the rhetorical appeal to the reader's sensibility, by means of which Burke activates a host of ideological and cultural attachments, is as important — and as open to analysis — as the mode of rational argument.

The question I have raised here is initially a question of reading (in what terms and at what levels of significance should a political discourse such as Burke's be read?), but it is also inescapably a question of Burke's historical role (what were the conditions which required the changed and charged manner of the *Reflections*?). As such it relates directly to the long debate on the meaning of his career. The Burke who emerges from most discussions of this problem is somehow less troubling and troubled a figure than his writings, in their complex interplay of competing attitudes and feelings, usually suggest. This is true even of Macpherson (1980) who provides a convincing explanation of Burke's ideological role without always indicating how tense and contradictory, historically, that role was. In Macpherson's view, what unifies the various phases and campaigns of Burke's career is his work as a political economist and his commitment to the principle of a self-regulating capitalist market. What occurred in the 1790s was a change in style rather than substance. Burke's use of the language of Christian Natural Law was not a reversion to a traditional conservatism but a brilliant rhetorical manoeuvre, made necessary by the revolutionary threat to property, and designed to sanctify the operations of the market. Burke saw that in Britain the capitalist order had, by his time, become 'traditional'. His achievement was that he was able to revive the Christian Natural Law, once hostile to the morality of the market, by providing it with a new capitalist content.

Macpherson's suggestive and provocative analysis is a useful corrective to the view that by 1790 Burke had become an anachronism, an ideological Canute striving vainly to stem the tides of change. But although it is true to say that Burke consistently championed the cause of the 'free' market, it should be added that he did so from a particularly exposed and increasingly unstable position. As a consequence of his own social experience and political career, Burke owed allegiance to two closely allied classes: the landed and politically dominant aristocracy, and the professional, mercantile and manufacturing bourgeoisie. Although both of these classes could certainly be described in Burke's period as 'capitalist', there were significant differences in their modes of social, economic and cultural life. The tension of Burke's position, as one whose task was to articulate and reconcile these differences, is expressed most memorably in the *Letter to a Noble Lord*, but its influence is not confined to that work. It also accounts for Burke's surprisingly impassioned denunciations of the conduct of ambitious new men in India. When, in the *Speech on the Nabob of Arcot's Debts* (1785), he described Paul Benfield with revealing irony as 'a specimen of the new and pure aristocracy created by the right honourable gentleman [Pitt], as the support of the crown and constitution, against the old, corrupt, refractory, natural interests of this kingdom' (IV, 308), Burke showed how fearful he was that this unbridled (because unattached) ambition which he so well understood could threaten the stability of the alliance between classes. The outraged aristocratic humanism of this speech, and its attack on middle-class administrators and adventurers whose origins were not unlike those of Burke himself, clearly anticipates the anti-Jacobin rhetoric of the 1790s. The corollary of this vein of denunciation, of course, is Burke's reverence for tradition, a deeply rooted sentiment which is occasionally elevated to theoretical status in the language of Natural Law.

Considered from this point of view, the more memorable rhetorical episodes of the *Reflections* and other works of the 1790s can be seen as a genuine expression of cultural alarm, the true language of a man *plus royaliste que le roi* who had staked his career on the continued hegemony of the landowning class. It is the dominance of a specifically agrarian form of capitalism, and the social and cultural life which arises from it, that Burke is concerned to uphold. Thus in the *Reflections* he laments a situation in which the 'landed interest' of France has fallen prey to a metropolitan alliance forged between the 'monied interest' and a set of insubordinate literary men. In making his defence of property Burke puts forward arguments which he claimed were broadly consistent with political principles he had held throughout his career. It is true that the *Reflections* does not mark a complete break in his discourse. For one thing, the elevated but distinctly unhyperbolical mode of the *Thoughts* did not altogether disappear in the 1790s. For another, as I have just suggested, elements of the anti-Jacobin rhetoric are clearly present in the earlier work. Yet the general change in manner is unmistakable. The position Burke was defending may have been the same, but it had to be defended in different terms in order to meet a new and more sinister threat. 'New things in a new world! I see no hopes in the common tracks,' Burke declares in the *Letter to William Elliot* (1795), a pamphlet which combines cultural nostalgia and political realism in a way which is characteristic of his final works. The circumstances of the 1790s called for an experiment in ideology, a more urgent and wide-ranging response than before. At the same time those circumstances (including the break with the Foxite Whigs) led to Burke's political isolation and exposure, a pressure which brought the instability of his social role increasingly into the open.

As Aers (1983) has shown, Burke's position in the 1790s is curious and suggestive: it is his very familiarity with the desires and expectations of the Jacobinised intellectual that allows him to apprehend the nature of a threat to which the men of property with whom he allied himself were slow to react. The point is made explicit in the *Letter to a Noble Lord* when Bedford is warned of the danger posed by those ambitious intellectuals who, unlike Burke, whose career had been founded on a connection with a group of aristocratic Whigs, are 'independent of any interest, which if it operated alone would make them much more tractable'. Continuing in his pedagogic style, Burke declares that he is

> better able to enter into the character of this description of men than the noble Duke can be. . . . I can form a tolerable estimate of what is likely to happen from a character, chiefly dependent for fame and fortune, on knowledge and talent, as well in its morbid and perverted state, as in that which is sound and natural.   (VIII, 55-6)

Burke's recognition of the subversive potential of writers and thinkers who have no attachments within (and hence feel no obligations towards) the dominant culture is made more urgent by his sense of the weakness and myopia of the men of property themselves. His despair at the complacency of the English aristocracy colours much of his correspondence of the 1790s. In the sustained crisis of that period Burke experienced a complex tension of belonging: on the one hand, there was his understanding of the social position of intellectuals whose talent and ambition he shared but whose ideology he repudiated; on the other, his unswerving allegiance to the culture of propertied men who seemed to lack the necessary energy and intelligence to resist — to lack, he may even have suspected, the moral right to rule.

Burke was uncommonly well placed, at this sensitive point in the social order, to descry the signs of the times. Who better to sound the alarm to men of property than one who was acquainted with the psychology of dissent? As the representative of a mature and distinguished literary culture — the culture of Johnson, Hume and Gibbon — he had at his command a rich moral and historical vocabulary with which to articulate his sense of crisis. In his response to the French Revolution, and in its most characteristic literary effects — its moments of excess and illumination, its sudden shifts of tone, temper and style — Burke realised the potential and released the accumulated pressures of this social and cultural experience. He was empowered to conduct his uncompromising defence of privilege in a language which was, for the most part, more elaborate, audacious and animated than the discourse of English radicalism. Only Blake, who belonged to a tradition of which Burke was probably unaware, lived out the crisis of the 1790s more completely and proved a more powerful interpreter of his times. It is in performing a similar role, though with an entirely different set of assumptions, that Burke still claims our attention. Few would now read him as a 'philosopher', as the author of a coherent theory which contains political lessons of timeless worth. Yet his works offer more than a case of simple expediency, tricked out in a rhetoric which can be conveniently stripped away. The rhetoric, indeed, embraces Burke's whole response. It is the very art and impulse of his work, the shaping spirit of a political discourse in which he communicates a complex experience of history.

Notes

Chapter 1
Introduction: Literary Criticism and the Political Text
(pp. 1-16)
1. The best literary account remains that of Boulton (1963); for 'Natural Law', neo-conservative interpretations of Burke's political thought see especially Stanlis (1958) and Canavan (1960); among more recent political studies, those of O'Gorman (1973) and Macpherson (1980) are particularly helpful.
2. The most comprehensive modern biography is that of Cone (1957-64); still useful on Burke's literary relations are Bryant (1939a) and Copeland (1949).

Chapter 2
The Legal Idiom
(pp. 19-33)
1. Blackstone (1765-69), IV, 244. In later editions this remark was revised to read 'committed near Waltham in Hampshire'.
2. *PH*, XXVIII, 146-7; see also Radzinowicz (1948-68), I, 339-41.

Chapter 3
The Politics of Taste
(pp. 34-50)
1. For differing approaches to this question see Wood (1964), Wilkins (1967), pp. 119-51, Boulton (1968), and Paulson (1983), especially pp. 57-73.
2. For further discussion of the imagery of light in the political writings of the period see Paulson (1983), pp. 43-7, 58-60.
3. Melvin (1975) offers a detailed analysis of Burke's theatrical presentation of revolutionary events.

Chapter 4
The Triumph of Economy
(pp. 51-72)
1. In the following remarks on the character of eighteenth-century economic discourse I am indebted to Tribe (1978).

Chapter 6
The Conditions of Performance
(pp. 95-107)
1. *Hansard*, 5th series, Vol. CCCXCIII, 403-74.
2. For more detailed surveys of parliamentary procedure and architecture see Thomas (1971) and Hastings (1950). On the parliamentary oratory of the period see Thomas (1971) pp. 187-228, Reid, L. (1949 and 1969) and Butt and Carnall (1979) pp. 370-83.

Chapter 7
Preparation and Delivery
(pp. 108-117)
1. For pioneering work in this area see Bryant (1939b, 1952 and 1966).
2. See the important textual work undertaken in Langford's edition of the *Writings and Speeches*, and especially his helpful remarks on sources for Burke's speeches (II, 30-40).
3. Eg. MSS 215-63, 263*, 3711. Thomas (1959b) provides an introductory survey.
4. Fitzwilliam MSS (Northampton), A. xxvii. 67, 43, 66.
5. Eg. MS. 222, pp. B 91-137, 210-11; a version is printed in Cavendish (1841-43), II, 14-24, 37.
6. For principles of transcription see Prefatory Note, pp. xi-xii above.

Chapter 8
Performance and Text
(pp. 118-136)
1. Cavendish to Burke, 1 Feb. 1775, Fitzwilliam MSS (Sheffield), Bk 1/639.
2. Fitzwilliam MSS (Northampton), A. xxxvi. 21, 17; printed in *Writings and Speeches*, II, 381-90.
3. For Burke's preliminary drafts see Fitzwilliam MSS (Northampton), A. xxxvi. 18, 19.
4. Richard Burke to Richard Champion, 22 Dec. 1774, ibid., A. xvi. 2. It is possible that Burke means that the speech had been revised in proof.
5. Richard Burke to Richard Champion, 4 Jan. 1775, ibid., A. xvi. 3.

Chapter 9
The Political Identity of Wilkes
(pp. 139-165)
1. My account draws on literary and historical research included in the following studies: Sutherland (1959), Rudé (1962), Boulton (1963), pp. 11-72, Mansfield (1965), Bryant (1973), pp. 44-66, Brewer (1976), pp. 163-200, and Dickinson (1977), pp. 195-231.
2. See Bibliography, 2 (iii) for a select list of the pamphlets on which this part of the study is based.
3. Pope to Arbuthnot, 26 July 1734; see Pope (1956), III, 418-20.
4. For questions of attribution in the *North Briton* see Nobbe (1939).

5. *A Letter on the Public Conduct of Mr. Wilkes* (1768), pp. 74-5. This pamphlet is appended to [J. Wilkes?] , *A Letter to the Right Honourable George Grenville* (1769), pp. 59-81.

Chapter 10
Legal Argument and the Middlesex Election
(pp. 166-185)
1. For an informed legal view of the case of the Middlesex Election see Holdsworth (1938), pp. 540-4.
2. The ministerial pamphlets under attack are *Serious Considerations on a Late Very Important Decision of the House of Commons* (1769) and *The Case of the Late Election for the County of Middlesex* (1769). The latter was probably written by Jeremiah Dyson but has sometimes been attributed to Blackstone.
3. References in this paragraph are to *A Fair Trial*, pp. 143, 146, 151, 160.

Select Bibliography

1. MANUSCRIPT SOURCES

BRITISH LIBRARY
Add. MS. 24223. Minutes of Proceedings in the Trial of Warren Hastings.
Egerton MSS 215-63, 263*, 3711. The Parliamentary Diary of Sir Henry Cavendish.

NORTHAMPTONSHIRE RECORD OFFICE
Fitzwilliam (Milton) MSS. Burke Papers.

SHEFFIELD CITY LIBRARIES
Wentworth Woodhouse Muniments. Burke Papers.

2. PRINTED WORKS

(i) *Burke*
The Works of the Right Honourable Edmund Burke, ed. F. Laurence and W. King, 16 vols (London, 1803-27)
The Speeches of the Right Honourable Edmund Burke, in the House of Commons, and in Westminster-Hall, 4 vols (London, 1816)
The Writings and Speeches of Edmund Burke, ed. P. Langford and others; in progress (Oxford, 1981-   )
A Philosophical Enquiry into the Origin of Our Ideas of the Sublime and Beautiful, ed. J. T. Boulton (London, 1958)
The Correspondence of Edmund Burke, ed. T. W. Copeland and others, 10 vols (Cambridge and Chicago, 1958-78)

(ii) *Other Printed Works*
Aers, D. (1983), 'Coleridge and the Egg that Burke Laid: Ideological Collusion and Opposition in the 1790s', *Literature and History*, 9, pp. 152-63
Anderson, P. (1964), 'The Origins of the Present Crisis', *New Left Review*, 23, pp. 26-53
Barnett, A. (1982), *Iron Britannia*, London
Blackstone, Sir W. (1765-69), *Commentaries on the Laws of England*, 4 vols, Oxford
Bond, E. A. (ed.) (1859-61), *Speeches of the Managers and Counsel in the Trial of Warren Hastings*, 4 vols, London

Boswell, J. (1934-50), *The Life of Samuel Johnson, LL.D.*, ed. G. Birkbeck Hill, revised L. F. Powell, 6 vols, Oxford

Boulton, J. T. (1963), *The Language of Politics in the Age of Wilkes and Burke*, London

Boulton, J. T. (1966a), 'The Letters of Edmund Burke: "Manly Liberty of Speech"', in H. Anderson, P. B. Daghlian and I. Ehrenpreis (ed.), *The Familiar Letter in the Eighteenth Century*, Lawrence, Kans., pp. 186-209

Boulton, J. T. (1966b), 'Edmund Burke's *Letter to a Noble Lord*: Apologia and Manifesto', in G. R. Hibbard (ed.), *Renaissance and Modern Essays Presented to Vivian de Sola Pinto*, London, pp. 73-81

Boulton, J. T. (1968), 'Arbitrary Power: An Eighteenth-Century Obsession', *Studies in Burke and his Time*, 9, pp. 905-26

Brady, F. (1962), 'Prose Style and the "Whig" Tradition', *Bulletin of the New York Public Library*, 66, pp. 455-63

Brewer, J. (1976), *Party Ideology and Popular Politics at the Accession of George III*, Cambridge

Bryant, D. C. (1939a), *Edmund Burke and his Literary Friends*, St Louis

Bryant, D. C. (1939b), 'Some Notes on Burke's Speeches and Writings', *Quarterly Journal of Speech*, 25, pp. 406-9

Bryant, D. C. (1952), 'Edmund Burke: New Evidence, Broader View', *Quarterly Journal of Speech*, 38, pp. 435-45

Bryant, D. C. (1956), 'Burke's *Present Discontents*: The Rhetorical Genesis of a Party Testament', *Quarterly Journal of Speech*, 42, pp. 115-26

Bryant, D. C. (1966), 'Edmund Burke: The New Images 1966', *Quarterly Journal of Speech*, 52, pp. 329-36

Bryant, D. C. (1973), *Rhetorical Dimensions in Criticism*, Baton Rouge

Butt, J., and Carnall, G. (1979), *The Oxford History of English Literature*, Vol. VIII: *The Mid-Eighteenth Century*, Oxford

Campbell, L. D. (ed.) (1800), *The Miscellaneous Works of Hugh Boyd . . . With an Account of his Life and Writings*, 2 vols, London

Canavan, F. P. (1960), *The Political Reason of Edmund Burke*, Durham N.C.

Canter, H. V. (1913-14), 'The Impeachments of Verres and Hastings: Cicero and Burke', *The Classical Journal*, 9, pp. 199-211

Cavendish, Sir H. (1841-43), *Debates of the House of Commons during the Thirteenth Parliament of Great Britain*, ed. J. Wright, 2 vols, London

Chapman, G. W. (1967), *Edmund Burke: The Practical Imagination*, Cambridge, Mass.

Cicero (1928), *The Verrine Orations*, trans. L. H. G. Greenwood, 2 vols, London

Cobbett, W. (ed.) (1806-20), *The Parliamentary History of England, from the Earliest Period to the Year 1803*, 36 vols, London

Coleridge, S. T. (1970), *The Watchman*, ed. L. Patton, in *Works*, Vol. II, London

Cone, C. B. (1957-64), *Burke and the Nature of Politics*, 2 vols, Lexington

Copeland, T. W. (1949), *Our Eminent Friend Edmund Burke*, New Haven

Copley, S. (1982), 'The "Natural" Economy: A Note on Some Rhetorical Strategies in Political Economy — Adam Smith and Malthus', in F. Barker (ed.), *1789: Reading Writing Revolution*, Colchester, pp. 160-9

Davies, T. (1781), *Memoirs of the Life of David Garrick*, 3rd ed., 2 vols, London

Defoe, D. (1969), *A Journal of the Plague Year*, ed. L. Landa, London

Defoe, D. (1971), *The Fortunes and Misfortunes of the Famous Moll Flanders*, ed. G. A. Starr, London

Dickinson, H. T. (1977), *Liberty and Property: Political Ideology in Eighteenth-Century Britain*, London

Fielding, H. (1967), *Joseph Andrews*, ed. M. C. Battestin, Oxford

Fielding, H. (1974), *The History of Tom Jones, a Foundling*, ed. F. Bowers, with introduction by M. C. Battestin, 2 vols, Oxford

Fielding, H. (1983), *Amelia*, ed. M. C. Battestin, Oxford

Fox, C. J. (1815), *The Speeches of the Right Honourable Charles James Fox*, 6 vols, London

Gandy, C. I., and Stanlis, P. J. (1983), *Edmund Burke: A Bibliography of Secondary Sources to 1982*, New York and London

Gibbon, E. (1956), *The Letters of Edward Gibbon*, ed. J. E. Norton, 3 vols, London

Hamilton, W. G. (1808), *Parliamentary Logick*, London

Harding, H. F. (1944), 'The Listener on Eloquence, 1750-1800', in *Studies in Speech and Drama, in Honor of Alexander M. Drummond*, New York, pp. 341-53

Hastings, M. (1950), *Parliament House*, London

Hay, D. (1975), 'Property, Authority and the Criminal Law', in D. Hay and others, *Albion's Fatal Tree*, London, pp. 17-63

Higonnet, P. (1980), 'The Politics of Linguistic Terrorism and Grammatical Hegemony during the French Revolution', *Social History*, 5, pp. 41-69

Hogarth, W. (1753), *The Analysis of Beauty*, London

Holdsworth, Sir W. (1938), *A History of the English Law*, Vol. X, London

Johnson, S. (1905), *Lives of the English Poets*, ed. G. Birkbeck Hill, 3 vols, Oxford

Johnson, S. (1968), *Johnson on Shakespeare*, ed. A. Sherbo, in *Works*, Vol. VIII, New Haven and London

Johnson, S. (1971), *A Journey to the Western Islands of Scotland*, ed. M. Lascelles, in *Works*, Vol. IX, New Haven and London

Johnson, S. (1977), *Political Writings*, ed. D. J. Greene, in *Works*, Vol. X, New Haven and London

Junius (1978), *The Letters of Junius*, ed. J. Cannon, Oxford

Kramnick, I. (1977), *The Rage of Edmund Burke: Portrait of an Ambivalent Conservative*, New York

Locke, J. (1967), *Two Treatises of Government*, ed. P. Laslett, 2nd ed., Cambridge

Macpherson, C. B. (1980), *Burke*, Oxford

Mansfield, H. C. (1965), *Statesmanship and Party Government: A Study of Burke and Bolingbroke*, Chicago

Melville, L. (ed.) (1913), *The Life and Letters of William Cobbett*, 2 vols, London

Melvin, P. H. (1975), 'Burke on Theatricality and Revolution', *Journal of the History of Ideas*, 36, pp. 447-68

Moritz, C. P. (1965), *Journeys of a German in England in 1782*, trans. R. Nettel, London

Namier, Sir L., and Brooke, J. (1964), *The History of Parliament: The House of Commons, 1754-1790*, 3 vols, London

Nobbe, G. (1939), *The North Briton: A Study in Political Propaganda*, New York

O'Brien, C. C. (1968), Introduction to E. Burke, *Reflections on the Revolution in France*, Harmondsworth

O'Gorman, F. (1973), *Edmund Burke: His Political Philosophy*, London

Paine, T. (1969), *Rights of Man*, ed. H. Collins, Harmondsworth

Parkin, C. (1956), *The Moral Basis of Burke's Political Thought*, Cambridge

Paulson, R. (1983), *Representations of Revolution (1789-1820)*, New Haven and London

Pocock, J. G. A. (1971), *Politics, Language and Time: Essays on Political Thought and History*, New York

Pope, A. (1956), *The Correspondence of Alexander Pope*, ed. G. Sherburn, 5 vols, Oxford

Prior, Sir J. (1826), *Memoir of the Life and Character of Edmund Burke*, 2nd ed., 2 vols, London

Punter, D. (1982), 'Fictional Representation of the Law in the Eighteenth Century', *Eighteenth-Century Studies*, 16, pp. 47-74

Radzinowicz, L. (1948-68), *History of the English Criminal Law and its Administration from 1750*, 4 vols, London

Reid, C. (1977), 'Language and Practice in Burke's Political Writing', *Literature and History*, 6, pp. 203-18

Reid, L. (1949), 'Speaking in the Eighteenth-Century House of Commons', *Speech Monographs*, 16, pp. 135-43

Reid, L. (1969), *Charles James Fox: A Man for the People*, London

Reynolds, Sir J. (1959), *Discourses on Art*, ed. R. Wark, San Marino, Calif.

Rudé, G. (1962), *Wilkes and Liberty*, Oxford

Samuels, A. P. I. (1923), *The Early Life, Correspondence, and Writings of Edmund Burke*, Cambridge

Smith, A. (1976a), *An Inquiry into the Nature and Causes of the Wealth of Nations*, ed. R. H. Campbell, A. S. Skinner and W. B. Todd, 2 vols, Oxford

Smith, A. (1976b), *The Theory of Moral Sentiments*, ed. D. D. Raphael and A. L. Macfie, Oxford

Speer, R. (1971), 'The Rhetoric of Burke's Select Committee Reports', *Quarterly Journal of Speech*, 57, pp. 306-15

Stanlis, P. J. (1958), *Edmund Burke and the Natural Law*, Ann Arbor

Sutherland, L. S. (1959), *The City of London and the Opposition to Government, 1768-74: A Study in the Rise of Metropolitan Radicalism*, Creighton Lecture, London

Thomas, P. D. G. (1959a), 'The Beginnings of Parliamentary Reporting in Newspapers, 1768-1774', *English Historical Review*, 24, pp. 623-36

Thomas, P. D. G. (1959b), 'Sources for the Debates of the House of Commons, 1768-74', *Bulletin of the Institute of Historical Research*, Special Supplement, 4

Thomas, P. D. G. (1971), *The House of Commons in the Eighteenth Century*, Oxford

Thompson, E. P. (1975), *Whigs and Hunters*, London

Thompson, E. P. (1980), *Writing by Candlelight*, London

Todd, W. B. (1964), *A Bibliography of Edmund Burke*, London

Tribe, K. (1978), *Land, Labour and Economic Discourse*, London

Walpole, H. (1894), *Memoirs of the Reign of King George the Third*, ed. G. F. Russell Barker, 4 vols, London

Waterhouse, E. (1941), *Reynolds*, London

Wilkins, B. T. (1967), *The Problem of Burke's Political Philosophy*, Oxford

Williams, R. (1972), *Drama in Performance*, revised ed., Harmondsworth

Williams, R. (1977), *Marxism and Literature*, Oxford

Williams, R. (1979), *Politics and Letters*, London

Williams, R. (1983), *Writing in Society*, London

Wood, N. (1964), 'The Aesthetic Dimension of Burke's Political Thought', *Journal of British Studies*, 4, pp. 41-64

Wraxall, Sir N. (1884), *The Historical and Posthumous Memoirs of Sir Nathaniel Wraxall*, ed. H. B. Wheatley, 5 vols, London

Young, A. (1898), *The Autobiography of Arthur Young*, ed. M. Betham-Edwards, London

(iii) *Wilkes and the Middlesex Election*

Listed below are the pamphlets and other works on which the third part of the study is based (entries for Burke, Johnson and Junius have been included in earlier sections). Pamphlets are arranged alphabetically by author, or by title where the author is unknown. Unless otherwise stated, the place of publication is London.

An Address to the Electors of Great-Britain, on the Choice of Members to Serve Them in Parliament . . . To which is added, The Test of Patriotism. By a Lover of his King and Country. 1768

Arnall, W., *Opposition No Proof of Patriotism: With some Observations and Advice concerning Party-Writings*. 1735, 1770

Blackstone, Sir W., *A Letter to the Author of 'The Question Stated'*. 1769

A Cautionary Address to the Electors of England : Being a Touchstone between the Constituents and Candidates. With a Word touching John Wilkes, Esq. 1768

Dialogue between the Two Giants at Guildhall, Humbly Addressed to John Wilkes, Esq; to which is added, A Versification of Two of Mr. W_____'s Election Pieces. 1768

Dowdeswell, W., *The Sentiments of an English Freeholder, on the Late Decision of the Middlesex Election.* 1769

[Dyson, J. ?], *The Case of the Late Election for the County of Middlesex, Considered on the Principles of the Constitution and the Authorities of Law.* 1769

Dyson, J., *A Word in behalf of the House of Commons: or, Remarks upon a Speech . . . on the Motion for Expelling Mr. Wilkes.* 1769

An Essay on Patriotism. 1769

A Fair Trial of the Important Question, or The Rights of Election Asserted; against the Doctrine of Incapacity by Expulsion, or by Resolution: Upon True Constitutional Principles, the Real Law of Parliament, the Common Right of the Subject, and the Determinations of the House of Commons. 1769

A First Letter to the Duke of Grafton. 1770

Forster, N., *An Answer to a Pamphlet entitled, 'The Question Stated' . . . With a Postscript, occasioned by a Letter in the Public Papers subscribed Junius.* 1769

Forster, N., *A Letter to Junius. By the Author of the Answer to 'The Question Stated'.* 1769

Forster, N., *A Defence of the Proceedings of the House of Commons in the Middlesex Election . . . By the Author of the Answer to 'The Question Stated'.* 1770

Forster, N., *A Letter to the Author of 'An Essay on the Middlesex Election': In which his Objections to the Power of Expulsion are considered . . . By the Author of 'A Defence of the Proceedings of the House of Commons'.* 1770

Grenville, G., *The Speech of a Right Honourable Gentleman, on the Motion for Expelling Mr. Wilkes.* 1769

Harlequin Premier: A Farce, as it is daily acted. 1769

Henderson, A., *A Letter to the Right Honourable the Earl of T— — e: or, The Case of J— — — W— — — —s, Esquire.* 1768

Henderson, A., *A Second Letter to the Right Honourable the Earl of T— — — — —e; In which the Proceedings relative to J— —n W— — — — —s, from March 28th to June 18th, are minutely considered.* 1768

The History of Jack Wilks, a Lover of Liberty. 2 vols. 1769

A Letter on the Public Conduct of Mr. Wilkes. 1768

A Letter to the Right Hon. Thomas Harley, Esq; Lord Mayor of the City of London. To which is added, A Serious Expostulation with the LIVERY, on their Late Conduct, towards John Wilkes, Esq; during the Election of the Four City Members. 1768

Macaulay, C., *Observations on a Pamphlet, entitled, 'Thoughts on the Cause of the Present Discontents',* 3rd ed. 1770

Meredith, Sir W., *The Question Stated, whether the Freeholders of Middlesex Lost their Right, by Voting for Mr. Wilkes at the Last Election? In a Letter from a Member of Parliament to one of his Constituents.* 1769

Meredith, Sir W., *Letter to Dr. Blackstone, by the Author of 'The Question Stated'. To which is prefixed, Dr. Blackstone's Letter to Sir William Meredith.* 1770

A Mirror for the Multitude; or, Wilkes No Patriot. 1769

A Narrative of the Proceedings against John Wilkes, Esq. from his Commitment in April 1763, to his Outlawry. 1768

No Liberty! No Life! Proper Wages and Down with Oppression. In a Letter to the Brave People of England. 1768

An Original Camera Obscura; or, The Court, City and Country Magic-Lanthorn. 1768

Phipps, C. J. (2nd Baron Mulgrave), *A Letter from a Member of Parliament to one of his Constituents, on the Late Proceedings of the House of Commons in the Middlesex Elections.* 1769

Reflections on the Case of Mr. Wilkes, and on the Right of the People to Elect their Own Representatives, to which is added, The Case of Mr. Walpole. 1768

Rous, G., *An Essay on the Middlesex Election: In which the Power of Expulsion is particularly considered,* 2nd ed. 1770

Scott, J., *The Constitution Defended, and Pensioner Exposed; in Remarks on 'The False Alarm'.* 1770

A Seasonable Address to the People of London and Middlesex, upon the Present Critical Situation of Publick Affairs. 1770

Serious Considerations on a Late Very Important Decision of the House of Commons. 1769

Shebbeare, J., *An Eighth Letter to the People of England: On the Power of Disqualification in the Commons; In which it is shewn, that the Subject is not sufficiently understood by those who have written on either Side of the Question.* 1770

Some Considerations upon the Late Decision of the House of Commons. 1769

A Vindication of the D———— of G————; In Answer to a Letter signed JUNIUS.

A Vindication of the Right of Election, against the Disabling Power of the House of Commons; Shewing that Power to be contrary to the Principles of the Constitution, inconsistent with the Rights of the Electors, and not warranted by the Law and Usage of Parliament. 1769

Wilkes, J., and Churchill, C., *The North Briton.* 3 vols. 1763

Wilkes, J., *A Letter to His Grace the Duke of Grafton.* Paris, 1767

[Wilkes, J. ?], *A Letter to the Right Honourable George Grenville, occasioned by his Publication of the SPEECH he made in the House of Commons on the Motion for Expelling Mr. Wilkes . . . To which is added, A Letter on the Public Conduct of Mr. Wilkes.* 1769

Wilkes, J., *A Letter to Samuel Johnson, L.L.D.* 1770

Index

Anonymous works are indexed according to title. Recent authorities are included only where they figure prominently in the argument.